DON'T CALL IT SPRAWL

In *Don't Call It Sprawl*, the current policy debate over urban sprawl is put into a broader analytical and historical context. The book informs people about the causes and implications of the changing metropolitan structure rather than trying to persuade them to adopt a panacea to all perceived problems. Bogart explains modern economic ideas about the structure of metropolitan areas to people interested in understanding and influencing the pattern of growth in their cities. Much of the debate about sprawl has been driven by a fundamental lack of understanding of the structure, functioning, and evolution of modern metropolitan areas. The book analyzes ways in which suburbs and cities trade goods and services with each other. This approach helps us better understand commuting decisions, housing locations, business locations, and the impact of public policy in such areas as downtown redevelopment and public school reform.

William T. (Tom) Bogart has been Dean of Academic Affairs at York College of Pennsylvania since 2002. From 1990 to 2002, he was a member of the Case Western Reserve University (CWRU) faculty in the Weatherhead School of Management. While at CWRU, he served as chair of the Department of Economics and as a research associate of the Center for Regional Economic Issues. His work was recognized with the Outstanding Dissertation Award from the National Tax Association. Previous publications include *The Economics of Cities and Suburbs* (1998). He lives in York, Pennsylvania, with his wife and daughter.

DON'T CALL IT SPRAWL

Metropolitan Structure in the
Twenty-First Century

William T. Bogart
York College of Pennsylvania

CAMBRIDGE UNIVERSITY PRESS
Cambridge, New York, Melbourne, Madrid, Cape Town, Singapore, São Paulo

Cambridge University Press
32 Avenue of the Americas, New York, NY 10013-2473, USA

www.cambridge.org
Information on this title: www.cambridge.org/9780521860918

First published 2006

Printed in the United States of America

A catalog record for this publication is available from the British Library.

Library of Congress Cataloging in Publication Data
Bogart, William T.
Don't call it sprawl : metropolitan structure in the twenty-first century / William T. Bogart.
   p. cm.
Includes bibliographical references and index.
ISBN 0-521-86091-1 (hardback) – ISBN 0-521-67803-X (pbk.)
1. Metropolitan areas – United States. 2. Cities and towns – Growth – Economic
aspects – United States. 3. City and town life – United States. 4. Urban transportation –
United States. 5. City planning – United States. I. Title.
HT334.U5B64 2006
307.76'40973–dc22   2005038008

ISBN-13 978-0-521-86091-8 hardback
ISBN-10 0-521-86091-1 hardback

ISBN-13 978-0-521-67803-2 paperback
ISBN-10 0-521-67803-X paperback

For Mary – past, present, and future
and
Elizabeth – a big part of that future

CONTENTS

ACKNOWLEDGMENTS

This is my favorite part of the book to write. I have benefited from the generosity of many people and my only fear is that I will omit someone. The seed for this book was planted while I was visiting the University of Michigan, germinated upon my return to Case Western Reserve University, and came to fruition after my move to York College of Pennsylvania. My colleagues at all three places are to be thanked for creating such supportive environments for inquiry.

This book includes empirical research on the structure of several metropolitan areas. Dan McMillen generously shared data on suburban employment centers in forty-eight metropolitan areas that he had worked very hard to create. Howard Maier of the Northeast Ohio Area Coordinating Agency allowed me to obtain the data from the 1994 household survey that feature prominently in the discussion in Chapters 4 and 8. My largest debt is to my former student turned coauthor, Nate Anderson. My move from Cleveland to York had the usual degree of confusion, including my inability to find my data from our earlier collaborative work. Nate took time from his demanding schedule to re-create the data files on Cleveland, Indianapolis, and St. Louis that are used in the analysis in Chapters 4 and 5. He also patiently read and responded to numerous drafts, ideas, and other musings.

Ed Parsons at Cambridge University Press has been a consistent supporter of my work and I am grateful for his encouragement throughout this project. Three anonymous reviewers made many helpful suggestions that improved the book. Jaclyn Keys provided timely and effective assistance with the index. Christine Dunn copyedited the manuscript in a way that preserved my voice while improving its clarity.

The book incorporates parts of some previously published articles, usually in substantially revised or abridged form. I am grateful to the following individuals and organizations for permission to reprint material: *Case Western Reserve University Law Review*, Blackwell Publishing, Edward Elgar Publishing, Lincoln Institute for Land Policy, Dick Netzer, and the

National Tax Association. Paul Gottlieb and Nate Anderson allowed me to draw on unpublished joint research.

This book, like my previous one, is dedicated to my wife, Mary. She has endured daily progress (or lack of progress) reports on this work for years and always managed to keep her enthusiasm, even when mine might have waned. Our daughter, Elizabeth, also contributed by reminding me to keep working on my homework, just as she does, even when it's hard. Any mistakes, omissions, or misinterpretations are completely my responsibility.

I   THE WORLD OF TODAY

Marco Polo describes a bridge, stone by stone. "But which is the stone that supports the bridge?" Kublai Khan asks. "The bridge is not supported by one stone or another," Marco answers, "but by the line of the arch that they form." Kublai Khan remains silent, reflecting. Then he adds: "Why do you speak to me of the stones? It is only the arch that matters to me." Polo answers: "Without stones there is no arch."

Italo Calvino (1972, 82)

T HIS IS A BOOK ABOUT THE FUTURE OF METROPOLITAN AREAS IN the United States. The current state of technology and the existing pattern of land use will determine much of that future over the next few decades. To illustrate this point, consider the prosaic yet easily overlooked fact that all of the adults who will be alive in the next twenty years have already been born. Therefore, it is first necessary to understand the present and the past before looking directly at the future.

Consider housing, for example. Approximately 2 percent of the housing stock in the United States consists of new construction each year. Put another way, more than 80 percent of the housing stock is more than ten years old. The decaying manufacturing districts, public housing projects, and office blocks in some central cities were once brand-new construction. The new construction today is the old building of tomorrow, and the options available to us are restricted by our choices today and in the past.

How would you describe the place where you live? If you are similar to most Americans, you live in a metropolitan area. By definition, then, you live in or near a relatively large city. But to understand the place you live, it is not sufficient to look only at the city, even if you live there. Conversely, one cannot ignore the city. In fact, what really matters are the relations among the parts of the city. For example, the commercial districts of the city interact with suburban employment centers, and the manufacturing areas typically found along the fringes of the metropolitan area interact with residential neighborhoods large and small. We can't describe these relationships, though, without first identifying the nature of the parts of the metropolitan area. What is even more challenging is that the set of relationships is not stable. Instead, it continues to evolve as businesses open and close, houses are bought and sold, and land is converted from one use to another.

The excerpt from Calvino is the most succinct way I know of describing how I approach the study of urban areas. Much of this book will be spent looking in some detail at the parts of the metropolitan area. The overarching goal of this text is to create a framework for understanding how those parts interact with each other today, in ways that have both antecedents in the past and potential for the future.

No one would describe most North American cities as picture-postcard places, but they too are not cities in the accepted sense, or at least not in the traditional sense. Socially fragmented, recklessly entrepreneurial, relying almost completely on the automobile, and often lacking a defined center, they are without many of the conventional trappings of urbanity that have characterized cities in the past. According to their detractors, they are not real cities at all. At least they are not real cities if one assumes that real cities have cathedrals and outdoor plazas, not parking garages and indoor shopping malls; that they have sidewalk cafés, not drive-through Pizza Huts, and movie theaters, not cineplexes; that real cities are beautiful, ordered, and high-minded, not raucous, unfinished, and commercial.

Witold Rybczynski (1995, 32)

There is a substantial and growing concern about urban sprawl. In fact, this concern has been present since at least the 1950s, and everyone from politicians to academics to popular commentators chime in on the subject regularly. The list of books and articles warning of the dangers of sprawl is voluminous, including novels such as *The Crack in the Picture Window* (Keats 1956), think-tank reports such as *Once There Were Greenfields* (Benfield, Raimi, and Chen 1999) and the famous "costs of sprawl" study (Real Estate Research Corporation 1974), and popular works such as *The Geography of Nowhere* (Kunstler 1993). The excerpt from Rybczynski is representative, although he goes on in his book to demonstrate why he disagrees with much of the sentiment. Much of this concern is directed toward the fact that by the late twentieth century cities looked different from cities at the beginning of the century. Only a few people have asked the question: What should we expect a metropolitan area to look like today? This question leads to the uncomfortable answer that the metropolitan area implicitly or explicitly desired by the antisprawl writers is no longer a possibility. We are creating a new world.

The world we live in today is *metropolitan*. I prefer this word to *urban*, because the line between the city and its surroundings is less clear-cut than it was in earlier times. The term also harks back to the idea of the

Greek polis, or city-state, which accounted for much of the known world to its inhabitants. Similarly, the vast majority of daily life for twenty-first-century Americans takes place within their metropolitan area of residence, and their travels usually involve going from one metropolitan area to another.

According to the 2000 census, 80.3 percent of the U.S. population lived in metropolitan areas. Until the Industrial Revolution, it was impossible to support more than about 15 percent of the population in urban areas without importing food. In only 200 years, we have gone from a world in which the dominant life-style was rural and agricultural to a world in which the dominant life-style is urban and employed in the service sector.

The metropolitan life that is the legacy of the Industrial Revolution has not remained static. Instead, the nature of cities has changed even as the overall population has shifted from rural to urban living. The transformation of cities from the small dense walking cities of the early Industrial Revolution to the even denser transit-oriented settlements of the early 1900s to the sprawling auto-centric places of today was not immediate. Places such as Dallas, Houston, Los Angeles, and Atlanta became stereotypes of low-density automobile cities, supposedly in contrast to cities such as Cleveland and Boston that developed earlier. But careful analysis illustrates that much of the difference between these newer cities and the older cities is superficial. One academic study, for example, found that by 1990 the relative dominance of downtown Cleveland was similar to that of downtown Los Angeles and that the distribution of employment throughout the Cleveland metropolitan area was quite similar to that in Los Angeles (Bogart and Ferry 1999).

Because the best data are only available from the census every ten years, there is a substantial lag in acquiring and analyzing data. Many of the data used in this book are from 1990. This is a weakness in that the world has continued to evolve, but it is an even greater strength because it illustrates my point that the world had already changed by 1990. Much of the popular and policy discussion in the last decade has not been grounded in reality.

WHY MY VIEW IS DIFFERENT

Three themes distinguish the view of metropolitan areas that I advance from much of the popular and even academic work concerned with urban sprawl. The first theme is the interdependence among the parts of a metropolitan area. The second theme is that mass transit is a historical anomaly. The third theme is that lags in investment mean that the existing metropolitan structure will always be inefficient on the basis of the existing technology.

Interdependence

Much of the public debate about metropolitan economic structure has to do with whether the role of downtown is being eroded and how to restore the downtown's previous economic dominance. Along with this debate has been a steady questioning of whether investments in downtown tourist attractions and office buildings have come at the expense of the inhabitants of city neighborhoods (especially poor ones). A major federal initiative of the 1990s, the creation of so-called *empowerment zones,* echoes the many state government enterprise zones that seek to focus investment and employment growth in specific parts of the city.

New urbanists have promoted the idea of *job-housing balance.* The goal is to reduce the use of automobiles by creating neighborhoods where the number of jobs equals the number of housing units. In that case, people can walk to work rather than drive. If sufficient retail opportunities are included, people can also do much of their shopping in their neighborhood rather than elsewhere.

All of these debates and initiatives are fundamentally misguided. The modern metropolitan area is not a set of islands – downtown, neighborhood, edge city, empowerment zone – that can be neatly separated and analyzed. Rather, it is a complex web of relationships among these various places. People live in one place, work in another, shop in yet another, and enjoy recreation someplace else. According to Peter Hall (1998, 867), even planned suburbs built in Sweden in the 1950s and 1960s had "a two-way commuter flow that completely contradicted the planners' analysis." To understand how a region works, we must focus on these relationships among areas in addition to describing areas in isolation.

As an economist, the type of relationship that I focus on is trade in goods and services. Everyone is familiar with the idea that the United States exports and imports goods and services to and from other countries. A less familiar idea is that importing and exporting also occur at a smaller geographical level. When you drove to work this morning from your house in Suburb A to your job in Suburb B, you represented an export of labor services from Suburb A and an import of labor services to Suburb B. Similarly, when you ate at a downtown restaurant, you were importing restaurant services from downtown to Suburb A. One of the advances in urban economic theory in the recent past has been the systematic application of the analytical tools developed to explain international trade to understanding intermetropolitan and even intrametropolitan trade. In this book, I will explain metropolitan structure using these tools, and I'll illustrate them using evidence from metropolitan areas throughout the United States as well as detailed data on trade in labor services among the parts of the Cleveland metropolitan area.

Cars versus Mass Transit: Which Is the Historical Anomaly?

Prior to the 1830s, there was no mass transportation. Instead, the dominant means of transport was a type of ubiquitous personal transportation – walking. (If you were rich enough, you might own a cart, a horse, or even a carriage.) This transportation mode was ubiquitous because you could use it to get from one part of a metropolitan area to any other part of the metropolitan area. It was personal because it involved one person making the decision about the time and route of travel.

Since the early 1900s we have increasingly relied on another form of ubiquitous personal transportation – the automobile. In 2000, the census reported that 75.7 percent of commuting trips were taken by people driving alone, with another 12.2 percent car pooling. In other words, fewer than one out of every eight commuters made the journey to work in an alternative way to a private automobile. Even in 1960, more than 60 percent of commuting trips were by private automobile. Noncommuting trips, which represent more than four-fifths of all personal trips, are even more likely to be taken using a private automobile.

Between the middle 1800s and the early 1900s, the dominant form of transportation was mass transit. This evolved from the horse-drawn omnibus of the 1830s to the electric subway and internal-combustion engine bus of the 1940s, but it retained the same basic features throughout. One feature was service to only a limited fraction of the metropolitan area, along railroad tracks, trolley lines, or bus routes. A second feature was a schedule and route not under the control of the passengers.

Why did mass transit come to dominate personal transportation, and even more important, why did it lose its dominance? The short answer is that people are willing to trade convenience and control for increased travel speed. Before the 1830s, when omnibus routes were first developed, the fastest and most convenient means of transport was to walk. After the car was developed, people could again conveniently and quickly arrange for their own transportation. Between those times, though, was a period where the huge speed advantage of mass transit offset its disadvantages in convenience and control. Throughout this book, we will examine how the metropolitan structure resulting from mass transit continues to influence both the built environment and the policy discussion long after mass transit's dominance has faded.

Ongoing Technological Obsolescence

We live in a world of rapid and continuing technological change. In such a world, it is natural to wonder why our cities are not "state of the art." The answer does not necessarily lie in bad planning or corrupt government or benighted developers, but rather in the difference between technological obsolescence and economic obsolescence. Consider the following example: the computer you buy today is no longer the best available next month, but that doesn't mean that you buy a new computer every month. The same principle applies to urban structure.

A good rule of thumb is that office buildings have a physical life expectancy of about eighty years and an economic life expectancy of about sixty years. Houses are built with an expectation that they will have a life of about forty years. There are exceptions, of course, but these rules help explain what we see. The urban area that we live in reflects a weighted average of the new construction of the past. Thus, much of the construction is technologically obsolete, from the office building that is insufficiently wired to accommodate computer networks to the house that reflects the demographics and preferences of the 1950s instead of the 2000s. A city is largely an anachronism, a relic left over from another time.

The current metropolitan structure was implied as early as the 1920s, with the widespread introduction of the truck and private automobile. Why, then, did it take until the 1960s (and the 1990s in some places) for urban sprawl and metropolitan area structural transformation to become issues of popular concern? Because investment does not occur immediately. The structures in our cities in the 1930s, 1940s, and 1950s had been overwhelmingly built for a world of mass transit; only gradually did the new construction become dominant.

This sense of inappropriateness is exaggerated in a place that has been growing slowly or declining and is mitigated in rapidly growing areas. The nature of human perception magnifies the difficulty in discerning urban structure. As an area evolves from rural to urban, it does not do so smoothly and quickly. Rather, there is a succession of abrupt changes, each bringing seemingly endless delays. If we could be gifted with Rip van Winkle's ability to move twenty years at once, we could easily detect the new urban pattern that has replaced the former rural pattern. (Imagine what cicadas think as they emerge every seventeen years to a noticeably different world.) Unfortunately, we actually live those twenty years one zoning-hearing-traffic-delayed-new-neighbor-store-opening-store-closing day at a time. Compounding the problem, there is never a final point at which we can say that the urban area is completed. Instead, we've no sooner finished developing than it is time to renovate, reuse, or rethink some part of the plan.

Urban areas are the heart of innovative activity in the economy. Jane Jacobs famously asserted (1961, 188), "Old ideas can sometimes use new buildings. New ideas must use old buildings." The old buildings she refers to provide an environment with relatively low overhead in which those new ideas can be nurtured and brought to fruition. Those new ideas in turn imply both new buildings and new relationships among buildings, in the fullness of time.

We are only now seeing the full apotheosis of the car and truck. There is a further implication of this theme. If personal computers, for example, really do herald a new spatial relationship among people and companies, then it may be decades before we notice a major change in the way our cities are structured. In this book, I will use evidence on the pattern of growth to illustrate the extent to which we are "living in the past."

WHAT DOES A TYPICAL METROPOLITAN AREA LOOK LIKE?

"From now on, I'll describe the cities to you," the Khan had said, "in your journeys you will see if they exist."

But the cities visited by Marco Polo were always different from those thought of by the emperor.

"And yet I have constructed in my mind a model city from which all possible cities can be deduced," Kublai said. "It contains everything corresponding to the norm. Since the cities that exist diverge in varying degree from the norm, I need only foresee the exceptions to the norm and calculate the most probable combinations."

"I have also thought of a model city from which I deduce all the others," Marco answered. "It is a city made only of exceptions, exclusions, incongruities, contradictions. If such a city is the most improbable, by reducing the number of abnormal elements, we increase the probability that the city really exists. So I have only to subtract exceptions from my model, and in whatever direction I proceed, I will arrive at one of the cities which, always as an exception, exist. But I cannot force my operation beyond a certain limit: I would achieve cities too probable to be real."

Italo Calvino (1972, 69)

Implicit in all discussions of metropolitan structure is the notion of a typical metropolitan area. This concept is inherently limited, as each city has unique features. Despite the concerns about homogenization expressed by critics of modern metropolitan form, it is still possible to distinguish differences among cities even when they share many common features.

Pace Calvino, my professional training inclines me to describe a typical city using the approach of Kublai Khan. What are the features of a typical twenty-first-century metropolitan area in the United States?

- Employment in Centers Reaches 30–40 Percent (and less than half of this is downtown): The majority of employment is dispersed throughout the metropolitan area. While downtown remains the largest center for employment, its dominance of the metropolitan landscape has been attenuated. The employment centers, including downtown, are relatively specialized, meaning that they are not carbon copies of each other but instead have unique and evolving characteristics.

- Twenty-Five-Minute Average Commute (and 85 percent commute fewer than forty-five minutes): Despite popular concerns over long commutes, commuting times have stayed almost constant for decades. The distance commuted has increased, but the distribution of time spent commuting hasn't changed, as the growing use of cars combined with the decentralization of employment has dispersed congestion from the downtown throughout the metropolitan area.
- Density: The average person in a metropolitan area lives where there is a population density of about 3,000 people per square mile (4.6 people per acre) and works where there is an employment density of about 4,000 people per square mile (6.2 people per acre). About one-third of the people live within five miles of the central business district (CBD), and only about 40 percent of the employment is within five miles of the CBD (Glaeser and Kahn 2004).
- Metropolitan Area Size: More than half of the metropolitan population in the United States is found in metropolitan areas of more than 1.5 million people. At the same time, more than one-fourth of the metropolitan population lives in metropolitan areas with a population of fewer than 350,000.
- Congestion: The measured extent of congestion has increased. A typical urban rush-hour commuter can expect to spend forty-seven hours per year "stuck in traffic," according to the latest study by the Texas Transportation Institute (Schrank and Lomax 2005).
- Plans for Building or Renovating a Stadium for Professional Sports: In addition to the ongoing demands for professional sports facilities, many cities continue to add or renovate convention centers, museums, aquariums, and other venues designed to attract business travelers and tourists both from within the metropolitan area and from other metropolitan areas.
- At Least One College or University that Attracts Students from Beyond the Metropolitan Area: In some cases, the college is the original attraction around which a city developed, such as in Ann Arbor, Michigan (home of the University of Michigan). In other cases, the growth of a city has led local business and political leaders to promote the creation or expansion of an existing school, such as in Tampa, Florida, where the University of South Florida has mushroomed as the Tampa–St. Petersburg area has grown. A quality college is a *sine qua non* both for business location purposes and as an amenity for residents.
- Segregation by Race and Income: The typical metropolitan area remains quite segregated by race, but the level of segregation has been falling since 1970. This reflects the important changes in the legal environment between 1940 and 1970 resulting from the civil rights movement. There has been extensive segregation by income

throughout history, and that segregation continues today. What has changed over time is the way in which this income segregation is enforced.

MENTAL MODELS OF METROPOLITAN AREAS

The dominant intellectual approach to describing cities during the twentieth century was the *monocentric city* model. In a monocentric city, all commercial and industrial activity takes place in the central business district, while the rest of the city consists of residential areas. This description was reasonably accurate as recently as 1950 in most cities. Even the monocentric city model was a simplified description of the urban form of twentieth-century cities. Chicago was in many ways the canonical monocentric city, and it was where the so-called Chicago school of urban sociology developed, which emphasized a model of urban areas as concentric circles with distinct land uses. Even Chicago, though, had as many as six distinct commercial subcenters as early as 1910 (Schwartz 1976, 23). Interestingly, these were located at transit intersections, foreshadowing the future *edge cities* at the intersection of major highways.

Even by 1960 observers such as Jane Jacobs and Jean Gottman had discerned a new structure for metropolitan areas, although popular interpreters of their work have neglected this insight. This new structure was called the *polycentric city*, in recognition of the multiple centers of economic activity that now comprised the metropolitan area. While some people have recognized this change for more than forty years, it still has surprisingly little impact on the design of public policy. With notable exceptions, such as Phoenix's *urban villages* planning concept, most metropolitan areas remain wedded to a picture of the world in which the downtown of the central city is the dominant employment center. Local governments and private individuals devote great resources to reverse the exodus of businesses from the downtown. Some of this activity is appropriate, but much of it has an impact resembling that of King Canute's orders to the tide.

While there is now some general recognition that the polycentric model is a more accurate depiction of reality than the monocentric city model, the world has evolved beyond the basic polycentric model to a more diffuse system. The best analysis indicates that less than 50 percent of all metropolitan employment is located in employment centers, with the rest being distributed throughout the metropolitan area (Anas, Arnott, and Small 1998).

It is possible to overemphasize how dramatic the change has been. Consider, for example, the following quote from Gottman (1961, 397).

"A distinguished European [de la Blache 1921], visiting the United States in 1912–13, was deeply impressed by the marked sprawling of American cities":

> In America the city has spread out with heretofore unknown proportions. . . . The American city has a transportation apparatus that makes it possible to specialize its various wards, to separate the "town" of business from the "town" of the *home*, to place between them vast parks, to keep the countryside within itself. "The locomotive," Anthony Trollope wrote half a century ago, "is here a domestic animal." What would he say nowadays? Swarming all around, indefinitely expanding its suburban districts, the city is the most perfect expression of Americanism.

Changes in the location of employment have implications for understanding individual behavior. In a monocentric city, accessibility to work is equivalent to accessibility to shopping and cultural activities, because all are located downtown. In a polycentric city, the picture becomes more complicated, because people now need access not only to their jobs but also to the services produced in other employment centers. In addition, businesses in one employment center often consume services produced in other employment centers, such as a suburban corporate headquarters using a downtown accounting firm.

The increasing percentage of two-worker households makes the accessibility question even more complicated. When two people work in two different places, their total commute is the same in a variety of locations, although one person might have a longer commute in one location than the other person. When my wife and I married in 1992, she worked in Mentor, Ohio, about thirty miles east of where I worked in Cleveland, Ohio. We looked for houses in between our two jobs, but our total one-way commute each day was bound to be about thirty miles. The only question was which one of us would have the longer commute.

Even with only one worker, the simple tradeoff of accessibility to downtown versus housing price is not completely satisfying as a description of the choices made by households. Randall Crane (1996) discusses the impact of the potential for suburban employment on household preferences for location relative to the workplace. The key point of his analysis is that a household will not minimize its current commute, but instead will take into account the possibility that the commute could change while the household remains in the same residence.

The relative importance of commuting in household location decisions has fallen because of these trends in employment location. Commuting accounts for fewer than 20 percent of all personal trips, and the percentage has been falling for several decades. Accessibility can no longer be simply measured as the distance or time from home to downtown, but must include several workplaces, shopping areas, cultural centers, and so on.

In his book on metropolitan structure, Deyan Sudjik writes (1992, 308), "For the affluent, the home is the center of life.... From it, the city radiates outwards as a star-shaped pattern of overlapping routes to and from the workplace, the shopping centre, and the school. They are all self-contained abstractions that function as free-floating elements. Each destination caters to a certain range of the needs of urban life, but they have no physical or spatial connection with each other in the way that we have been conditioned to expect of the city."

David Levinson (1997) uses evidence on the commutes of people who recently moved to argue that these broader considerations imply that minimizing the commute is not the goal for most people. Hence, the publicity regarding the amount of congestion, while interesting, is largely irrelevant. In addition, concerns about congestion seem overblown given that average commuting times have not changed since the late 1960s. David Levinson and Ajay Kumar (1994) use travel survey data from Washington, DC, to show that the pattern of commuting times stayed almost constant in the metropolitan area between the years 1968 and 1988, despite the tremendous growth over those two decades.

Even the polycentric city model is insufficient to capture the richness of the interconnections in the modern metropolitan area. When only about half of all employment is concentrated into employment centers, the diffusion of production, consumption, and trade throughout the metropolitan area has gone to a new level. Rather than focus narrowly on bilateral trade between bedroom suburbs and downtowns, we are now forced to consider a complicated web of trade in goods and services among a wide range of economies within the metropolitan area. I call these local economies *trading places* to capture both their diversity and their interaction with each other. As Witold Rybczynski (1995, 232) says, "The old hierarchy of center and periphery, of downtown and suburb,... is being replaced by a system of roads and highways and, one could add, by a system of telephone wires, television cables, and computer links. What was once a composition of well-defined physical places has been replaced by vague zones of influence; accessibility, not permanence, is what characterizes the metro area."

What has been described as urban sprawl is perhaps best understood as a time of transition from the monocentric metropolitan areas of the early twentieth century to the interrelated trading place metropolitan areas of the twenty-first century. In other words, urban sprawl represents the chaotic time of transition from one equilibrium metropolitan structure to another. Part of the difficulty in recognizing this pattern is that the transition takes place over a period of years, so that the daily (and even annual) experience of many people encompasses only the chaos. William Fischel (1985) discusses this idea in the context of concern over lost farmland near urban areas. In fact, only 4 percent of the United States is developed for urban purposes. However, most people see nothing but urban areas, and so when even a small amount of farmland nearby is converted, it can represent a large fraction of the farmland with which the people are familiar. Jean Gottman (1961) provides a thoughtful analysis of how agriculture near urban areas shifts from land-intensive to capital-intensive activities rather than disappearing. For example, a farmer will sell off cornfields that use a great deal of land but continue to manage a dairy or poultry operation, only now importing the feed rather than growing it himself.

The most important feature of local land use in efficiently generating this new structure is arguably flexibility. If the land-use regime is flexible, then as the new structure begins to emerge people can make the most appropriate use of land instead of being forced into a configuration based on an obsolescent structure. Richard Peiser (1989) finds that cities that allow early development at low densities have a final density that is higher than cities that force early development to be built at a higher density. This illustrates the value of flexibility in a time of structural transition. Not only is the planner's approach of zoning in advance of development based on a flawed paradigm, it is ineffective at accomplishing the goal of relatively high-density development compared to a more flexible, "sprawl-friendly" regime.

NEW METROPOLITAN STRUCTURE: ATLANTA AND LOS ANGELES (AND CLEVELAND AND PITTSBURGH!)

The world that I describe will hardly surprise people inured to shocking ideas about sprawling cities such as Los Angeles, Houston, or Atlanta. But what many popular commentators have missed is that these cities are not the exception but the rule. Let's first examine some figures comparing the extent of commuting in the Atlanta metropolitan area with the extent of commuting in metropolitan Pittsburgh. Then I will illustrate how even a staid Midwestern city such as Cleveland looks, for economic purposes at least, very similar to that quintessence of sprawl, Los Angeles.

Atlanta and Pittsburgh

The extent of interconnectedness in the modern metropolis is hard to exaggerate. Atlanta is a good place to see this phenomenon at the county level, as it consists of relatively small counties closely linked to each other. In fact, the city of Atlanta includes parts of six counties. By 1990, more than half of the commuters in the region worked outside of their county of residence. Surely, though, this is just an extreme case, because Atlanta is notorious as the epitome of sprawling development.

Pittsburgh is not notorious, though, which lets us judge the extent to which Atlanta is an exceptional case rather than a model. A recent study by the RAND Corporation (Sleeper et al. 2004) of Allegheny County, which surrounds and includes Pittsburgh, illustrates the ubiquity of intrametropolitan trade. Note that while Atlanta is in parts of six counties, the county that includes Pittsburgh has more than 120 municipalities. This illustrates the diversity of local government structure across the United States, an issue to which we will return later. On average, only 13 percent of workers in the county live in the municipality of their workplace. Only the city of Pittsburgh has more than 30 percent of its workforce living within its boundaries. Most municipalities are *both* importers and exporters of labor. Thus, even in municipalities where the number of jobs equals the number of residents, the so-called *jobs-housing balance* beloved of urban planners, there will be considerable cross-commuting.

Los Angeles and Cleveland

Los Angeles is the stereotypical automobile-dependent, centerless city decried by critics of modern metropolitan structure. It has been castigated in fiction as a city designed by the devil (Hoyle 1967) and in nonfiction as a postmodern hell (Davis 1992). Cleveland, on the other hand, is just one more stop in "flyover country," a Midwestern town known more for football (and its suburb of Euclid among students of zoning) than for path-breaking urban structure.

By 1990 Cleveland looked in overall statistical terms quite similar to Los Angeles. For example, in 1990 about 32 percent of total employment in the Los Angeles metropolitan area was concentrated in employment centers, defined as areas with both dense employment and large total employment. (All data about employment centers in Los Angeles are taken from Giuliano and Small 1991.) In 1990, only 31 percent of total employment in Cleveland was concentrated in employment centers. (Data about employment centers in Cleveland are taken from Bogart and Ferry 1999.) To put it differently, one could argue that in 1990 employment in Cleveland was *more* diffuse than employment in Los Angeles. Despite its reputation as a sprawling place, Los Angeles by some measures is quite compact. Data from the U.S. Census Bureau indicate the Los Angeles urbanized area has the highest density of any metropolitan area in the country, and it has also gotten denser in the last fifty years.

An alternative measure of centralization is the extent to which employment is concentrated in the downtown of the largest city in the metropolitan area. In Los Angeles, in 1990 about 10 percent of total metropolitan area employment was located downtown. In Cleveland, about 16 percent of total metropolitan employment was located downtown. By this measure, Cleveland is more concentrated than Los Angeles. This is a difference, though, between five out of six jobs in Cleveland *not* being downtown and nine out of ten jobs in Los Angeles not being downtown, not really the stuff of dramatic variation in metropolitan structure.

Moreover, the number and size distribution of employment centers in the two metropolitan areas follow a common statistical regularity, the so-called *rank-size rule*. This rule says that the size of an employment center is inversely proportional to its rank in terms of employment, that is, the second largest employment center is about one-half the size of the largest, the third largest employment center is about one-third the size of the largest, and so on. Not only does the rank-size rule accurately describe the employment distribution of the current employment centers, but it also is a good description of the employment distribution of "prospective" employment centers, areas with dense employment but with total employment below a threshold level.

The employment centers in Cleveland and Los Angeles also seem to have similar economic functions as measured by the way that they specialize. Although the exact way of measuring specialization is not the same in the studies of the two metropolitan areas, the conclusion that the employment centers specialize and that they can be described as falling into one of a few categories is common.

The discussion in this section has focused on a few cases, but the results are consistent across the entire range of metropolitan areas that have been studied. The conclusion to draw from careful analysis of the data is that as early as 1990 there was a clear pattern in the structure of metropolitan areas in the United States. As ever more detailed data from the 2000 census are analyzed, that pattern will be even clearer. For example, a study by Edward Glaeser, Matthew Kahn, and Chenghuan Chu (2001) found that only 22 percent of employees in the 100 largest metropolitan areas worked within three miles of the city center, while 35 percent of the employment was more than ten miles from the city center.

Why Cleveland?

The previous section is the first of many detailed discussions of Cleveland found in this book. A natural question is whether Cleveland is representative of twenty-first-century metropolitan structure. I use Cleveland as an illustration for three reasons.

The first reason is prosaic. I have considerable familiarity with the metropolitan area. My experience is important because every city has idiosyncrasies that are difficult to discern from afar but become second nature to those living and working there. Having spent twelve years in Cleveland, I am well aware of the special features of the policy terrain. Further, I am able to use detailed data for the area that are not universally available. While there continues to be progress in developing nationally comparable data at the metropolitan level, this analytical tool remains a goal rather than a reality. There is still, unfortunately, no substitute for local knowledge when analyzing trade flows within a metropolitan area.

The second reason is that Cleveland is more representative than one might at first expect. We just saw that as early as 1990 its overall structure was comparable to that of Los Angeles. Also, most of the metropolitan population in the United States lives in small and medium-sized regions, so that Los Angeles, New York, and Chicago are more correctly thought of as outliers than as typical. In 2000, there were 232.6 million people living in 362 metropolitan areas. One quarter of them lived in eight metropolitan areas with populations exceeding 4.7 million (the population of Houston–Baytown–Sugar Land, Texas). Another quarter lived in 225 metropolitan areas with population fewer than 335,000 (the population of Brownsville-Harlingen, Texas). Half of the people lived in the thirty-four metropolitan areas with a population of 1.5 million or more (the population of Indianapolis, Indiana). Cleveland, or more formally the Cleveland-Elyria-Mentor, Ohio, metropolitan area, was the twenty-third largest in the country, with a population of 2.1 million.

The third reason is that people in Cleveland didn't know that they were living in a new world until after the fact. A Lexis-Nexis search for "sprawl" in the *Plain Dealer*, the main Cleveland newspaper, finds only forty-six articles and nine headlines from 1993 to 1995, with the first headline not appearing until 1994. Between 1996 and 1998, there were ninety-three articles and thirty-eight headlines that included the word *sprawl*, indicating an increased interest in the topic. By the time there is general public awareness of a change, the change has already occurred. One justification for this book is to provide people with an alternate language for understanding the change that has already occurred, rather than vainly trying to describe the world in terms more appropriate to a city in 1910.

IT'S NOT *SPRAWL* OR *EDGE CITIES*: IT'S *TRADING PLACES*

> And so a growing number of people have begun, gradually, to think of cities as problems in organized complexity – organisms that are replete with unexamined, but obviously intricately interconnected, and surely understandable, relationships.
>
> Jane Jacobs (1961, 438–9)

Sprawl connotes the absence of structure. It seems to imply that people and buildings have been randomly distributed over the landscape, without any underlying logic or structure. This idea is not foreign to critics of the world we live in, nor is the counterargument that the structure has changed and that the critics are applying an outdated template to current events.

A few years ago I coined the term *trading places* to describe the parts of the metropolitan economy. This phrase is more evocative of the actual structure of urban areas for several reasons.

1. Municipalities, employment centers, neighborhoods, and the other components of metropolitan areas are small open economies. They are "open" in that they buy goods and services produced elsewhere (import) and sell goods and services to other places (export). They are "small" in that they cannot determine by themselves the price of the goods and services they buy and sell. Rather, national or even world markets set the prices. By definition, a small open economy is a *trading place*.

2. A previous type of urban structure was the monocentric city, in which the central city was dominant and all other parts of the metropolitan area were satellites. Now, we find suburban employment centers not only to be growing faster than downtowns, but to have a total economic mass that dwarfs that of the downtown. Hence, the downtown and the rest of the metropolitan area have *traded places* in the urban hierarchy.

3. In the movie, *Trading Places*, the lead characters (played by Dan Aykroyd and Eddie Murphy) are apparently in conflict but in fact share a deeper common interest in getting revenge on the plutocrats who upended their lives to settle a one-dollar bet. This situation is echoed in most metropolitan areas, where each local government is faced with the challenge of competing with other parts of the metropolitan area while at the same time sharing an interest in the success of the region as a whole.

4. Cities are not static. Every day, people and goods move throughout the city. Over time, the very structure of the city evolves. *Trading places* is an active phrase, reminding us of the kinetic nature of metropolitan areas.

Trading places include the central business district of the monocentric city and the employment centers (edge cities and so on) that have become familiar in recent decades. Another example of a trading place is the bedroom suburb of the monocentric city; it locally produces and consumes housing and local government services, exports labor services, and imports everything else. Trading places also include the various diffused employment opportunities that make up the majority of jobs in the metropolitan area of the twenty-first century.

PLAN OF THE BOOK

The metropolitan area of the twenty-first century is not a finished product, but an ongoing evolutionary process. Economists evaluate whether a change is an improvement using the concepts of efficiency and equity, and these ideas are introduced in the next chapter and used throughout the book. Chapter 2 goes on to contrast two alternative frameworks for public policy. The first framework is the use of massive public investment to alter the structure of metropolitan areas. I call this framework the "crusading" approach because it is reminiscent of the unrelenting attack by a true believer. The second framework is to use the momentum of existing trends to create a better metropolitan area. This is the "persuading" approach because rather than directly confronting the opponent, it attempts to redirect the opponent's momentum in a more desirable direction.

Chapter 2 emphasizes that the evolution of metropolitan areas is driven by individual decisions that evolve over time, not determined in advance by a plan. Much of the general discussion of urban sprawl takes place against a backdrop of utopian visions of urban structure. Utopian plans are often reactions to perceived problems with the current structure, so the utopias evolve even as the actual structure evolves. In turn, the utopian ideas influence what is built, so there is a profitable dialectic between the two. An important dimension of metropolitan areas that is neglected or downplayed in almost every utopian vision is the way that an area will evolve over time. This omission has led many planners to underestimate the importance of flexibility in planning. One important moral from examining the past is that today's new construction is tomorrow's blight, and we should focus not only on current conditions but also on the long-term evolution of metropolitan areas.

The book will put the present that we are experiencing in the context of both the past that led to it and the future that we are creating. In Chapter 3, I briefly survey the history of metropolitan decentralization, from the invention of mass transit in the 1800s to the widespread use of cars and trucks in the 1920s and the well-known expansion of the suburbs after World War II. The experience of the last fifty years has not represented a radical departure, but it is instead an ongoing evolution with roots that can be traced back over a century. For example, large-scale residential decentralization is a phenomenon that dates to the invention of mass transit in the mid-1800s, and most of the public policy and market changes that made post–World War II suburbanization possible were in place by 1940.

Chapter 3 continues to introduce analytical tools as well. The reasons for trade are described, as are some approaches to measuring trade. The concept of urban sprawl is shown to be difficult to pin down, despite the valiant efforts of scholars and others.

I have already emphasized the importance of trade in understanding metropolitan structure. In Chapter 4 I carefully examine the nature of metropolitan employment centers. Although these centers do not account for the majority of employment, they are still the dominant parts of the metropolitan landscape. They have the tallest office buildings and the biggest traffic jams, and they garner the most popular and scholarly attention. In recent years there has been a great deal of effort placed into identifying and characterizing these employment centers. In addition to recapitulating results that have appeared in print before, this chapter contributes some new results on the pattern of specialization and diversification among employment centers.

Moving from these general results, I present new analysis of intra-metropolitan trade in the Cleveland metropolitan area. Most of the trade in goods and services within a metropolitan area is done using cars and trucks. I focus on driving decisions by individuals, using data from household travel surveys to analyze commuting (trade in labor services).

Downtown, while not as dominant as it was in the past, still has unique features. In Chapter 5, I consider the role of downtown in the twenty-first-century metropolitan area, beginning with analysis of the trading place nature of downtown. This chapter discusses the effectiveness of selected policies intended to improve the economy of the downtown. In keeping with the emphasis of this book, I emphasize the connections between downtown and the rest of the metropolitan area. Special attention is paid to the role of downtown as a destination for visitors from elsewhere in the metropolitan area and from other metropolitan areas, as well as the design and implementation of policies designed to attract permanent residents to the downtown. One challenge to redeveloping downtown is land-use regulation, which is the subject of the next chapter.

Chapter 6 introduces the idea that zoning is a trade barrier and describes how to integrate the political theory of the determination of zoning with the economic theory of the effects of zoning. Because zoning is a trade barrier, it changes the way that the trading places of the metropolitan area interact with each other. Similar to any trade barrier, there are winners and losers as a result. This chapter also presents ways that local tax policy can interact with zoning policy to affect development decisions. An interesting question is whether zoning has the major impact that popular rhetoric ascribes to it, and several ways of identifying the effects of zoning are introduced. Finally, alternative policies that accomplish the same goals as zoning are analyzed.

Economists define urban areas as regions with a relatively high density of population and economic activity. With all those people in a relatively small space, there are opportunities for them to get in each other's way. This is congestion, and it's the major costly spillover (negative externality) associated with metropolitan areas. In addition, there are environmental stresses from both ongoing urban activity and the conversion of rural land to urban uses. One of the strongest arguments advanced against the new structure of metropolitan areas is that urban sprawl increases pollution and congestion. Chapter 7 critically examines this question, focusing especially on the extent to which employment decentralization and residential decentralization have worked together to alter commuting patterns while leaving the average commuting time almost unchanged for a generation. Negative externalities also arise from garbage and sewage, and these externalities can be analyzed using the same tools that we apply to congestion. Policy approaches that directly target pollution and congestion are suggested as more effective instruments than land-use regulation.

Urban sprawl is often criticized for creating or exacerbating segregation. While in the United States we must always confront the issue of racial segregation, there are other types of segregation to consider as well, including segregation by income, age, and religion. Chapter 8 focuses on the provision of local government services and the relation between government activity and various dimensions of segregation. There is strong advocacy by many observers for ameliorating the impact of economic segregation by pooling the resources of a metropolitan area, either through annexation/consolidation or through a system of tax-base sharing. This chapter uses the trading place analytical framework combined with detailed information about commuters in the Cleveland metropolitan area to examine the impact of alternative reform proposals on municipal finances. One of the surprising results is that the type of metropolitan area tax-base sharing used quite prominently in Minneapolis–St. Paul would have a significantly harmful impact on Cleveland relative to the current system. This illustrates the difficulty in crafting urban policy reforms that are politically viable.

Chapter 9 summarizes the themes of the book and draws out some implications for the future. One important conclusion is that we can expect dramatic change to occur slowly. This apparent oxymoron is the result of the dominance of the existing built environment in determining the character of the metropolitan area. However, the built environment is constantly in flux, and over time relatively small changes accumulate, leading to a noticeably different world. Some of these differences are good, some are bad, and most have both good and bad features. Important changes that occur over a long time are not easily categorized as sprawl or smart growth, and it is folly to think that such labeling combined with facile policy suggestions will lead to a utopia. Whether one is happy with a particular outcome or not, don't dwell too much on a static picture, as the metropolitan structure will not remain fixed.

2 MAKING THINGS BETTER: THE IMPORTANCE OF FLEXIBILITY

A s children we were told that "sticks and stones may break my bones but names will never hurt me." The world in which we live is often described as sprawl, a loosely defined or indefinable set of problems to be solved. This automatically creates pressure on public policy to solve the problem, in this case by changing the form of the city. On the other hand, if the world in which we live is better defined as a city-state composed of trading places, then there are different implications for policy. So as adults we know "sticks and stones may break my bones but names can lead to bad public policy."

One reason it is important to be as clear as possible in describing problems is because a distorted presentation by partisans can lead to support for potentially inappropriate public policy. I like to illustrate the problem with the following example. In a book published by the Natural Resources Defense Council titled *Once There Were Greenfields: How Urban Sprawl Is Undermining America's Environment, Economy, and Social Fabric* (Benfield et al. 1999), the authors hold up Los Angeles as "the best-known example of sprawl in America" (9). To emphasize the problem presented by Los Angeles, they point out that "Greater Los Angeles is now said to occupy space equivalent in size to Connecticut" (10). This sounds damning indeed. However, when one learns from the 2000 census that Los Angeles County, with a land area of 4,061 square miles, has a population of 9.5 million while the state of Connecticut, with a land area of 4,845 square miles, has a population of 3.4 million, the picture is a bit more confusing. Did the authors mean to imply that Los Angeles would be better with one-third of its current population? Surely not, and they probably didn't mean to condemn Connecticut by the comparison either. Even more confusing is that the land area of the entire Los Angeles metropolitan area, 33,966 square miles, dwarfs Connecticut, which makes the comparison even less appropriate. The Pittsburgh metropolitan area, at 4,624 square miles, is closer in size to Connecticut. There is little to be gained, though, by rhetorically comparing sprawl in Pittsburgh to an implied better situation in Connecticut. However, by using only part of the picture, and by slanting the comparison, one can drum up support for whatever policy one likes.

Another example of policy distortion is found in some of the tenets of smart growth and the new urbanism. It is important for the health of a metropolitan area that it include a variety of options that are easily accessible to its citizens, but easily accessible should not be defined to exclude the primary source of personal transportation, the automobile. Walkable mixed-used neighborhoods should be removed from their fetishistic role to a more appropriate place in the metropolitan idea map. The walkable mixed-used neighborhood should be maintained as a viable land use if people choose it, but it should be recognized that the viability of the residential part of the neighborhood will depend on access to jobs and commercial activities elsewhere in the metropolitan area and the viability of the nonresidential parts of the neighborhood will require exporting their services as well. Thus, the neighborhood becomes a different sort of trading place within the mosaic of the city-state, and not one that is necessarily superior or favored.

There is no shortage of policy proposals for improving metropolitan areas. Every year, and particularly every election year, brings a rediscovery of an urgent need resulting from urban sprawl along with a possible way to remedy the need. This overflow can make it difficult for the serious analyst of urban areas, much less the casual observer, to organize his or her thinking. Economists have a general approach to the design of public policy. Public policy should address problems directly. If the urban form is not the problem, then it is important to identify the problem and design solutions appropriately. This chapter will introduce some of the general themes of the book, and we will examine specific problems and policies in later chapters. First, let's take a look at the general framework that economists use for analyzing whether changes are desirable.

EFFICIENCY AND EQUITY: HOW ECONOMISTS EVALUATE OUTCOMES

Every profession has a set of standards by which to judge outcomes. Economics is no exception to this rule. The two broad criteria used by economists are *efficiency* and *equity*, and within those broad criteria there are some important subdivisions. While I don't want to distract our attention from the main goal, it is important to have a common language for addressing policy issues. Thus, we will briefly develop these concepts so that we can use them in the remainder of the book.

Efficiency

"I'm angry. Waste always makes me angry. And that's what all this is. Sheer waste," says Rhett Butler in *Gone With the Wind*. This is a succinct statement of the economic concept of efficiency. Economists are fascinated, even obsessed, by the question of whether people make decisions to use the scarce resources available to them in ways that are not wasteful.

There are two main dimensions of efficiency. The first, *productive efficiency*, deals with the question of whether goods and services are being produced without wasting resources. The second, *allocative efficiency*, deals with the question of whether goods and services are distributed among individuals so that there are no mutually beneficial trades remaining.

To see these concepts in practice, consider the case of housing. If houses are being produced without wasting resources, then the housing market is judged to be productively efficient.

Now consider a situation where I would rather live in your house than mine and you would rather live in my house than yours. That is not allocatively efficient. We would both be better off if we swapped houses. Of course, there are some complications. What if after paying for the expenses of moving my household items I no longer prefer your house? In that case, the original situation might be allocatively efficient. Alternatively, you might prefer my house enough to be willing to pay me enough money that I am once again willing to trade even after considering expenses.

As this example shows, even a simple situation can rapidly become complicated. Once we realize that our decisions can have an impact on others, the question of efficiency becomes even trickier. If your neighbor would rather have you living next door than me, then our swapping houses might not be efficient after taking his or her preferences into account. It is not guaranteed, though, that he or she will be consulted regarding our proposed housing swap. This is an example of what economists call an *externality*, and externalities are pervasive in urban settings. For example, the extent to which my neighbors maintain their houses will affect the way that I maintain my house, and vice versa. But I won't necessarily take the impact on them into account when making my own decisions about how much effort to expend, although these decisions are important to all concerned. As Hesiod says in *Works and Days*, "A bad neighbor is as great a misfortune as a good one is a great blessing." The Code of Hammurabi, the oldest known laws in the world, includes a set of penalties for creating negative externalities. For example, "If any one open his ditches to water his crop, but is careless, and the water flood the field of his neighbor, then he shall pay his neighbor corn for the loss." Even worse, if you don't maintain your dam and it breaks, then you might be sold into slavery and your land divided among your neighbors. And you thought your homeowners' association was strict!

Congestion is another example of an externality, as I do not take into account the impact my decision to drive has on your ease of travel. Instead, I only consider whether or not driving is more beneficial to me than any alternative choice. While the negative externality of congestion reduces the overall net benefits of driving, it is important not to forget that there are private benefits from the transportation services provided. Whether or not my driving is efficient depends on whether the net benefits exceed the total costs, including both the costs to me and the externalities created.

An important feature of externalities such as congestion is that their complete elimination might not be efficient. If no one drove on a road, then it would be uncongested. But this is a great loss of potential benefits from transport. If the net benefits of the activity are positive *and* the person choosing to undertake the activity faces the full costs, then it is efficient to undertake the activity. In Chapter 6 and especially in Chapter 7, we will explore in some detail modern policy responses to externalities and the extent to which they are efficient.

Equity

Even if a situation is efficient, it is not necessarily fair. In the case of public policy, the question of fairness looms large. Economists, while they tend to focus on efficiency, are not ignorant of fairness. The concept of equity is used to analyze the extent to which a situation is fair.

As with efficiency, equity has multiple dimensions. There are three that will be emphasized here. First comes *horizontal equity*, which means that people in equal situations are treated equally. This is trivial, except when it comes to defining what we mean by an equal situation and what it means to be treated equally. Second comes *vertical equity*, which analyzes the extent to which people in different situations are treated differently. The usual application of vertical equity is to income. If high-income people pay more as a fraction of their income than low-income people for a policy, then the policy is called *progressive*. The opposite situation is called *regressive*. The third dimension of equity has to do with the time that fairness is evaluated. An analysis of equity concerned with fairness before some decision is made is called *ex ante equity*, while an analysis made after the decision is called *ex post equity*. A (fair) raffle illustrates this concept. If you and I both hold a raffle ticket, then the situation is fair *ex ante* because we have an equal chance of winning the prize. An *ex post* analysis will find an unfair situation, though, because one of us has a prize while the other does not.

It is sometimes complicated to determine whether a situation is fair. Consider the case of identical people in identical houses, one of whom pays higher property taxes. This seems horizontally inequitable. But wait, the identical houses are in different municipalities, and the one paying higher taxes also receives a broader range of services. Now it's fair, but it seems like a trick to call the houses identical when they are in different municipalities. So let's put them in the same municipality. Surely, now the situation is unfair. But if the person paying higher taxes paid a lower price for the house because of the higher property taxes, then the people are treated equally once again. The person who owned the higher-tax house when it received its higher assessment is worse off as a result, but when the higher taxes are reflected in the purchase price of the house then future owners are as well off as their lower-tax neighbor.

POLICY DESIGN IN ACTION: A REGIONAL PLAN

Robert Nelson's book, *Economics as Religion*, makes an important contribution to the (post)modern debate about the nature and use of the social sciences. One of his central themes is the seeming immunity of certain tenets of the faith to any countervailing evidence. A second theme is the lack of recognition of the elements of faith that serve as axioms of any analysis.

Throughout this book, I will review a few of the myths that underlie the regional planning efforts of today, which are clear to me because they differ from the myths that I subscribe to both consciously and unconsciously as an economist. It will be helpful to begin with an examination of a specific report that diagnoses the problems facing a region along with providing solutions in the form of regional planning. I will adopt an unconventional approach for a scholar and not provide the complete citation to the report until the end of this section, when it will help me to make an important point about the discipline of regional planning.

The title of the plan is "What's Ahead for Cleveland" by John T. Howard and it is published by the Regional Association of Cleveland. This plan is relatively short and is written for the general reader, as is often the case with these documents. It begins with a diagnosis of the problems facing the area. One important problem is an inefficient transport system. For example, the author finds that "[m]ore than half the workers in the city spend more than half an hour each day, getting from home to work" (11), and this problem results because the work locations are too far away from housing locations. He also finds that the city cannot be expected to grow the way it did in the past, and that this is true "of all American cities" (17). As a result, it is important to better plan the region to improve the quality of life for all the residents.

The plan comes in several dimensions. The first section, "Planning for Tomorrow's Industry," recognizes that business location decisions are changing, which creates a challenge for the downtown but also an opportunity to increase the quantity of downtown housing. The second section, "Planning for Tomorrow's Play," suggests ways to improve recreational opportunities. The analysis recognizes that "the family is not as important as it used to be" (26) in structuring the lives of individuals. The third section, "Planning for Tomorrow's Highways," points out the problems with the popular checkerboard or grid road system and argues for cul-de-sacs as a way to reduce through traffic in residential areas. This section also argues for increased off-street parking for businesses and constructing more bypasses around business districts. The fourth section, "Planning for Tomorrow's Homes," describes the problems of houses located only a few feet from each other, including small yards that children can't play in and front porches too close to the street. Fortunately, there is a recently constructed public housing model, the Cedar Central Apartments, that have "nearly the only modern apartments, meeting modern minimum standards, in all the Cleveland region" (45–6). The author also finds grounds for optimism in the demonstrated ability of private enterprise to perform planning over a broad area, as evidenced by the "dozens of large-scale housing developments built within the last few years."

Some of the diagnoses and prescriptions could be taken from just about any regional planning study in the country, but even people with a casual acquaintance with the field are probably shocked to learn that a regional planner is advocating cul-de-sacs and large private housing developments. Howard can be forgiven for not conforming to the current shibboleths, though, as his report was published in 1941.

The plan does include one element that remains up to date, even as many of the specific proposals are now viewed as misguided or even dangerous. In the concluding section, the reader is admonished that "[n]othing should be constructed unless it fits into the Plan" (61). The regional planner of today couldn't agree more.

CRUSADING POLICY VERSUS PERSUADING POLICY

My idea is to go just outside centers of population, pick up cheap land, build a whole community and entice people into it. Then go back into the cities and tear down whole slums and make parks of them.

> Rexford Tugwell, creator of the New Deal's Greenbelt demonstration suburbs, quoted in Jane Jacobs (1961, 410)

There are many issues posed by this new kind of city. . . . But what the planner cannot do is to cut across the direction of events. The only plausible strategy

is to attempt to harness the dynamics of development to move things in the
direction that you want.

Deyan Sudjik (1992, 309)

The quote from Tugwell epitomizes what I call *crusading policy*. A crusading policy is one that seeks to destroy an unpleasant reality and replace it with a preferred reality. A more academic sounding term might be *replacement policy*, but the image I want to keep in mind is the fervent crowds shouting "Deus lo volt (God wills it)." I sometimes like to call crusading policy *karate policy*, after an expert breaking rocks with his bare hands.

Sudjik, on the other hand, presents what I call *persuading policy*. In this type of policy, the goal is to use the existing momentum but to deflect it in a better direction, which is why I also refer to it as *judo policy* in contrast to the karate policy introduced earlier. An academic name for this might be *adaptive policy*. Like the judo expert who can achieve wonders if his or her opponent is strong and moving quickly, a persuading policy can achieve its greatest results when there is extreme development pressure that can be channeled.

Perhaps the most famous confrontation between crusading policy and persuading policy came in New York City in the early 1960s. Robert Moses wanted to build a highway through lower Manhattan that would have eviscerated the Greenwich Village area. Jane Jacobs helped to mobilize opposition to the proposal based on the argument that there was already a vibrant community in place, unrecognized by the urban planners.

Moses and his colleagues were not unique in missing or misinterpreting the nature of community in neighborhoods. Herbert Gans, in *The Levittowners,* carefully identified the internal logic of places that seemed to planners to be sterile suburban neighborhoods. And Moses could arguably be used as an example of persuading policy in the way that he used development pressure on Long Island to facilitate both road construction and park creation.

One challenge to the practitioner of persuading policy is that it must be reinvented every time it is applied. Because every metropolitan area is different in both its economic characteristics and its political landscape, one cannot simply replicate policies that worked elsewhere. This heterogeneity is a challenge to serious analysts of urban development, as positive press coverage of a successful (or seemingly successful) initiative spawns imitators in settings that might be less favorable.

While I think that urban sprawl is not a useful concept for describing the world or prescribing public policy, even those who disagree with me are better served using a persuading approach instead of a crusading approach. Persuading policy does not necessarily favor decentralization, nor does crusading policy necessarily oppose it. This neutrality characterizes the economist's approach: "Tell me what you want to do, and I'll tell you how to do it." (Or as the cynic would say, the economist's response is "I'll tell you why it can't be done.") One can construct "pro-sprawl" crusading policy or "anti-sprawl" persuading policy. In fact, and ironically given her initial efforts as an opponent of urban planners, the Jane Jacobs example is the fountainhead from which today's smart-growth movement springs.

There are two general dimensions along which crusading policy proposals differ from persuading policy proposals. First, crusading policies tend to be static rather than dynamic. Second, crusading policies tend to treat people as passive inhabitants of an environment rather than as active participants in and creators of a changing environment.

Static Analysis versus Dynamic Analysis

To build political support for any policy, it is vital to describe the new and better world that results from implementing the policy. "And I saw a new heaven and a new earth: for the first heaven and the first earth were passed away; and there was no more sea. And I John saw the holy city, new Jerusalem, coming down from God out of heaven..." (Revelation 21:1–2). The author of Revelation was able to end on that note, and generations of politicians and planners have followed suit. However, the world does not end the day after the new convention center, streetcar line, or shopping mall opens. Not all of the benefits are immediately evident, nor are all of the benefits stable and permanent.

The best analysis of metropolitan structure has emphasized the dynamic nature of cities. Robert Fishman (1987) describes the new world of "technoburbs" that have replaced the purely residential suburb with a more complicated mix of uses. He also emphasizes that these technoburbs are not the end of an evolutionary process, but just another stage. Similarly, Joel Garreau's edge cities (1991) are acknowledged by him as just the latest way that Americans have found to develop urban areas.

Utopian authors and policy analysts that prescribe for a better world typically neglect the continuing passage of time. Like John, they prefer to end with the vision of the creation of a new city, leaving the future as an indefinite continuation of that glorious present. Myron Orfield (1997) recommends metropolitan revenue sharing and changes in state-financed infrastructure as a politically viable way to a better world. In focusing on political viability, he is an advocate of persuading policy. However, what happens after the new regional order is established? Presumably, there will be a new area of decline. One response is that regional tax-base sharing, by automatically increasing payments to declining areas, will serve a homeostatic function. However, this is a crude assumption, and it requires that whatever problems arise in the future can be solved by the policies developed to address current problems.

David Rusk (1995) advocates metropolitan area government as the remedy to urban decline, which he ascribes to inequalities resulting from the inability of cities to annex their surrounding area. This is more of a crusading policy, unless one is willing to assume that suburban residents will simply voluntarily subsume their identity into a regional government. (Alternatively, that city residents will agree to lose their political autonomy and trust to the kindness of suburban residents that often have strikingly different demographic and political characteristics.) Suppose, though, that Rusk is correct that annexation is the best approach. At what point does it stop? For example, as of 2004 there are thirty-nine metropolitan areas that cross state boundaries, with eight that include parts of three states and two (Philadelphia and Washington, DC) that include parts of four states. Should these new regional governments be allowed to cross state lines? If not, then what policies should be followed in these circumstances? In addition, this number understates the potential number of metropolitan areas that cross state boundaries. The entire Atlantic seaboard is arguably a single integrated economic area, as first recognized by Jean Gottman in *Megalopolis* more than forty years ago. Is it optimal for the regional governments to begin and end at state borders? And what happens if an area is declining? Should a city be able to detach parts of itself that have become rural?

Flexibility

> Recognition of the value of flexibility involves merely recognition that an urban economy is a live organism. . . . No design can be judged until pictured in a state of adjustment; our most acute distresses, and our most intriguing opportunities, are accompaniments of adjustment.
>
> Edgar M. Hoover (1968, 281)

The long-run nature of real-estate investments underscores the importance of flexibility. If a building, road system, or other infrastructure is too rigid then it runs the risk of locking in mistakes for a long time. Granted, it would be ideal to lock in an ideal pattern, and allowing flexibility can undermine this happy occurrence. But one has to wonder whether what is ideal for one time period remains ideal in the future. Paul Hohenberg and Lynn Lees (1985, 292) cite the example of Paris. Defensive walls were built in the 1840s that were no longer needed. The large amount of space consumed by the walls preserved land for circumferential boulevards that are now considered *de trop* (if I may be permitted). Richard Peiser's (1989) research on the ultimate density of development under prescriptive and adaptive zoning approaches has already been discussed, again suggesting that even if the goal is to increase density, requiring high-density development from the outset is not necessarily the ideal approach for achieving the goal. Indeed, sometimes mistakes are required by planners, rather than occurring due to the absence of regulation. Using observations on close to 100,000 dwellings, Alice Coleman (1990) documents the way that urban planners designed housing in England that increased social dysfunction. Because the problems were caused by the design, it is doubly difficult to come up with policies that improve social outcomes.

Once we move beyond the realm of mistakes, the principle of flexibility becomes even more evident. Levittown, New York, is a cliché of suburban homogeneity. While the houses as constructed were identical, they have evolved according to the tastes of their owners. Barbara Kelly (1993) documents the astonishing diversity that resulted from the gradual transformation of the houses and yards. Instead of a Procrustean bed of conformity, such as that imposed today by planners and neighborhood associations, the mass-produced house instead served as a blank slate on which people could realize their own individual visions. This process began quite early in Levittown's history. William Dobriner (1963, 122) found, "The clash of dissident internal forces has rendered the community a heterogeneous assemblage of urban families." This is hardly consistent with the popular caricature, which unfortunately still tends to dominate the discussion of the suburb.

A final, homely, example of the need for patience in evaluating urban outcomes is found in my own experience. I lived for twelve years in Shaker Heights and University Heights, Ohio. These two suburbs exemplify the type of place that new urbanists aspire to create. One reason for their charm is the profusion of tree-shaded streets. When we look at photographs from the time that the houses were built, though, we see small trees that have just been planted vainly trying to block the view of fields standing just beyond this latest extension of the urban area. In other words, these modern paragons of traditionalism were born in an atmosphere of sprawl, and only gradually took on their current nature. In fact, the 1941 Cleveland regional plan described earlier named University Heights as a place on the outskirts of the city with plenty of space available. The current inner-ring suburbs were once seen as part of the urban fringe, and a time traveler from 2000 might well have decried them as urban sprawl. Perhaps we should accord some time to the more recently constructed areas before judging them devoid of charm.

We should also be careful not to judge a neighborhood as successful based on the experience of a point in time. In fact, the Hoover quote that opens this section is part of a caution about the dangers of constructing too much in one place at one time. Simply put, if all of the houses in an area are newly constructed at the same time, then they will likely be obsolete at the same time. This risk of today's new development becoming tomorrow's slum has been a theme in both public policy and fiction. Frederick Pohl and C. M. Kornbluth's (1955) science-fictional description of a thinly veiled Levittown, Belle Reve, transforming into a Hobbesian nightmare, Belly

Rave, is a salutary warning. Their oracle is not limited to just one place, though. "The festering slums of Long Island were another New York problem; Boston had its Springfield, Chicago its Evanston; Los Angeles its Greenville" (31). While their worst predictions have fortunately remained fiction, their insight into the potential problem of tract developments is still important.

The real question is whether an area is being renewed through housing turnover or not. Every house will eventually pass to a new owner, whether due to voluntary sale, abandonment, or even the death of the previous owner. An area can remain vibrant if these transitions are accompanied by maintenance and renovation of the existing stock. When is this likely to occur? The basic economic model of household lifetime income shows us that incomes increase during one's working life. Thus, you are likely to want to "trade up" for a better house as your income increases, or as your family grows and changes. To whom will you sell your house? One answer is to someone your own age with the income to purchase that house. This is likely to lead to a gradual reduction in the average income of the neighborhood, although I do not necessarily consider that a fault. A second answer is a younger version of yourself. In that case, the neighborhood is likely to retain its original character. Regardless of who the home is sold to, the key question is whether it will be maintained by the homeowner. This will be a decision that is made repeatedly by a myriad of individuals, so it is a natural point for us to consider the way that individuals make these decisions.

The Role of People: Passive Inhabitant versus Active Participant

> City planners are geared to providing new opportunities, but usually those that *they* find desirable, and without concern about how other people feel. Often, they deny that people have aspirations, arguing that they do not know what they want, and will therefore be receptive to whatever the planner considers superior.
>
> Herbert Gans (1967, 291)

Economists view people as active participants in decisions about work, housing, and public services. Planners tend to view people as passive inhabitants of an area, using whatever residential, commercial, and recreational possibilities are provided. This contrast is the underlying reason that the professions tend to have different attitudes toward sprawl – benign neglect tinged with concern for externalities by economists, concern leading to wholesale design pronouncements by planners.

The contrast between people as active participants and passive inhabitants is fundamental to the design of policy. Crusading policy assumes that people will follow orders and stay in place, whereas persuading policy recognizes that people have goals of their own and seeks to channel that energy.

Public policy is especially difficult in urban settings because of the weight of past decisions in shaping both the built environment and the culture. To understand why this matters, we must take a brief tour of modern investment theory. (A thorough, albeit technical, introduction to this topic is found in Dixit and Pindyck 1994.) Any activity that involves immediate costs in the expectation of future benefits can be classified as an investment. Examples include skipping dessert today in the hope of staying healthy next year, attending college to earn a higher salary in the future, or moving to a house in a better school district so that your children have an opportunity for a superior education.

Investment decisions have three common elements. First, there is some irreversibility to them. If you move to a school district for your daughter's first-grade year, and the year is a disappointment, you can't relive the year in a different school. Second, there is control over the timing of the investment. You don't have to make the decision to move now or forever stay in one place, because if you decide not to move now you can revisit the decision next year. Third, there is ongoing uncertainty. Even if your daughter had a good first-grade experience, you are still left with the question of how second grade will work out.

These three factors combine to imply that people should be wary when making investment decisions. If one could costlessly reverse an investment decision, one would be more willing to take a chance. If one had to make decisions that could not be delayed, then one might be inclined to act in cases where waiting for more information might be preferable. And if there came a time when all uncertainty was resolved, then one could make a decision in the certainty that the benefits would outweigh the costs.

Given these conditions, a person will wait to make an investment decision until the expected net benefits exceed the irreversible costs by an amount great enough to account for the possibility of future decreases in net benefits. Why invest at all? Because the longer you wait, the more net benefits you give up. At some point, it becomes worthwhile to make the move. But there can be a considerable period of "optimal inertia," where it would make sense to invest in the absence of irreversibility and uncertainty but it would not make sense in the presence of irreversibility and uncertainty.

The school example we have been returning to makes this point clear. Unless you are reasonably certain that the new school will be substantially better, you will be unwilling to incur the irreversible financial and other costs involved in relocating. But every year that you wait is a lost year for your daughter to benefit from the better educational opportunity. And once you decide to move, a small improvement in the school you moved from will be insufficient to induce you to move back. Rather, only a drastic improvement will change your mind.

Although the theory of investment under uncertainty has only been formally developed over the past thirty years, observers of cities understood its implications before then. A historian, Shigeto Tsuru (1963, 53), provided the following statement about investment and urban structure, which is still timely more than forty years after it was first published. "When a structure which contributes to external economies of a city is by nature lumpy and is at the same time durable for good reason, the marginal type of adjustment to a new situation, characteristic of a large part of rational economic action, has to be ruled out. Once a structure is built and completed, we will have to put up with it for some time even when we find that it stands in the way of something newer and better."

This principle of optimal inertia helps us to understand the difficulty with crusading policy in a different way. In order for people to undertake major investments (e.g., moving to an urban neighborhood or changing their commute from car to streetcar), they must be convinced that the new situation will be substantially better than their current one. Crusading policy tries to move a rock from one side of a mountain range to the other by going directly over the mountain, whereas persuading policy is content to follow the pass between the mountains. Even if the ultimate goal is the same, the persuading approach is more likely to be successful, and almost certain to be more efficient.

ENTREPRENEURSHIP IN METROPOLITAN AREAS

The city is a complex organism, never entirely comfortable, always a place with its dark corners and suffering. But it is precisely that edge of danger and instability that makes the city such an extraordinarily powerful force. In the final analysis it is in its role as an engine for change that the city is at its most alive.

Deyan Sudjik (1992, 31)

Joseph Schumpeter (1950, 132) describes entrepreneurs as people who "reform or revolutionize the pattern of production by exploiting an invention." The key to entrepreneurship is in developing or applying ideas that are not foreseen by others. These new developments are the way that a capitalist market economy develops and evolves. Why then is it so difficult when planning urban areas to leave room for the unexpected? When I was born in 1964, no one outside of Arkansas had heard of Wal-Mart or its founder, Sam Walton. Now his legacy "doth bestride this narrow world like a colossus, and we petty men walk under his huge legs" or at least up and down the aisles of the store.

It is not possible for us to foresee the ideas that people will create. Because urban structure is a complicated result of the effects of these ideas, it is important to be able to efficiently incorporate them into the existing structure. The challenge is how to create a structure that is able to change in unforeseen ways. This is vital because metropolitan areas are always "losing" jobs, so that the difference between growth and decline is the relative success in encouraging entrepreneurial job creation. One study of thirty-four metropolitan areas (Eberts and Stone 1992) found that the average job loss from closings and contractions over a three-year period was 20.5 percent, with a minimum of 13.3 percent. Even the metropolitan area with the largest gain in net employment, San Diego, lost 20.9 percent of the jobs that existed at the beginning of the study period. Trying to improve the economic health of a region without focusing on entrepreneurship is impossible.

The fragmentation decried by policy proponents such as David Rusk and Myron Orfield can be a double-edged sword. On the one hand, it creates the possibility of flexible systems of adaptation to local conditions. On the other hand, it can become a source of rigidities if residents and officials are unwilling to adapt to changes in conditions.

The challenge of adaptability can be addressed in (at least) two ways. The first approach is to resist the urge to overdefine the present. For example, one can limit harmful outcomes directly by addressing the outcome rather than by minutely specifying the exact nature of the land use throughout a region. If new harmful outcomes are discovered or if new technologies reduce existing harmful outcomes, then one does not have to completely rethink land-use controls, a lengthy and politically contentious process.

The second approach is to create a process that encourages flexibility. This is politically daunting because of the urge of people to conserve what it is about a place that attracted them, even if it is possible that a change would be an improvement. William Fischel (2001) provides a book-length analysis of both the inclination of "homevoters" to be averse to risks and the consequences that result. This conservative principle can be useful in curbing the worst abuses of criminals and the not-completely thought-through ideas of entrepreneurs, but it can also be the enemy of community advance.

Paul Bairoch (1988) ascribes the advent of the Industrial Revolution in smaller towns in England (not the most urban of European countries at the time) to the unwillingness of entrenched interests in the more developed areas to accommodate these new ways of doing business. While in the short run this approach made sense, at least to the entrenched interests, in the long run it led to leading cities becoming mere afterthoughts in a new economy. The current political leaders of cities will profit by encouraging their citizens to learn from the example of Norwich (the second city in England at the time of Shakespeare, left behind in the Industrial Revolution) that one cannot legislate away the future. The example of Bristol, which was a leading city during the time of Shakespeare and enjoyed further growth and success during the Industrial Revolution, indicates that success in one period does not prohibit success in the future. Closer to home, Boston has continually reinvented itself over the past few centuries as technology and society have evolved. The most important factor, according to analysis by Edward Glaeser (2005), is the large and diverse pool of skilled workers in Boston. They create an environment that can adapt readily to the decline of some industries and the rise of others as technology and markets evolve.

THE PRESENT AS A WEIGHTED AVERAGE OF THE PAST

> City planners quite understandably find more satisfaction in building than in preserving. Even if the city architect is a man of genius, it is to be expected that he will deem nothing that already exists to be as good as what he would build if only he were allowed.
>
> Wolf Schneider (1963, 361)

The built environment at the end of a year is almost identical to the built environment at the beginning of the year. We live in a world that is continually, but slowly, changing. A small change every year, though, will eventually generate a large change. Much of the public response to sprawl has been due to enough small changes occurring for everyone to realize that we are not building cities the way that we used to.

How much of today's environment is a relic of a past set of circumstances? In most cases, it is difficult to obtain data to answer that question. However, a provocative book by Robert Lang (2003) includes data that allow some insight. Lang's book focuses on what he terms "edgeless cities" to distinguish them from the edge cities made famous by Joel Garreau in the book of the same name. He emphasizes that metropolitan areas can no longer be characterized simply as one or a few employment centers, because decentralized employment dominates many cities. This theme is already familiar to the reader of this book, as I introduced it in Chapter 1. The important thing that Lang does is collect data on the location and construction date of office space in thirteen metropolitan areas (Atlanta, Boston, Chicago, Dallas, Denver, Detroit, Houston, Los Angeles, Miami, New York, Philadelphia, San Francisco, and Washington, DC). This gives us a window into how quickly urban areas are changing compared to each other, as well as how fast the central cities are changing relative to the suburbs.

In the median metropolitan area studied by Lang, 23.9 percent of the office space was constructed before 1980, 53.6 percent was constructed between 1980 and 1989, and the remaining 23.1 percent was constructed between 1990 and 1999. There is considerable variation around these central tendencies. For example, the metropolitan areas with the highest fraction of recent construction are Detroit (30.2 percent) and Atlanta (29.9 percent), while those with the smallest fraction are New York (12.3 percent) and San Francisco (12.1 percent).

If we take the median of the metropolitan areas and simulate the growth rates that would have yielded the percentage of space built at different times, then we can see the difference between the 1980s and 1990s quite clearly. The median metropolitan area had about 160 million square feet of office space by 1999. As noted previously, the new construction is skewed heavily toward the 1980s. This would imply an average annual growth rate (assuming that there is no demolition of existing space) of 12.5 percent during the 1980s in contrast to the 2.6 percent in the 1990s. The average for the entire period of about 7.4 percent thus includes two very distinct eras. Although the precise figures vary from city to city, the overall pattern remains the same.

Neither Lang nor other observers cite the 1980s as the main period of divergence between central cities and suburbs, so more analysis is clearly needed to understand this pattern. People who remember the time know that tax and regulatory changes in the late 1970s and early 1980s conspired to inspire substantial overbuilding of commercial property. This in turn led to the savings and loan crisis of the late 1980s and early 1990s.

Despite Lang's recognition in the book that cities are dynamic places, his definitions of places are all static and he doesn't really consider transitions from one type of place to another. This is a common failing in the literature, as we will see in the next chapter when we consider various measures of the extent of urban sprawl.

The correlation between the growth rate in office space for the central city and the growth rate for the suburbs is 0.7 in the thirteen metropolitan areas studied by Lang. The suburban growth rate is larger in every case. In other words, the growth rate of the central city and suburb are closely related, supporting the idea of an integrated metropolitan economy. Given the historic pattern of development, it is unsurprising that the central city growth rates are lower, as there is a larger base of already-constructed space.

What is most remarkable is that more than two-thirds of the office space available in 1999 already existed in 1990, whether the metropolitan area is rapidly growing or slowly growing, Sun Belt or Rust Belt, geographically constrained or open to expansion. An ambitious plan to reshape a metropolitan area in a decade needs to take into account that the vast majority of the shape of the metropolitan area will not change in a decade.

UTOPIAN METROPOLITAN STRUCTURE

It is futile to plan a city's appearance, or speculate on how to endow it
with a pleasing appearance of order, without knowing what sort of innate,
functioning order it has.

Jane Jacobs (1961, 14)

The built environment of the past continues to exist into the present,
making urban areas anachronisms even in their own time. The past plays
an even stronger role, though, in the legal environment and culture of
a region. Because the past is different for each state, and often for each
metropolitan area in a state, the present that exists is different for each
state. Because the present is tomorrow's past, these differences will continue to accumulate into the future. It is naïve to expect a common template to be appropriate for planning these different futures.

One of the interesting features of most utopian urban plans is how
divorced from space *and time* they are. They will typically depict a stylized
city, one that seems to have no particular existence and no history, rather
than engaging in the more difficult reality that there is not a *tabula rasa*,
but rather an evolutionary opportunity. With plans, it's often not only a
matter of "you can't get there from here," but also "you aren't starting
from where you think you are."

Much of twentieth-century metropolitan development can be thought
of as achieving the goal of Ebenezer Howard (1902) to create a "garden
city." Howard's concern was the extraordinary growth of the large cities
of the late nineteenth century, and he proposed the garden city concept as
a way of encouraging people to stay out of the large cities.

Howard proposed a city with a maximum population of 32,000, occu-
pying 6,000 acres of land (with 5,000 acres reserved for agriculture).
The city was to be roughly self-sufficient, not only in agriculture and
industry, but also in culture, with each city including a museum, parks,
library, and school. He proposed linking the various garden cities within a
metropolitan area using an interurban railway. However, it is not obvious
to me what the reason for this is. If people are neither commuting nor
buying and selling from other cities, then what purpose does the railway
serve?

The urban structure we see now can be thought of as an implementation
of Howard's plan, albeit with some important changes. For example, the
highway has replaced the railway. The garden cities are not self-sufficient;
rather they interact on a regular basis with the remainder of the metropolitan area. This is consistent with Howard's linkages, and also consistent
with an economic justification for those linkages. There is a combination
of specialization in employment centers and diffuse employment throughout the region. Howard's population density of thirty-two people per

urban acre is higher than the typical gross densities of a relatively densely populated suburb by a factor of about four (20,480 people per square mile versus 5,000 to 6,000 people per square mile).

The metropolitan area that has most explicitly followed the idea of the garden city has been Phoenix, Arizona. In its 1985 General Plan, the city bases its future growth around several "urban villages," which are patterned on Howard's garden cities. The plan states "Each [urban village] would become relatively self-sufficient in providing living, working, and recreational opportunities for residents" (Leinberger and Lockwood 1986, 52). As with Howard, this idea conflicts with the economic justification of metropolitan growth, which is to provide opportunities for mutually beneficial trade among the residents of a metropolitan area. Hence, any attempt to actually implement a consistent urban village or garden-city planning structure is doomed to fail. It will either be inefficient if it succeeds at creating self-sufficiency, or it will be an inefficient way of promoting the interactions among specialized parts of the metropolitan area that are the basis of the twenty-first-century metropolitan economy.

One response is that stricter controls on development and greater emphasis on mass transit and walking could create the sort of jobs-housing balance that planners beginning with Howard and continuing to the present have desired. However, the difficulty in doing so is not restricted to the United States. Even in planned suburbs built in Sweden in the 1950s that were designed to have about half of their residents working locally, there was considerable cross-commuting (Hall 1998, 867). It is unlikely that the United States in the twenty-first century will be as amenable to central planning and mass transit as Sweden was in the mid-twentieth century.

Utopia is a moving target. Just as the actual structure of urban areas evolves, the vision of the ideal urban structure evolves. What is most interesting is that the ideal city of one time is often a reaction to the existing city, which in turn is the realized version of an earlier ideal. The cul-de-sacs and bypasses extolled in the 1940s in reaction to the street grids of the 1920s have in their turn inspired an ideal of connectivity. Earlier in this chapter, we saw how the ideas of 1941 seemed strangely inappropriate in a new century that has seen many of those ideas implemented.

In his novel *Looking Backward*, Edward Bellamy described the perfect world that the United States had become by 2000. He did so, though, from the vantage point of 1887, during the prime of the monocentric city. All retail activity has been moved from the inefficient small shops with their variety of merchandise to a centralized store that sells the same items in every neighborhood in the country. In fact, customers don't even carry their purchases home from the store, but order them for speedy home delivery. Yes, the perfect world envisioned in the late nineteenth century included Wal-Mart and the Internet, albeit only imperfectly described.

Today, of course, there is a backlash against such centralization, at least when it comes to approving zoning changes for superstores.

The utopian vision (or visions) of today no doubt contain the seeds of the actual world of tomorrow. In addition, there are probably hidden drawbacks to those visions that will only become clear once they are implemented. This conclusion provides all the more reason, then, to value the opportunity to modify and refine a situation when circumstances have changed.

3 ARE WE THERE YET?

T HE FOUR-MILE JOURNEY FROM ATHENS TO PIRAEUS WAS AN ALL-
day affair in 400 BC (Hall 1998, 38) The radius for a one-day activity these days is closer to 100 miles. Thus, a metropolitan area effectively encompasses 625 times the area of classical Athens. The population
of "greater Athens" in those days was about 200,000 to 300,000. Our
largest metropolitan areas are about 100 times as populated, illustrating
both that density has decreased and that this day's journey rule of thumb
is reasonable. Interestingly, the word *metropolis*, literally "mother city,"
originally referred to the city that was the founder of a colony. Just as
the colonies of Ancient Greece had an independent life but also an ongoing relationship with their mother city, the trading places of the modern
metropolitan area have a special relationship with the central city, albeit
one that does not preclude their own sphere of independence.

To the Greeks, the ideal polis was self-sufficient. How, then, does one
reconcile the current structure of trading places with an earlier autarkic
archetype? Again, by reference to scale. The suburb of the twenty-first
century includes a land area and population similar to that of a classical
Greek polis. But the suburb does not encompass the entire world to its
inhabitant in the way the polis did. On the other hand, the collection
of trading places in a region does constitute the relevant world for most
people. In fact, for most people only a small fraction of all the trading
places are prominent in their mental maps. Thus, one way to describe
a metropolitan area is that it encompasses an area that is self-sufficient
from an individual's point of view. In other words, it has most of the
things that a person wants within its boundaries. This does not preclude
obtaining goods and services elsewhere, any more than the Greek ideal
did. Pericles boasts in his funeral oration (Cahill 2003, 41), "the City
[Athens] is so large and powerful that all the wealth of the world flows
into her, so that our own Attic products seem no more familiar to us
than the fruits of the labors of other nations." Emphasizing metropolitan
self-sufficiency recognizes the relatively limited horizons people possess.

Although driving has replaced walking, increasing the amount of space that we can cover quickly, our mental world remains limited by travel time.

Pursuing these thoughts even further, consider the American way of shopping. No longer do people haggle in a marketplace. But people continue to comparison shop, only now by going from store to store. Again, we are using space in a different way, but the relative amount of time is about the same. The dense market has sprawled and metastasized, and instead of threatening to walk away during a heated negotiating session, we merely continue browsing or get back in the car.

The development of urban structure, then, can be viewed as a progression of autarkies. The difference between the twenty-first-century AD household and the fifth-century BC household is the scope and scale of goods available within a day's journey. The true measure of the revolution in transportation is that people are unaware of how far products have traveled. From an individual's point of view, products might as well have spontaneously generated in the local supermarket or mall. The political challenge is how to engage that person to control and encourage the infrastructure that enables the retail revolution to occur. Without large parcels of land on which to build, current retail practices that emphasize truckload deliveries are impossible. To maintain local autarky, there must be sufficient convenient transportation (read *roads* and *parking*) for the residents of the polis to come to market.

The evolving metropolitan structure thus involves changes not only in the way that people travel, but also a change in the fundamental organization of business. Thus, any attempt to control urban structure has to address these fundamental organizational questions or else it is fated for failure or irrelevance. It is not enough to focus on one dimension, such as the means of commuting, when the nature and location of the jobs to which people are commuting is changing. It is certainly a mistake to emphasize a metropolitan shape that doesn't conform to the mental maps that most people carry. For the resident of the twenty-first-century metropolitan area, the world consists of parking lots connected by roads, not markets connected by walking paths (classical Athens) or CBDs connected by mass transit (nineteenth- and twentieth-century cities).

EVOLVING METROPOLITAN STRUCTURE

Before Copernicus, the dominant view of the solar system was that the sun and the other planets orbited the earth. Increasingly ingenious explanations were invented to justify this theoretical construct in the face of anomalous empirical observations. Finally, Copernicus demonstrated that there was a more sensible way of understanding the world.

A fundamental misunderstanding of how metropolitan areas work has hampered the current debate on the causes and consequences of urban sprawl. This misunderstanding is analogous to the pre-Copernican fallacy that the earth is the center of the universe, and everything else revolves around the earth. In the discussion of urban sprawl, the downtown or central city takes the place of the earth in the Ptolemaic cosmology, and the rest of the metropolitan area is defined only in relation to the downtown.

It is possible for the basic structure of a metropolitan area to change over time. Such a change has been occurring in U.S. metropolitan areas for the last 100 years, and the change is coming to fruition at the beginning of a new century. To plan for future urban growth, it is vital to recast our understanding of how our urban areas operate. It is time for a Copernican revolution that puts the downtown and the central city in their appropriate place – not unique and solitary, but rather one important part of a system.

Metropolitan structure over the last 150 years has changed in ways that can be summarized in two words: *decentralization* and *specialization*. (Yes, there has been declining urban density since about 1850. The patterns observed in the second half of the twentieth century are continuations of ongoing trends, not dramatic breaks with the past.) The monocentric city of the late 1800s and early 1900s exemplified these two words. Unlike in previous urban structures, residences were separated from businesses by the newly acquired ability of workers to live a streetcar ride away from the CBD. Thus, the boundaries of the city expanded, and the parts of the city became specialized. The downtown or CBD was the place where industrial, commercial, and retail activity occurred, while the residential areas were almost exclusively devoted to housing.

Mass transit was not invented until the 1800s. According to urban economic historian Paul Bairoch (1988, 428), the first omnibus was instituted in Nantes to bring people to a hot bath warmed by excess steam power produced by a mill. This beginning as an adjunct to private enterprise continued throughout the period during which mass transit flourished.

Real-estate developments in the early twentieth century were often initiated by a person who controlled a streetcar line. The houses, by increasing the traffic on the line, increased in value, while the direct access to the workplace provided by the streetcar made the houses more valuable. Even the famous Red Car trains of Los Angeles were not profitable in their own right, but were supported by the land development operations of their owners.

By helping people move beyond walking distance of commercial and industrial activity, the streetcar was a tool of specialization. By moving people from downtown hyperdense housing to the more-spread-out suburbs, they were a tool of decentralization. The communities built by such luminaries as J. C. Nichols in Kansas City and the van Sweringens in Shaker Heights, Ohio, were the urban sprawl of their day, greatly expanding the scale of the city while instituting new policies such as deed restrictions that are still controversial today.

Explosive urban growth is not unique to the period after World War II. The Industrial Revolution enabled cities to grow beyond previous limits by providing rapid transportation and abundant food. New locations could change from wilderness to metropolis if the transport network and their industrial mix permitted. Consider the two homes of the National Basketball Association's Lakers franchise, Minneapolis and Los Angeles. Both grew from fewer than 2,000 people in 1850 to more than 300,000 in 1910.

The widespread adoption of the truck in the 1920s allowed businesses to move away from the railheads and docks of the CBD. Beginning with manufacturing businesses, which desired the lower land prices and fewer neighbors afforded by a more rural setting, firms that could do so fled the city. Automobiles allowed residential decentralization throughout the metropolitan area, continuing the trend that had begun along streetcar lines in the late 1800s. Because the developments were no longer tied to streetcar lines, one impact of automobiles has been to increase the density of development in areas unserved by transit.

The Great Depression and then World War II imposed a two-decade delay on the full realization of the world of the car and truck. However, the twin themes of decentralization and specialization continued in full force throughout the second half of the twentieth century.

The result was something new in the world. Here is how two historians of European cities described the outcome (Hohenberg and Lees 1985, 197–8): "Growth was rapid, unplanned, and largely unregulated. Calculation was applied only to the logistics of transporting bulky products. Otherwise, the settlements had little form, less amenity, and no systematic relationship to one another. As they spread, devouring the countryside and its central places, they gradually merged into an entirely new type of major urban concentration. This bore no name and appeared hard put to find one."

This description, while familiar, is incomplete. As we will continue to see, there was a system, but it was one that emerged at a different scale and through a different process than in the past. Instead of walking scale around the downtown or transit stops, now the components of the metropolitan area covered large areas. The metropolitan area expanded to an extent impossible in the past.

THEORIES OF METROPOLITAN STRUCTURE

It is not my intent to provide encyclopedic coverage of every theory of urban structure. But because these theories undergird so much of the ongoing popular discussion, it is important to introduce some of them. We'll begin with the most prominent theory, the monocentric city model; move quickly through the polycentric city and central place theory; and then be in a position to introduce the fundamentals of trade as a prologue to the full exploration of trading places in the following chapter. Trading place analysis includes these previous approaches, so that it provides an overarching context for them rather than replacing them with something completely new. Because of the considerable empirical support for the previous approaches, this is prudent. It is also appropriate in a scientific sense, as good theories should incorporate the insights of previous work while adding new ideas that can explain more phenomena.

Monocentric City

Those who owned, managed, and financed the industrial and warehouse districts did much of their work in the downtown office buildings, but they too moved their homes away from [the] city center during this same post-fire period. The higher the downtown became, the greater the horizontal spread of the residential neighborhoods that housed its daytime inhabitants: skyscraper and suburb created each other. The process was aided by the same transportation technology that had given the city its hinterland. Middle- and upper-class Chicagoans who could afford to do so turned to the rail-road as an ideal way of removing their residences from the crowds, noise, and pollution of the downtown and factory areas. The result was Chicago's extraordinary suburban growth in the decades following the fire. "Chicago, for its size," declared the *Chicago Times* with the usual local jingoism in 1873, "is more given to suburbs than any other city in the world. In fact, it is doubtful if any city, of any size, can boast of an equal number of suburban appendages."

William Cronon (1991, 347)

The monocentric city model, in various guises, is the underlying rhetorical framework for urban policy discussions everywhere. Whenever one hears about the urban core or the suburban fringe, the speaker is implicitly relying on a monocentric view of the world.

The model is relatively simple but has proved to be incredibly adaptable. The key assumptions are that all employment is located downtown, in the CBD, and that households travel to work in the CBD from their homes. This pattern of business location is typically justified by the presence of a transport node, such as a port or railroad station, in the CBD. Firms value proximity to the transport node, and people value proximity to their jobs. Thus, the value of land depends on proximity to the CBD, with land values declining as one moves farther away. This negative relation between land value and distance to the CBD is known as the rent gradient, and it is one of the most often investigated concepts in urban economics.

Usually, the model is constructed so that firms outbid households for land in the CBD. In that case, we are left with the classic monocentric model, with an urban core (CBD and surrounding employment area) and suburban fringe (the rest of the metropolitan area, consisting only of residences). More complicated versions of the model include multiple business and residential land uses, so that both the CBD and the suburbs are divided into various specialized regions.

How quickly does land value decline with distance from the CBD? It depends on the cost of transport and on the ability of people and firms to substitute capital for land. In plain English, substituting capital for land means building taller buildings. In the extreme case, we have skyscrapers of thirty stories or more. So not only does land value decline with distance from the CBD, but so too does the capital-land ratio and the density of development.

The skyscraper and the specialized (in nonresidential activities) CBD were the result of a related set of technological advances. Steel-frame construction made it possible to build tall buildings. Electricity made it possible to provide light in the interior parts of the building. The elevator facilitated transportation within the building, while the telephone connected people on different floors as well as in different buildings. Finally, the streetcar brought thousands of people quickly from scattered suburban residences to the concentrated work sites.

The skyscraper represented an unprecedented concentration of capital and labor on a piece of land. This raised the value of land in the CBD, to the point that relatively unintensive uses of land were not economically feasible. Because no change can happen overnight, there was not an immediate transformation to a city of high-rise buildings, but the trend was clear. The disparity between rapid interurban transport by train and the congestion-prone intraurban transport, particularly for freight, reinforced the extreme value to firms of being downtown.

The confluence of factors that made the monocentric city the template for U.S. cities was powerful but short-lived. The heyday of the monocentric city was about 1890 to 1930. Perhaps the climax of the monocentric city was the competition between the Chrysler Building and the Empire State Building in the late 1920s to be the tallest skyscraper. Unfortunately, the incipient changes in urban structure combined with the onset of the Great Depression left the Empire State Building less than fully occupied, which changed its symbolism from triumph to futility.

Ironically, the analytical tool describing monocentric cities was not fully developed until after metropolitan structure had ceased to be monocentric. The monocentric city model is generally attributed to William Alonso, Richard Muth, and Edwin Mills, who developed it in a series of articles and books during the 1960s. By then, geographers such as Jean Gottman had already identified metropolitan structure as "nebulous" and dispersed rather than centered on the CBD.

Despite this empirical flaw, the monocentric city model has long flourished because there is no competing analytical framework that is both elegant and plausible. Worse, though, the model has been misinterpreted as inconsistent with the trading place world of today. As we will see in Chapter 4, the monocentric city model remains a powerful tool for understanding what is happening near trading places. Put simply, it is a terrible global description of metropolitan structure, but a terrific local description.

The monocentric city was both created and rendered obsolete by technological change. As long as bulky freight traffic required either railroad or water transport, manufacturing firms needed to be located near train stations or ports to obtain raw materials and distribute finished goods. The invention of the truck facilitated the exodus of industrial firms. Given their desire for land to create a horizontal assembly line and to provide insulation for their negative externality-producing activities, this exodus came quickly. The development of the automobile made it possible for their workers to follow them beyond the service area of streetcars. The telephone, which had already helped workers scattered throughout the CBD to speak with each other, proved itself adaptable over even longer distances.

Polycentric City

> Today what we have seen in Megalopolis can hardly be fitted into any of the orderly patterns elaborated by theoreticians. There is too much flow, flux, and constant change within the region. There are too many relationships that link any given community or area of some size to several other areas, cities, and hubs. Perhaps the best comparison of its structure, at a time when astronomical comparisons are in fashion, would be with the structure of a nebula. The expression "nebulous structure" is apt to convey the confusion spreading before us in place of the more neatly organized systems to which we were accustomed in the past. Some central cities are rapidly losing their former "centrality" to become suburbs or satellites or in some ways dependencies of communities that do not seem to have either the size or the functions associated with the concept of "central place" and that are multiple instead of one!
>
> Jean Gottman (1961, 736)

An intermediate stage between the monocentric city and the trading place city is the polycentric city, literally a structure with more than one center. Gottman contrasts the solar system of the monocentric city with the nebula of the polycentric city. As we have already seen in Chapter 1, there are multiple centers of employment in modern metropolitan areas but these centers account for only about half of the total employment.

Employment centers are excoriated on the one hand as contributing to the decline of the CBD and praised on the other hand as islands of density in the sea of urban sprawl. Joel Garreau (1991) popularized them in the form of edge cities in the book of the same name. Although Garreau was concerned with only a subset of these centers, his phrase is often applied broadly to describe centers of economic activity outside the historic CBD.

One strength of the polycentric city model is that it allows scholars to recognize the changed reality of metropolitan structure without abandoning the analytical elegance of the monocentric city model. Rather than orient all of the space in the metropolitan area to the CBD, the metropolitan area is organized relative to a group of mini-CBDs. Each subcenter becomes a local peak in the rent gradient, density gradient, and capital-land ratio. Locations are defined by their distance to multiple centers, instead of only their distance to the CBD. These subcenters are usually at an advantageous transport location, whether near an airport or simply at the intersection of two major roads. The most familiar case is the subcenter that develops at the intersection of a circumferential highway (beltway) and a radial road from the CBD. I'll bet you can find one or more in your metropolitan area.

Dan McMillen and William Lester (2003) provide the most interesting study of subcenters to date. Rather than analyze a single point in time, they consider the evolution of subcenters in Chicago from 1970 to 2000. They find nine subcenters in 1970, increasing to thirteen in 1980, fifteen in 1990, and thirty-two in 2000. The subcenters are growing and their employment mix is changing. In particular, there has been a marked decrease in manufacturing employment in the subcenters, reflecting both the secular decline in manufacturing employment over this period and the ongoing decentralizion of manufacturing beyond the urban area.

Using employment projections for 2020, they also forecast the future evolution of these employment centers. Interestingly, they predict a decrease in the number of subcenters from thirty-two to twenty-four, but not because of a move back to the CBD. Instead, the number decreases because subcenters grow and merge, while others lose employment to the extent that they no longer qualify as centers.

Central Place Theory

Most maps emphasized the demography of human settlement more than anything else, the hierarchy of metropolis, town, and country. That hierarchy revealed itself on paper with place markers and typefaces of different sizes.... Villages, of which there were many, were marked with small dots and had one or two roads linking them to the surrounding countryside. Towns earned larger letters for their names and had one or two rail connections in addition to a few roads. Large cities, of which there were only a few, usually had access to water transport, several railroads, and many roads. And the great city – the metropolis, Chicago – in addition to its million or more inhabitants had railroads, highways, and watercourses that seemed to reach everywhere.

William Cronon (1991, 267)

There is a tradition in regional science that is older than either the monocentric city or polycentric city approaches. This analytical tradition focuses on the link between production and consumption, emphasizing that some goods and services are more amenable to widespread distribution from a central location while other goods and services are more amenable to local production and distribution. Not only does this approach have a long history, but it is also the fundamental building block for the most sophisticated mathematical analysis currently being applied to metropolitan structure. A book by Masahisa Fujita, Paul Krugman, and Anthony Venables (1999) is a quite accessible introduction to this research literature, as long as you are comfortable with microeconomic theory expressed in the form of differential equations.

The area over which a producer can successfully provide a product at the lowest price is called the *market area* for the product. If the product is either easily transported or produced with large fixed costs, the market area will be larger.

Central place theory links the idea of market area with a hierarchical approach to urban structure. The assumption is that large market area is related to large employment, so that larger cities will export to smaller cities. This will continue until one reaches rural areas, which export their products to provide the food that makes the large cities possible, closing the loop.

Changing labor productivity has weakened this relationship. For example, much manufacturing has moved to rural areas while continuing to serve an extended market area. The fundamental insight about the systematic variation that results from the link between production and consumption continues to be true, however.

SPECIALIZATION AND TRADE

If we are going to explore trading places systematically, we must begin by considering what conditions lead to trade and how to measure the extent of trade. Trade results when an economy produces more or less of a good or service than it wishes to consume. The economy exports the products in which local production exceeds local demand and imports the products in which local production falls short of local demand.

I have been deliberately vague about the area doing the trade. We are used to discussions about trade at the international level, that is, among countries. But there is trade at a variety of other levels as well. For example, metropolitan areas export and import goods and services. I wrote the first draft of this section while sitting near Fort Myers, Florida, in March. It was a lovely, sunny day and I went to the beach as a reward for my hard work. Back home in York, Pennsylvania, there was a snowstorm on that same day. On behalf of York, I imported the service of sunny days at the beach and Fort Myers exported that service. When a person from Fort Myers purchases a college education from York College of Pennsylvania, then York returns the favor.

Specialization is both a cause of trade and, as we shall see, a symptom of trade. Thus, we will begin our look at trade by first considering specialization. Interestingly, much of the measurement of trade is indirect, as the trade is difficult to observe. What is often measured is the degree of specialization rather than the actual extent of trade.

Why not just do everything for ourselves? Because it is more efficient to do only some things ourselves and to exchange the product of our labor for goods and services produced by others. There are cost advantages in concentrating production, which means that there is specialization.

The first type of cost advantage is *internal economies of scale*. This term describes a situation in which costs decrease when output is increased by a company in a location. Thus, the cost advantage is internal to the firm making the decision. Internal economies of scale can lead to trade among otherwise identical places because it makes sense only to incur any fixed costs of production once for each product rather than twice. Internal economies of scale are especially important in helping create employment centers within metropolitan areas. A firm that employs hundreds or even thousands of workers can be an anchor for a variety of related firms. All of those people have to eat lunch, for example. Internal economies of scale are at the heart of central place theory.

The second type of cost advantage is known, naturally, as *external economies of scale*. Urban economists also refer to these situations as *agglomeration economies of scale*, because the cost savings are the result of companies locating near each other. The link to urban structure, which emphasizes both density of activity and the relative locations of various activities, is immediate.

Agglomeration economies of scale are an example of an externality, and so they can lead to a situation where the outcome is inefficient. Because one firm does not necessarily take into account the cost savings it provides to other firms, it might choose an inefficient location. An empirical question, which we will return to in Chapter 4, is the extent of specialization in various parts of metropolitan areas. If there is considerable specialization, it suggests (but does not guarantee) that agglomeration economies of scale are present and that firms are taking advantage of them.

The theoretical work of Fujita et al. (1999), alluded to earlier, suggests that agglomeration is the appropriate configuration only for a limited range of transport costs. If transport costs are too high, then any production cost advantage is dissipated, so that diffused production is optimal. If transport costs are too low, then there is no benefit from proximity that offsets the congestion costs. Their model, similar to most that deal with complicated issues of location decisions by multiple firms, is extremely stylized. But the fundamental insight obtains even when the further complications of reality are allowed. We should be surprised not at the fragmentation of the CBD but rather that it came together in the first place. It was extremely naïve to expect a metropolitan area to go from a monocentric structure to a set of "mini-CBDs." Instead, we see agglomerations that form for specific purposes, while the revolution in transport costs resulting from the car and truck has allowed firms and households to move away from congestion.

The deagglomeration has not been uniform. Some types of work continue to require walkable centers, while others don't. Interestingly, retail agglomerations continue to evolve, with the high street, strip mall, regional mall, power center (big box), and now the life-style center co-existing.

The automobile and the truck make it possible to decentralize. This is both obvious and profound. It is obvious because the automobile, unlike the streetcar, subway, or railroad, is not tied to a specific right of way. Even the bus is tied to a route, which will tend to concentrate people both spatially and temporally. A private car, though, can travel whenever its owner desires wherever there is a road available. The truck frees businesses from rail depots and port facilities on rivers, lakes, and oceans. Now a business that deals in bulky materials or products is free to move away from the city if it wants to.

This is a profound change, though, because of the implications of cars and trucks for economies of scale. Critics of modern urban form often point out that cars take up considerably more space than their passengers would occupy if they filled a bus or streetcar. However, parking for cars can be provided at both relatively small scales and large scales, while stations for subways or streetcars require a certain minimum scale to be efficient. And if the subway is operating at only a fraction of capacity, then each passenger is actually using *more* space than an automobile driver. In the case of business, contrast a loading dock in a suburban plant with a cargo-handling facility at a port. Again, the truck frees business from the tyranny of economies of scale.

The freedom from transportation economies of scale makes it possible to decentralize. This decentralization, though, can reduce economies of scale that result from the proximity of economic activity. It is not clear to what extent the decentralization of firms and households has reduced the efficiency of metropolitan areas. After all, the quintessential illustration of agglomeration, Silicon Valley, occurred in the late twentieth century in an area served almost exclusively by private automobiles.

PATTERNS OF TRADE

The amount and pattern of trade depend on the relative production and consumption in each location. Fundamentally, trade requires that production cost advantages outweigh the costs of transporting the product from one place to the other. Note that the costs of transport can include not just the physical hauling of products, but also taxes, regulations, and other intangible costs. For example, a company from the United States that wants to sell products in Canada not only needs to get the product there, but it also needs to be sure that the label meets Canadian standards, including being written in French as well as English.

As transport costs decrease, the amount of trade in products that are already traded can increase. In addition, products that it was previously uneconomical to trade can become tradable. This, in turn, can lead to further specialization of both of the economies involved in the trade.

Measuring Specialization and Trade

The most straightforward approach to measuring trade is to observe the flows of goods and services from place to place. Unfortunately, this is very difficult to do within a metropolitan area. This difficulty arises for two reasons. The first reason it is difficult to observe trade is that there is no tariff (tax on imports) or other regulatory barrier to most forms of trade. Thus, there is no government that has a direct interest in collecting the information.

The second reason is that much of the trade is in services rather than manufactured products. When I drive to a restaurant, I am importing dining services to my home location. When I drive to my office, I am exporting labor services from my home location. But there is not a tangible product that one can observe crossing municipal boundaries. In Chapter 4, I will present a way to capture this information, at least for the case of commuting. For now, though, we must recognize that widespread direct measures of the extent of intrametropolitan trade are rare at best.

If we can observe the actual trade flow, it is helpful to characterize it concisely. One common way of characterizing the amount of trade is known as the *gravity model*. In this model, the volume of trade between two economies is proportional to the size of the economies and inversely proportional to the distance, time, and transport costs between them. The gravity model has been and continues to be a workhorse because it is flexible yet concise. I will use it in Chapter 4 to describe the pattern of intrametropolitan trade in labor services.

If direct measures are ruled out, then we are left with indirect measures of the extent and pattern of trade. This brings us back to using data on specialization in places to infer the pattern of trade.

The most commonly used indirect measure of trade is the location quotient (LQ). The LQ compares employment by sector (manufacturing, retail, etc.) within a subarea, such as a suburb, with employment by sector within a larger area, such as a metropolitan area. Algebraically, the LQ is given by the following formula:

Let: e_i = total workers in sector i in metropolitan area
e_j = total workers in suburb j
e_{ij} = workers in sector i in suburb j
e = total workers in metropolitan area

Then define the LQ as

$$LQ_{ij} = (e_{ij}/e_j)/(e_i/e)$$

An LQ less than 1 implies a lower concentration of sectoral employment in the suburb than in the metropolitan area. In this case, we infer that the suburb is an importer in the sector in question. Conversely, if the LQ is greater than 1, we infer that the suburb is an exporter.

Consider the following simple example. The suburb of JustDesserts employs a total of twenty-three people, all in the restaurant sector. The metropolitan area of BalancedDiet employs a total of 124 workers in the restaurant sector out of a total employment of 300. In this case, e_i = 124, e_j = 23, e_{ij} = 23, and e = 300. The LQ is therefore $(23/23)/(124/300)$, or 1.00/0.41, which equals 2.44. In this case, we would infer that Just-Desserts is an exporter of restaurant services to the rest of BalancedDiet.

The LQ makes a number of strong assumptions in order to be so compact. First, it assumes that the larger region (metropolitan area in the example) is self-contained, so that there are no imports to or exports from the metropolitan area. If the metropolitan area is a major exporter in a sector, then the sectoral percentage of employment will be relatively high (compared to other metropolitan areas). Thus, we might incorrectly infer that a suburb is an importer in that sector rather than an exporter because it has a small percentage of employment relative to the metropolitan area, even though it is large relative to the rest of the broader national economy. Second, it assumes that consumption in a location is proportional to employment. This is especially unsatisfying for within-metropolitan-area analysis, because of the widespread pattern of commuting from one suburb to another. Third, it assumes that all workers in all locations are equally productive. If there are agglomeration economies of scale, then we would expect workers in more specialized areas to be more productive. Thus, the LQ will tend to underestimate the extent of exports from those areas.

Despite all of these restrictions, the LQ is both familiar and useful. Similar to the gravity model, it is a workhorse of trade analysis, and it will once again prove its worth in the metropolitan context.

The discussion to this point has focused on the production side of exports. It could also be the case that people and regions differ systematically in their consumption. The next section introduces the main approach economists have used to study systematic consumption differences within metropolitan areas. However, we can speculate that the current structure of trading places might just be an intermediate step toward a fully integrated metropolitan economy. This would be an echo of an earlier type of metropolitan structure as the monocentric model implies complete lack of production specialization in the CBD. The future might be lack of production specialization throughout the metropolitan area, depending on whether the current agglomeration economies continue to persist. However, there will continue to be considerable consumption specialization, both across metropolitan areas in the form of local amenities, such as climate, and within metropolitan areas due to variations in local amenities, including the quality of local public services.

Specialization in Local Consumption Goods: The Tiebout Model

In order to think carefully about local amenities in a trading place world, it is helpful to refresh our mastery of some basic concepts. We can usefully think of the suburbs in a metropolitan area as *small open economies*, which is another way of saying that for economic purposes they are small countries. They are "open" because they import and export goods and services to other economies. They are "small" in the sense that their individual actions are unlikely to have a dramatic effect on the entire market for goods and services.

Countries import some goods and services, export some goods and services, and locally produce and consume some goods and services. The United States, for example, imports VCRs from other countries, exports corn to other countries, and consumes soft drinks that are produced within the United States. What are the analogous products for the suburban economy? The most common export is labor – people that live in a suburb and work in another suburb or downtown. A typical import is retail services from a regional shopping mall. (The shopping mall represents an export activity for the suburb in which it is located.) Important locally produced services include housing and local government services.

Just because every suburb produces housing and local government services does not mean that every suburb is identical. Quite the opposite, in fact: local government services and the quality and density of the local housing stock are among the primary ways that suburbs are distinguished from one another. The dominant approach among economists when it comes to analyzing suburbs focuses precisely on these differences. This approach is called the *Tiebout model*, after the economist who first proposed it in a 1956 journal article. This article has spawned an enormous amount of research literature, and I recommend that the interested reader look at the book by William Fischel (2001) for a modern interpretation and extension of Tiebout's work.

The Tiebout model assumes that people are free to choose the town in which they reside. Towns compete for residents by offering a bundle of public services financed by local taxes. Individuals then "vote with their feet" and choose the combination of taxes and public services that is most appealing to them. The conclusion of the model is that suburbs will tend to consist of people who have similar tastes for public services, and further that the system will be efficient in that the local taxes are essentially a price for local public services. This link between economic behavior (purchasing houses) and political outcomes (uniform demand for local public services) is important for understanding municipal decisions, and we will return to it in Chapters 6 and 8.

The Tiebout model has been the basis for most economic research focused on local governments for the past fifty years. There is considerable evidence that suburbs are relatively homogeneous. It is difficult to measure individual preferences for public goods, but we know that these preferences are correlated with other characteristics, such as age and income. Much of the literature has focused on measuring these other characteristics and examining whether suburbs in metropolitan areas with a more fragmented local government structure are more homogeneous.

The Tiebout process is only one reason that suburbs will tend toward homogeneity, in particular that they will attempt to exclude low-income households. In an academic article (Bogart 1993), I identified four reasons for exclusion: fiscal zoning (exclude households that pay less in taxes than they consume in public services), public goods (exclude households that increase the cost of producing public services), consumption (exclude households that generate negative externalities, especially in housing), and political economics (exclude households that are likely to have systematically different preferences for public services than the politically dominant residents). It is impossible to distinguish among these reasons based solely on the observation that certain types of households (typically low income) are being excluded.

An important assumption of the Tiebout model is that people are free to locate without worrying about their commute. This assumption of accessibility flies in the face of anecdotes about long drives and gridlock. However, the evidence is that commuting times have remained roughly constant or fallen slightly over the past few decades, with the commute in most metropolitan areas averaging about twenty-five minutes. Hence, the assumption that households are free to locate without regard to their workplace is consistent with the observed patterns of commuting. Bruce Hamilton (1989) points out that this empirical relation undermines the logic of the monocentric city model, in which households are assumed to trade off commuting time for land prices. If all parts of the metropolitan area are equally accessible for commuters, then commuting is not a sufficient explanation for intrametropolitan variation in land prices. Genevieve Giuliano and Kenneth Small (1993) find that commuting costs are not a major determinant of location in Los Angeles, and they use this finding to criticize both the monocentric city model and the emphasis on jobs-housing balance.

The primary implicit assumption driving a great deal of popular discussion of commuting is that people value proximity between their residence and workplace as measured by distance. If all parts of the metropolitan area are equally accessible, then this assumption is inappropriate for describing the world. In addition, because the important decision is about time rather than distance, a great deal of attention is focused on the wrong question. Because the issues related to urban sprawl are so fraught with controversy, it is doubly important not only to check the logic but also to note the facts.

The most important theoretical addition to the original Tiebout model was also provided by Bruce Hamilton (1975, 1976) who argued that communities could use zoning to ensure that people were unable to free ride and enjoy local public services. The most common local tax is the property tax, which varies according to the value of your house. So households have an incentive to own a below-average-market-value house in a town that supplies a high level of local public services. Fiscal zoning, in which towns set a minimum house value, solves this problem in an efficient way. The property tax is effectively transformed into a lump sum tax, and households sort themselves into homogeneous municipalities. While this is efficient, it is not necessarily equitable, as households that are unable to afford houses in municipalities with high-quality public services (read schools) are disadvantaged. It is illegal for towns to set a minimum house value, but the combination of zoning, subdivision regulations, and building codes can have much the same effect in practice.

There is considerable evidence that suburbs specialize in producing local government services for their residents. Because one facet of the local amenities is the restrictiveness of zoning, it is unsurprising that not every suburb will have extensive employment opportunities for its residents within its borders. Chapter 4 will present evidence on how much specialization exists in the production of traded goods, which indirectly indicates these differences in the nontraded local government activities.

Public services are referred to as *nontraded* because they are only available to the residents of the community. For example, only residents are allowed to send their children to the local public schools, and there are often restrictions on the use of public recreational facilities as well. On the other hand, *traded* goods and services are available to anyone within the metropolitan area. For example, a shopping mall provides retail services to households throughout the region, not just to people that live in the town where the mall is located. But a shopping mall can only be located in places where local zoning ordinances permit. Chapter 6 will look in more detail at the way that zoning influences the pattern of trade among the trading places that comprise a metropolitan area.

WHAT IS URBAN SPRAWL?

> It's a world of looping freeways and roads accompanied by a random placement of homes, shopping malls, and businesses. All visible sense of order and structure is lost.
>
> Alex Marshall (2000, 41–2)

The preceding quote is taken from a book called *How Cities Work*. Unfortunately, the author in this passage undermines my confidence that he actually understands how cities work because he doesn't see order or structure. The statement is not even made apologetically, as the author is merely expressing the widely held belief of many observers of U.S. metropolitan structure. I disagree with the description and will devote considerable time to explaining what the underlying order of the city is and how it can be altered through public and private actions. Let's begin, though, with a brief visit to the true world of chaos – the attempts to define and measure urban sprawl.

Scholarly Definitions

There has been no shortage of attempts to name and characterize the new metropolitan structure. Robert Lang (2003, 31) identifies forty-four different names in what he refers to as a "partial list," including his own contribution of "edgeless city." While "trading places" is not in the list, perhaps it will make the cut in some future edition. Don't worry, I'm not going to comment on forty-four different approaches. In fact, I'll stick to mentioning a few of the better ones published after Lang's book and discussing why they aren't completely satisfactory.

A recent survey of the academic literature by George Galster et al. (2001) found six different general approaches to defining urban sprawl, ranging from aesthetic judgment to source of externality. They argue that sprawl is not useful as a description unless it can be quantified in some way, and they propose the following definition (685): "Sprawl is a pattern of land use in an urbanized area that exhibits low levels of some combination of eight distinct dimensions: density, continuity, concentration, clustering, centrality, nuclearity, mixed uses, and proximity." Although the paper is interesting and I agree with the basic point regarding an objective definition of sprawl, this particular approach still seems incomplete. There is a clause that is implicit in the definition but omitted, namely "at a point in time." The definition proposed by Galster et al. is a static definition, which is inconsistent with the dynamic nature of urban structure and the ongoing evolution of metropolitan areas.

Edward Glaeser and Matthew Kahn (2004) emphasize the simultaneous development of metropolitan areas that are both decentralized and low density. They also document the extent to which these two dimensions are correlated. Population decentralization and employment decentralization are closely correlated. In general, though, they find that there is not a consistent correlation among various measures of sprawl. This calls into question the Galster et al. approach of combining several measures into a single index, as it is not clear that a single underlying concept is being measured.

Thomas Nechyba and Randall Walsh (2004) use a similar definition to Glaeser and Kahn, "the tendency towards lower city densities as city footprints expand." Their article finds that sprawl is beneficial overall, as it permits or reflects increased housing consumption at lower housing prices. There are efficiency and equity concerns, including congestion and pollution, loss of open-space amenities, and uneven public service provision. They also bemoan the lack of an economic model of urban areas that can properly incorporate these issues. I agree with them that a general framework is needed, but I disagree about its absence. That's what this book is about, after all.

Popular Definitions

Academics are not the only ones who have tried to corral the concept of sprawl. If anything, there are more efforts outside the scholarly literature than within it. For example, *USA Today* (El Nasser and Orenberg 2001) developed a simple sprawl index based on population density. They include two equally weighted criteria: the proportion of 1999 metropolitan population living in urbanized areas (with a population density of at least 1,000 people per square mile), and the change from 1990 to 1999 in the proportion of metropolitan population living in urbanized areas.

They analyze 271 metropolitan areas, and the index for each criterion is the rank, with more density giving a lower rank and thus less sprawl. This popular approach has the same underlying analytical framework and the same limitations as the various academic approaches outlined in this section. For example, a metropolitan area that declines in density from 1990 to 1999 is likely to conform to the definitions of sprawl used by Glaeser and Kahn or Nechyba and Walsh.

Because the concept of urban sprawl is often left undefined, it is possible that the term can be used in situations that don't justify it. This possibility is magnified when combined with the general ignorance about some of the technical terms bandied about by sprawl *cognoscenti*. A recurring theme in newspapers across the United States has the following generic form: "Urbanized Area Increases by Big Percentage While Population Increases by Small Percentage." The *New Orleans Times-Picayune* warned on September 21, 2003, that the population of St. Tammany Parish grew by 60 percent from 1982 to 2000 while the urban land area increased by 218 percent during the same time period. The *St. Louis Post-Dispatch* (February 9, 1997) provided similar statistics (17 percent increase in population since 1960, 125 percent increase in urbanized area) in a story headlined "Urban Sprawl Rots Cities."

It's not only newspapers that are emphasizing this type of result. For example, the Department of Housing and Urban Development found in a study published in 2000 that urban areas were growing at twice the rate of population between 1994 and 1997. David Rusk, former mayor of Albuquerque turned urban analyst, pioneered the use of this index in a 1997 study of 213 urbanized areas that found a 47 percent increase in population from 1960 to 1990 compared to a 107 percent increase in the land area.

The Rusk sprawl index, defined as the percentage change in urbanized land area divided by the percentage change in urbanized area population, is easy to calculate and seemingly straightforward to interpret. On its face, the index being greater than one seems to be clear evidence of declining population density, leapfrog development, transformation of rural to urban land – well, sprawl. What is omitted from the index is recognition that an increase in urbanized area does not necessarily indicate conversion of land from rural to urban use. Ironically, an increase in this sprawl index could result from smart-growth principles at work.

The U.S. Census Bureau defines an urbanized area as a central place of 50,000 along with contiguous census blocks with a minimum population density of 1,000 per square mile. (Note that 1,000 people per square mile is only 1.6 people per acre, which at an average household size of 2.6 is only about 0.6 households per acre, or one house for every 1.5 acres.) What the Rusk index overlooks is that the area newly classified as urban

might have already been occupied in prior years. If the smart-growth
principle of infill development is assiduously followed, it will result in an
increase in density, which in turn will cause some areas that previously
were below the census threshold to pass it.

Consider the following example. In time 0, the urbanized area includes
500 square miles with a total population of 1.5 million, or an average
density of 3,000 per square mile. This is a typical figure. In 2000, the
average density of urbanized areas was 2,670, down from 6,160 in 1920,
but an increase from its 1990 level of 2,589. By time 1, the urbanized
area has increased by 10 percent, to 550 square miles, while the population of the urbanized area has increased by only 3 1/3 percent, to
1.55 million. The metropolitan area thus has a sprawl index of 3, and
the readers of the local newspaper in time 1 can expect headlines. After
all, the urban population increase of 50,000 people consumed fifty square
miles, for an average density of only 1,000 people per square mile. (Compare this to the actual average density of 1,469 for areas built since
1969.)

Suppose, though, that the fifty square miles of the metropolitan area
that are newly "urbanized" had a population of 35,000 in time 0. The
average population density of 700 does not lead to its being classified
as urban, but it is hardly rural either. Our smart-growth public policy
is successful in maintaining the original density in the previously defined
urbanized area while channeling new growth (15,000 new residents) into
existing areas to create a critical mass. So what seems to be an obvious
instance of sprawl has turned into a more ambiguous situation.

The Rusk sprawl index illustrates again the overemphasis on a static
idea of a metropolitan area. Any statistical picture restricted to a single
point in time will neglect the past and the future of the region being
studied.

Sprawl from Space

Based on the examples and discussion in the preceding text, it seems
almost impossible to develop a satisfactory approach for looking at
metropolitan structure and characterizing the extent to which it is sprawl
or not. It seems as if one would need to compare detailed satellite imagery
for different times in order to understand how development patterns have
changed. Remarkable as it may sound, this is precisely the approach that
a group of researchers (Burchfield et al. 2005) has taken. Although their
research is new, the data on which it is based are from 1976 and 1992,
so the story they tell is a timely remedy to some popular misconceptions
about the late twentieth century.

They define *sprawl* as the percentage of undeveloped land in the square
kilometer surrounding the average residential development. Why a square

kilometer? Because only 0.3 percent of all development, and only 0.5 percent of recent development, is greater than 1 kilometer away from other development.

I want to highlight their finding that new development (constructed between 1976 and 1992) is *not* more sprawling than older development. However, the pattern of development is perfect for making it seem as if there is a dramatic change in sprawl. The typical development has about 50 percent open space in the surrounding square kilometer. The peak of development occurred where there was about 50 percent open space in the surrounding square kilometer. Many people were able to see the last half of their surrounding open space disappearing and (incorrectly) generalized from their individual situation to the overall situation.

Burchfield et al. directly analyze the dynamic nature of metropolitan areas, unlike almost every other study. Specifically, they find more sprawl connected with higher growth rates. As we discussed earlier, when conditions are more uncertain, then investors will tend to postpone investment. In this context, that means that developers will wait to develop land, because the rapid growth brings with it considerable uncertainty.

They also find that fragmentation of local government is not related to sprawl, unlike much of the conventional wisdom. They are not the first to point out the weak empirical base for this widespread belief. In a study cited earlier, Galster et al. (2001) use the extreme cases of Houston, Texas, and Lexington, Kentucky, to illustrate that unitary government over a large land area does not automatically lead to the type of development that anti-sprawl advocates desire. The decades-long development of the Irvine Company property in Orange County, California, provides a private-sector counterexample too.

One advantage of taking a satellite view is that it reminds us of the important role that nature plays in influencing the pattern of human development. The most significant determinant of sprawl in their analysis is the extent to which the terrain is rugged. Nature also interacts with public-service provision, as they find that places where water is easily obtained from wells sprawl more than places where it is not. If water must be delivered by a utility regulated by the state or local government, then development is more concentrated.

I would be remiss if I neglected to highlight a trading place aspect to their analysis. They find that the extent of decentralization depends on the sectors in which a city specializes. In other words, the pattern of trade influences the geographical nature of the trading places.

Although this new research is exciting, it is still only one study and its data-intensive approach is unlikely to replace the multiplicity of misleading sprawl indices. To repeat, the fundamental problem is that almost every measure of sprawl is static. Further, they are often inappropriate to apply broadly. Why not look for something more economically fundamental than arbitrary levels of conformity to a stylized pattern of land use? My argument is that trade patterns are more of an invariant across metropolitan areas than land use and more robust to metropolitan idiosyncrasies. Chapter 4 discusses some evidence on this issue.

Household Size and Population Density

One determinant of metropolitan structure that is overlooked in the popular discussion is the changing demographics of the United States. Some of the observed changes in population density can be explained by changes in household size rather than by changes in the density of housing units. In 1970, average household size was 3.11; whereas by 2000 average household size had declined to 2.59. Even if we had continued to build housing at the same density as in 1970, the change in household size implies a population density in 2000 that is only 83 percent of the 1970 figure.

The impact of changing household size can be most easily observed in older suburbs that were already built out several decades ago. For example, Royal Oak, Michigan, an affluent suburb of Detroit, went from a population of 85,499 in 1970 to 60,062 in 2000. Royal Oak did not lose population due to abandoned housing, as the number of housing units remained roughly constant. In fact, the municipality thrived during those three decades. To bring in the inevitable Cleveland example, the suburb of Shaker Heights was built out by 1970 and it remained an affluent and attractive location during the entire period. Shaker Heights had a population in 2000 of 29,405, almost exactly 80 percent of its 1970 population of 36,306. This change, similar to that of Royal Oak, parallels the decrease in household size.

Why are household sizes smaller? The answer lies at either end of the age spectrum. There are fewer babies per household on the one hand, and more independent senior citizens on the other. It's not clear that proponents of higher population density are advocating for a change in either one of these trends. Not all of the observed decrease in density is due to reduced household size, of course. However, the lack of public discussion of this factor in changing metropolitan structure further illustrates the way that the policy debate tends to focus on a static, rather than a dynamic, view of the urban area.

There is at least one study that attempts to decompose increases over time in the amount of urbanized area into changes in total population and changes in land use per capita. Leon Kolankiewicz and Roy Beck (2001) find that about half of the increase in urbanized area between 1970 and 1990 was due to the increase in total population, and the other half was due to an increase in the amount of land used per person. Interestingly, these results varied considerably from city to city, as some cities combined substantial population growth with changes in land use per capita, and other cities did not grow as rapidly. Consider that an urbanized area with a Rusk sprawl index of 1 will still increase in size by 10 percent if the population increases by 10 percent, and we immediately see why it is important to include demographic factors in our land-use analysis. Unfortunately, too few researchers and even fewer popular commentators are doing so.

SPRAWL AND THE URBAN FRINGE

We live in an urban world. An important phenomenon in that world is the transformation of land – sometimes gradual, sometimes sudden – from rural to urban uses. Defining the *urban fringe* is not easy, as it is an ill-defined concept and the fringe is always moving. For example, almost all of the urban land in the United States was urban fringe (or even more remote) as recently as 200 years ago. In fact, it is impossible to determine where the urban ends and the rural begins by visual inspection only. Consider the following point from Henry George (1880, 257), describing the effect of San Francisco on land values in remote Marin County in the 1800s. "But when we reach the limits of the growing city – the actual margin of building, which corresponds to the margin of cultivation in agriculture – we shall not find the land purchasable at its value for agricultural purposes, as it would be were rent determined simply by present requirements; but we shall find that for a long distance beyond the city, land bears a speculative value, based upon the belief that it will be required in the future for urban purposes, and that to reach the point at which land can be purchased at a price not based upon urban rent, we must go very far beyond the actual margin of urban use."

Once we identify the fringe, we are left with the question of who is helped or harmed, and how much, by the seemingly relentless advance of the city. It is easy for politicians to tell stories of rapacious land speculators destroying farmers' livelihoods, but thoughtful analysts have long known that the true picture is richer. In a book whose title is often cited by the opponents of sprawl, but whose lessons have not been learned by them, Jean Gottman (1961, 258–9) looks at the rural area surrounding urban concentrations as an intrinsic part of the metropolitan economy:

> Agriculture, by occupying more acres than do cities and suburbs, still dominates the landscape in large sectors of Megalopolis, but it is in constant retreat. On the fringe of advancing urbanization the farm has little survival power and ultimately gives way to more intensive uses of land. It is the main source of open space available for new housing, industry, highways, woods, and recreational areas. Compensating for the threat to its existence are the economic advantages of being close to a vigorous and expanding market. It is an odd yet logical coincidence that some of America's most efficient and prosperous farms are those about to be liquidated by the city. This threat of extinction has been cited as an agricultural problem, but actually the individual

farmer is enriched by the increased market price of his real estate. It is to the urbanized area that the threat is serious, because when existing open space between metropolitan complexes has once disappeared the present problems of congestion and communication will be compounded.

Not all of today's observers are as thoughtful as Gottman. However, when we look at data compiled by the U.S. Department of Agriculture (which certainly doesn't have a stake in promoting urban sprawl), the picture of urbanization destroying farming capacity is easily seen to be exaggerated. A recent edition of the annual *Natural Resources Inventory* (Natural Resources Conservation Service 2003) focuses on urbanization and development of rural land. Between 1982 and 2001, about 34 million acres (an area the size of Illinois) were converted to developed land. During that same period, the amount of prime farmland fell from 342 million acres to 330 million acres and the amount of cropland fell from 232 million acres to 209 million acres. Between 1997 and 2001, there were 9 million acres developed, 46 percent of which was converted from forest use.

Based on these data, it is clear that urbanization continues and that some of this development involves conversion of cropland. To some extent, it is a question of judgment whether or not the extent and quality of cropland are sufficient. Here is the judgment of a U.S. Department of Agriculture study (Vesterby and Krupa 2001, 22–3):

> Urbanization and the increase in rural residences do not threaten the U.S. cropland base or the level of agricultural production at present or in the near term. Urbanization rates of increase are relatively small and other land (such as forest, pasture, and range) can be shifted into crop production. Also, crop yields per acre continue to increase due to advances in technology. For these reasons, the U.S. cropland base should be sufficient to meet food and fiber demands (both domestic and foreign) for the foreseeable future.

There is an important economic aspect to the ongoing development of previously rural areas. The transition from agricultural to urban uses of land represents a change in the export activity of the trading place. With standard zoning, we have replaced one monoculture (e.g., corn cultivation) with another (e.g., a residential subdivision). This not only affects the use of the land, but the people, firms, and places with which the trading place interacts.

URBAN GROWTH AND STRUCTURAL CHANGE: THE NEVERENDING STORY

We like to think of ourselves as special and the problems of our time as unique. Even a cursory glance at the historical record will rapidly disabuse us of that conceit. The case of urban growth is no different from that of other issues. While having some features that are different in the twenty-first century than in the past, the concerns that are expressed about cities today echo those expressed about cities that today are looked at as exemplars of a better time.

In Chapter 2, we saw how a regional plan from more than sixty years ago still resonates today. Now we can extend the time horizon even further and take our geography across the ocean, to consider cities in Britain and Australia during the 1800s. Here is how Asa Briggs (1965, 21–2) summarizes the evolution of cities by using language that could easily be adapted to the experience of today:

> Some of the changes within cities were the product of conscious munici-pal policy. Most changes, however, were the result of a multitude of single decisions, public and private: inevitably there had to be bargains and com-promises. The general plan of the [Victorian] city continued to express all this. [At the end of the reign] the cities were confused and complicated, a patchwork of private properties, developed separately and with little sense of common plan, a jumble of sites and buildings with few formal frontiers, a bewildering variety of heights and eye-levels, a profusion of noises and smells, a social disorder with districts of deprivation and ostentation, and every architectural style, past and present, to add to the confusion.

Not only was the end result judged to be sprawl, but contemporary observers were amazed at the speed of transition from rural to urban use. The preceding passage continues (23), "The visitor to Birmingham could 'expect to find a street of houses in the autumn where he saw his horse at grass in the spring.'" The twenty-first-century suburbanite watching rows of townhouses grow like flowers during the warm months can sympathize with the experience of that earlier generation.

4 TRADING PLACES

We are caught in the tension between forces that encourage distinctiveness and forces that compel all communities toward identicality. Centrifugal forces broke down the huge ancient cities, the Londons and Tokyos and New Yorks, into neighborhood communities that seized quasi-autonomous powers. Those giant cities were too unwieldy to survive; density of population, making long-distance transport unfeasible and communication difficult, shattered the urban fabric, destroyed the authority of the central government, and left the closely knit small-scale subcity as the only viable unit. Two dynamic and contradictory processes now asserted themselves. Pride and the quest for local advantage led each community toward specialization: this one a center primarily of industrial production, this one devoted to advanced education, this to finance, this to the processing of raw materials, this to wholesale marketing of commodities, this to retail distribution, and so on, the shape and texture of each district defined by its chosen function. And yet the new decentralization required a high degree of redundancy, duplication of governmental structures, of utilities, of community services; for its own safety each district felt the need to transform itself into a microcosm of the former full city. Ideally we should have hovered in perfect balance between specialization and redundancy, all communities striving to fulfill the needs of all other communities with the least possible overlap and waste of resources; in fact our human frailty has brought into being these irreversible trends of rivalry and irrational fear, dividing district from district, so that against our own self-interest we sever year after year our bonds of interdependence and stubbornly seek self-sufficiency at the district level. Since this is impossible, our lives grow constantly more impoverished.

Robert Silverberg (1973, 169–70)

R OBERT SILVERBERG PERFECTLY CAPTURES THE STRUCTURE OF THE twenty-first-century metropolitan area as a set of relations among trading places. However, he is not an architect, urban planner, economist, lawyer, political scientist, or sociologist. His view is pessimistic, but that might just be a plot device – the preceding excerpt is from a short story in a science-fiction anthology.

The present situation represents a balancing between the forces of specialization and redundancy. There is local specialization in the production of goods and services for export to other areas, and there is local specialization in the production of goods and services for local consumption. There is also redundancy, not just in government services and utilities, as Silverberg observes in his fictional society, but also in the form of diffuse service employment in the form of McDonalds, Walgreens, Dominos, and urgent-care medical facilities.

Paradoxically, trade in goods and services increases *both* homogeneity and diversity. It allows more homogeneity in consumption relative to autarky, but it also permits greater diversity among the trading places. And this diversity in turn consists of multiple homogeneities, in the form of Tiebout suburbs, community associations, and specialized employment centers.

SPECIALIZATION IN PRODUCTION: EVIDENCE FROM EMPLOYMENT CENTERS

Economists, planners, and geographers have been chasing a theory of the structure of the metropolitan area as it evolved from the twentieth-century monocentric form to the twenty-first-century set of trading places. There are two important empirical questions that need to be addressed in choosing how much weight to place on the various theories as we synthesize them. First, how much employment is located in employment centers – areas with both large numbers of workers and high employment density – and how much is more diffused? Second, are the employment centers specialized or do they resemble each other in the mix of industries located there?

Answering these questions is a fundamental step toward developing a theory of the metropolitan economy. However, assembling the data needed for such work is still extremely difficult, so most studies only look at one metropolitan area at a time. While this is useful, it handicaps attempts to compare results across metropolitan areas, as different authors sometimes use slightly different methodologies. There are also inherent difficulties in generalizing from the largest metropolitan areas, such as Los Angeles or Chicago, which have been the subject of the most extensive analysis. I will use summary information from the analysis of employment centers in forty-eight metropolitan areas to introduce some general themes in the study of employment centers. I will then present some detailed analysis on patterns of trade in labor services (commuting) in the Cleveland metropolitan area.

When we consider how to model the joint phenomena of employment concentrations and diffuse employment, a natural place to begin is with the fundamental reason that cities form at all. Cities come at a cost, both pecuniary (higher land costs) and nonpecuniary (congestion and pollution). As we saw in Chapter 3, it is only worthwhile for activities to cluster in space if there is some advantage to doing so. The advantage comes from economies of scale, meaning that some activities are more productive if they occur at larger volume (or closer range) than at smaller volume. Economies of scale can be found in production; for example, 100,000 cars are cheaper to produce (per car) than is one car. They can also be found in consumption, for example, in Judaism a *minyan* (minimum congregation) requires ten people.

The question of what activities will take place in employment centers can thus be reframed as a question of the economies of scale to be found in those activities. Let us take a homely example, the clustering of religious activity, because I've already used the case of a minyan. The population density allowed within walking distance of a temple will limit the size of an Orthodox Jewish congregation. Of course, a wise congregation will account for this possibility when choosing a location. On the one hand, this reduces the possibility of a noticeable religious center, as the services exported will only go a short distance rather than throughout the metropolitan area. On the other hand, the concentration of Orthodox Jews within walking distance can lead to an area having a unique character, especially if other commercial activities (e.g., kosher food stores) located there serve a broader geographical region. Contrast this case with an evangelical Christian church that draws 2,000 people each week from throughout a metropolitan area for Sunday services. It has a larger geographical reach and physical footprint, but perhaps a smaller ability to create a local identity.

David Levinson (2003) has an interesting discussion of the approach that the famous planned community of Columbia, Maryland, took toward religious space. The town requires that any religious activity take place in an "interfaith center" rather than in a specialized building. This has led to self-selection among religious congregations regarding who chooses to locate in Columbia. Groups that need a dedicated facility choose alternative places instead of Columbia.

Before this discussion detoured into comparative religion, there was a basic ecumenical point about market area, economies of scale, and employment centers. Some activities have a limited market area, such as convenience stores. These activities are diffused throughout the metropolitan area. Some activities have a larger market area but limited economies of scale, in the sense of creating or needing agglomerations. One can easily think of some types of specialty shops or activities as examples. A popular attraction that draws people from throughout south central Pennsylvania and northern Maryland is MaizeQuest, a maze in a cornfield with some related activities, for example, a farmer's market. These related activities are a form of agglomeration. However, by its very nature MaizeQuest does not yield a lot of opportunities for clustering and concentrating employment, because dense economic activity would detract from the rural nature of the place. Finally, there are activities with a large market area and large economies of scale, and these activities form the basis for the identifiable employment centers. The office plazas of edge cities are the most prominent example, with the cluster of manufacturing and distribution facilities that crowd around airports as another easily observed type.

If employment centers are specialized, then it must be the case that they export their goods and services to other employment centers and import goods and services from other employment centers. It makes no sense, in such a world, to think that we can study the economy of a suburb in isolation. Rather, each suburb is part of a system of interactions, and the economic theory of trade is vital to understanding the modern metropolitan area. We now turn to evidence regarding the extent of specialization in employment centers. Later in the chapter, we will look in more detail at the flow of services through a metropolitan area.

Employment Center Specialization: Measurement and Implications

An employment center is an area with both a high density and high quantity of employment. I use the transportation analysis zone (TAZ) as the geographical unit of analysis. A TAZ is composed of one or more census blocks, with the borders being supplied to the U.S. Census Bureau by the metropolitan planning organization in each metropolitan area. The data are thus a snapshot of metropolitan structure in 1990. An interesting task for future research will be to link these snapshots (even at ten-year intervals) to better understand the dynamic processes driving metropolitan structure. The only example I know of that considers a relatively long period of time is the article by Daniel McMillen and William Lester (2003) that was mentioned in Chapter 3. They study employment centers in Chicago using historical data back to 1970 and projections forward to 2020 and find that the number of identified centers increases from nine in 1970 to a projected twenty-four in 2020. They also find that the sectoral composition of the employment in the centers changes over time and that existing centers continue to grow along highways. This is the type of research that needs to be done in many places to better understand the dynamic nature of metropolitan structure.

The most widely used methodology for studying employment centers was developed by Genevieve Giuliano and Kenneth Small (1991) in their study of Los Angeles. It requires identifying TAZs with dense employment, combining adjacent employment-dense TAZs into groups, and measuring total employment in the groups. An employment center is defined as a cluster of contiguous TAZs, all with gross employment density exceeding some minimum level and with total employment exceeding some minimum. One difficulty in comparing the various results is that the density and employment cutoffs vary from study to study, and in some cases even from place to place within the same study. Identifying employment centers in this way is quite labor-intensive, and most researchers have been content to focus on only one metropolitan area at a time. While understandable, this also reduces our ability to generalize about the experience of other metropolitan areas. Computational methods of identifying employment centers have advanced, and more recently researchers have been able to use a consistent methodology to identify subcenters in a large number of metropolitan areas.

Daniel McMillen (2003) describes a methodology that combines a pure statistical approach presented in McMillen (2001) with the employment cutoff approach of Giuliano and Small (1991). He defines an employment center as a set of contiguous TAZs that have significantly positive residuals in a nonparametric regression of employment density and a total employment of at least 10,000. This is a sophisticated alternative to an arbitrary employment density cutoff, with the additional advantage that saying "positive residuals in a nonparametric regression" will impress (or at least confuse) your friends. This methodology allows the density cutoff to vary within and across metropolitan areas to identify regions of relatively dense employment while still keeping the intuitively satisfying minimum employment cutoff. McMillen and Stefani Smith (2003) apply the methodology to identify employment centers outside the downtown for forty-eight metropolitan areas from throughout the United States. Because they don't include the downtown in their data, the results are not definitive for all the trading places in a metropolitan area. It is instructive, however, to consider the overall picture from such a wide range of cities. We will return in Chapter 5 for a more detailed look at the downtown in a few metropolitan areas.

The complete list of metropolitan areas and the number of employment centers identified by McMillen and Smith are found in Table 4-1. The important thing about this table is to see the range of cities represented in the list. All of the metropolitan areas are relatively large, but they are taken from across the United States and include both newer, growing cities and older, declining cities. In the forty-eight metropolitan areas, they find a total of 275 suburban employment centers. In Table 4-2, the frequency distribution of the number of suburban centers is shown. The range is from one to forty-six, but the vast majority of the cities have only a few centers identified. More than a quarter of the metropolitan areas have only one center (the modal number is one), more than half of the metropolitan areas have three or fewer centers, and 75 percent of the metropolitan areas have five or fewer.

Table 4-1. *Number of Suburban Employment Centers by Metropolitan Area*

Metropolitan area	Number of centers	Metropolitan area	Number of centers
Albany, NY	2	Miami, FL	1
Atlanta, GA	4	Milwaukee, WI	3
Baltimore, MD	5	Minneapolis, MN	7
Boston, MA	11	New Orleans, LA	1
Charlotte, NC	1	New York, NY	38
Chicago, IL	12	Norfolk, VA	5
Cincinnati, OH	3	Oklahoma City, OK	3
Cleveland, OH	3	Omaha, NE	1
Colorado Springs, CO	1	Orlando, FL	3
Columbus, OH	1	Philadelphia, PA	4
Dallas, TX	12	Phoenix, AZ	5
Denver, CO	5	Pittsburgh, PA	1
Detroit, MI	8	Portland, OR	3
Ft. Lauderdale, FL	2	Providence, RI	3
Hartford, CT	1	Rochester, NY	1
Honolulu, HI	1	Sacramento, CA	3
Houston, TX	8	St. Louis, MO	5
Indianapolis, IN	1	San Antonio, TX	5
Jacksonville, FL	3	San Diego, CA	6
Kansas City, MO	2	San Francisco, CA	12
Las Vegas, NV	2	Seattle, WA	14
Los Angeles, CA	46	Spokane, WA	1
Louisville, KY	2	Tampa, FL	4
Memphis, TN	1	Washington, DC	10

Source: See McMillen and Smith (2003) for details. They identify a total of 275 suburban employment centers in 48 metropolitan areas.

Diffusion of Employment throughout the Metropolitan Area

The monocentric city model postulated a concentration of employment in the CBD with the rest of the metropolitan area devoted to residential use. Polycentric models have extended the monocentric city model to account for the fact that there are multiple centers of employment, while maintaining the assumption that these multiple centers account for the bulk of metropolitan employment.

Less than half of metropolitan employment is located within employment centers, according to a literature survey by Alex Anas et al. (1998). Much of the research that they survey has focused on the large cities of Los Angeles and Chicago and the newer cities of the South and Southwest such as Atlanta and Houston. One contribution of the research reported

Table 4-2. *Frequency Distribution: Number of Employment Centers in a Metropolitan Area*

Number of centers	Number of metropolitan areas	Percentage	Cumulative percentage
1	13	27.1%	27.1%
2	5	10.4%	37.5%
3	9	18.8%	56.3%
4	3	6.3%	62.5%
5	6	12.5%	75.0%
6	1	2.1%	77.1%
7	1	2.1%	79.2%
8	2	4.2%	83.3%
10	1	2.1%	85.4%
11	1	2.1%	87.5%
12	3	6.3%	93.8%
14	1	2.1%	95.8%
38	1	2.1%	97.9%
46	1	2.1%	100.0%

Source: Data from McMillen and Smith (2003). Percentages are rounded to one decimal point.

Table 4-3. *Summary Statistics: Total Employment in Centers*

5%	25%	Median	Mean	75%	95%
10,277	12,716	17,283	21,556	24,261	46,118

Note: There are a total of 275 employment centers in 48 metropolitan areas. Employment centers are constructed to have at least 10,000 total employees. The maximum employment is 215,780; the center with the second highest employment has 91,354.

here is to investigate whether the generalizations made on the basis of these cities are also an accurate depiction of cities elsewhere in the United States.

The approach used by McMillen and Smith guarantees that the employment centers have at least 10,000 employees. Table 4-3 presents the summary statistics about total employment in the centers. The largest employment center has 215,780 employees, but most of them are much smaller. The mean number of employees is only 21,556 and the median is 17,283. The center with employment at the ninety-fifth percentile has 46,118 employees, so the overwhelming majority of the employment centers have total employment concentrated in a relatively small range. In addition, it is clear given the relatively small number of employment centers and the relatively small employment in the typical employment center that the share of total metropolitan employment accounted for by employment centers is also relatively small. This confirms the findings of Anas et al. and indicates that there are some general features of metropolitan structure that are common across metropolitan areas of widely disparate size, regional location, industrial specialization, and history of recent growth or decline.

Specialization of Employment Centers

A common criticism of metropolitan decentralization is that firms have been scattered throughout the metropolitan area without any pattern. Lewis Mumford (1961, 505) provides a scathing description of metropolitan structure in the United States as a "formless urban exudation." The existence of employment centers mitigates that criticism to some extent, because it provides evidence of significant employment concentrations rather than just diffuse employment. However, if the employment centers are no more than random agglomerations of firms, then some of the efficiency benefits from concentrated economic activity are lost. Edward Glaeser and Matthew Kahn (2004) compare employment and population density at different distances from the CBD and conclude that suburban employment is more diffuse than concentrated. They also point out that cars imply that agglomeration can take place over a larger geographical area than in a "walking city." In this context, it is telling to observe that Silicon Valley has grown up in a region overwhelmingly auto-dependent, while two famous East Coast agglomerations, the Route 128 corridor around Boston and the Route 1 corridor in central New Jersey, are named for roads.

Several studies have examined whether suburban employment centers are specialized in production. Regardless of methodology, the authors of the studies find a great deal of specialization. For example, Giuliano and Small (1991) use a statistical tool called *cluster analysis* to divide the thirty-two centers they find in Los Angeles into five types of centers: specialized manufacturing, mixed industrial, mixed service, specialized entertainment, and specialized service. Richard Bingham and Deborah Kimble (1995) also use cluster analysis to analyze edge cities in Ohio and characterize them as specializing in retail, social service, personal service, manufacturing, producer service, or wholesale. Los Angeles is unique in the role that it plays in the entertainment industry, which explains the main divergence between these two studies.

If we view a metropolitan area as a set of small open economies that specialize and trade with each other, then a natural approach is to use the LQ introduced in Chapter 3 to measure specialization in employment (and thus, presumably, in production). The LQ is the sectoral percentage of employment in an employment center divided by the same-sector percentage for the entire metropolitan area (alternately the United States). This method describes the specialization of the smaller geography as compared to that of the wider geography.

An alternative interpretation of the LQ is that it reveals information about trade patterns (Isserman 1980). If consumption of goods and services in each employment center is proportional to the metropolitan area's sectoral employment composition, then employment centers with relatively high employment in a sector presumably export that sector's output to the rest of the metropolitan area and beyond. Because employment centers typically include more employees than residents, it is an overstatement of within-center consumption to assume that it is proportional to employment. Thus, the specialization that I report within employment centers is an underestimate of the true extent of their specialization. In other words, the metropolitan area is even more orderly than I am able to demonstrate – and my results demonstrate a significant amount of order.

In previously published articles, I've implemented this idea by using LQs to measure the specialization of employment centers in several metropolitan areas in the Midwest (Cleveland, Indianapolis, and St. Louis). This section of the chapter summarizes the results of calculating LQs for the complete set of 275 employment centers in 48 metropolitan areas. I also construct an index of specialization that can be used to compare employment centers within and across metropolitan areas.

Strictly speaking, an LQ greater than one in a sector indicates that the employment center specializes in that sector and is a net exporter, while an LQ less than one indicates that the employment center is a net importer. However, to better identify areas that were clearly net importers and exporters, I focus on LQs that are greater than 1.25 or less than 0.75. In other words, I do not identify an employment center as specializing in a sector unless its employment in that sector is at least 25 percent higher than it would be if the center reflected the metropolitan area's employment pattern.

Table 4-4 summarizes the LQ analysis. The only sector with more than forty-nine employment centers having an LQ greater than 1.25 is finance, insurance, and real estate (FIRE), which has seventy. By contrast, the smallest number of employment centers with an LQ less than 0.75 is 165, again in the FIRE sector. Employment centers tend to be importers far more often than exporters. To put it succinctly, they specialize in production.

In most cases, the majority of employment centers fall into one of the extremes listed in Table 4-4. Begin with the first row, manufacturing. There are forty-nine centers that are identified as exporters, while 194 are identified as importers, for a total of 243 out of 275 in these categories.

Table 4-4. *Summary of Location Quotients by Sector*

Sector	Number of centers with LQ > 1.25	Number of centers with LQ < 0.75
Manufacturing	49	194
TCUW	47	176
Retail	38	198
FIRE	70	165
Other services	38	173

Note: There are a total of 275 employment centers in the 48 metropolitan areas. "FIRE" stands for "Finance, Insurance, and Real Estate," and "TCUW" stands for "Transportation, Communication, Utilities, and Wholesaling."

Table 4-5. *Correlation of Total Employment and Sectoral Location Quotients in Centers*

	Employment	Manufacturing	TCUW	Retail	FIRE
Manufacturing	−0.08	—	—	—	—
TCUW	−0.08	0.15	—	—	—
Retail	−0.21	0.05	0.35	—	—
FIRE	−0.09	−0.01	0.37	0.50	—
Other services	−0.12	−0.11	0.13	0.40	0.39

Note: There are a total of 275 employment centers in the 48 metropolitan areas. "FIRE" stands for "Finance, Insurance, and Real Estate," and "TCUW" stands for "Transportation, Communication, Utilities, and Wholesaling."

The sector that has the most evenly diffused employment by this measure is other services, and even that sector has 211 out of 275 employment centers identified as either exporters or importers.

Table 4-5 presents evidence on the extent to which the employment specializations are related to each other. The table includes correlation coefficients between total employment in each center and the LQs for the various sectors. The first result to notice is that total employment is negatively correlated with all of the LQs. This is consistent with the idea that larger centers are less specialized, which is a tenet of the monocentric city model. The second result is that there are a number of positive correlations among the various sectors. This is one reason that it is not a simple matter to characterize the specialization of employment centers, as they typically have a set of interrelated activities taking place within their boundaries.

Measuring Specialization and Diversity

The detailed list of specializations and employment concentrations is fascinating, but difficult to summarize. One standard way of comparing the sectoral employment composition of one area to another is to calculate what is known as an *index of specialization*. This measure, originally developed to analyze racial segregation, is applicable in a wide variety of situations.

Intuitively, the index of specialization measures the minimum extent to which we would have to alter the employment mix of the employment center to match that of the metropolitan area as a whole. Consider the following simple example. There are two employment sectors, manufacturing and services. The metropolitan area has 30 percent of its employment in manufacturing with the remaining 70 percent in services. The employment center has 20 percent manufacturing and 80 percent services. If we shifted 10 percent of the employment from services to manufacturing, then the composition of employment would match that in the metropolitan area. So the index of specialization in this case would be ten.

In our data, there are more than two sectors, but the approach is the same. Mathematically, the index of specialization is calculated as follows:

$$Index\ of\ Specialization = 100 * 1/2 \sum |MSA\%_i - Center\%_i|$$

The summation is taken over all of the employment sectors in the data. Returning to our simple example, we find that the absolute value of the difference in manufacturing is 10 percent, the absolute value of the difference in services is 10 percent, and so the calculated value of the index is $100 * 1/2 * (10\% + 10\%) = 10$, as we saw previously.

In Table 4-6, we see the extent to which the employment centers are specialized relative to a national norm. The index of specialization for the 275 employment centers averages about forty-five. Thus, almost half of the employment would have to be rearranged in the average employment center to match the sectoral composition of the United States as a whole. Once again, the evidence supports a description of metropolitan areas composed of specialized places.

SIZE DISTRIBUTION OF EMPLOYMENT CENTERS

One of the best-known and most robust empirical regularities about city sizes is Zipf's law, or the *rank-size rule*. Let a city's population be denoted as N, and let $S(N)$ equal the number of cities with a population of N or greater. In other words, $S(N)$ is the "rank" of the city in terms of population. The rank-size rule states that plotting the logarithm of $S(N)$

Table 4-6. *Summary of the Index of*
Specialization

Statistic	Value for 275 employment centers
Mean	44.7
Standard deviation	21.6
Median	38.8
Minimum	5.6
Maximum	85.6
25th percentile	21.6
75th percentile	67.1

against the logarithm of *N* will show a straight line, or more technically, that a regression of the logarithm of *S* on the logarithm of *N* will have a slope of −1. This rule has been found to be a reasonable description of the size distribution of cities in a wide variety of places and over a wide range of time periods.

Urban theorists have recently given renewed attention to Zipf's law for metropolitan area sizes as a restriction on the class of acceptable models of urban growth. Models that generate the rank-size rule as a feature have been proposed by a variety of researchers. Although a few studies have suggested that the rank-size rule also holds for employment centers within a metropolitan area, there has not yet been the same theoretical attention to this finding.

We begin by formally developing the relation between employment and rank that is analogous to the relation between population and rank described earlier. Let *N* be the total employment in the employment center and *S(N)* the number of employment centers in the metropolitan area with employment greater than or equal to *N*. We estimate the following regression, where α is a constant and ε is a random error term. The test of Zipf's law is whether β is equal to −1.

$$ln(\text{S}) = \alpha + \beta ln(\text{N}) + \epsilon$$

A coefficient in Table 4-7 on *ln*(Employment) less than 1 in absolute value implies that employment is more concentrated in larger employment centers than is predicted by the rank-size rule, while a coefficient greater than 1 in absolute value implies that employment is less concentrated in larger employment centers than is predicted by the rank-size rule.

Because the CBD employment is not included in the data, the analysis is not complete. However, the maintained hypothesis that the rank-size

Table 4-7. *Rank-Size Rule Regressions I*

Metropolitan area	Intercept	ln(Employment)	Adjusted R²	Rank-size rule
Boston	14.64	−1.31	0.95	No
	(0.97)	(0.10)		
Chicago	15.20	−1.36	0.92	No
	(0.15)	(0.12)		
Dallas	14.57	−1.27	0.91	No
	(1.17)	(0.12)		
Detroit	12.70	−1.13	0.94	Yes
	(1.07)	(0.11)		
Houston	11.76	−1.02	0.95	Yes
	(0.92)	(0.09)		
Los Angeles	17.76	−1.48	0.98	No
	(0.34)	(0.03)		
New York	13.68	−1.09	0.79	Yes
	(0.93)	(0.09)		
San Francisco	12.27	−1.04	0.96	Yes
	(0.65)	(0.06)		
Seattle	18.51	−1.68	0.91	No
	(1.44)	(0.15)		
Washington, DC	10.12	−0.83	0.97	No
	(0.53)	(0.05)		

Note: Standard errors in parentheses. The variable "rank-size rule" is "yes" if we do not reject the hypothesis that the coefficient on ln(Employment) equals −1 at the 95 percent significance level.

rule holds also implies that it holds for a subset of the data. To have a reasonable (although still small) sample size, I restrict my attention to metropolitan areas that have eight or more employment centers. This leaves us with ten metropolitan areas to consider.

Four of the ten metropolitan areas have an estimated relation between rank and size of employment centers consistent with the rank-size rule. But even a rejection of the "pure" rank-size rule relationship should not obscure the important point – there is a simple empirical regularity in the data on employment center sizes. With the exception of New York, the simple regression equation explains more than 90 percent of the variance in the dependent variable. Nine of the ten estimated coefficients for employment have an absolute value greater than 1, which implies that employment is less concentrated in large employment centers than predicted by the rank-size rule. The omission of the CBD from the data, though, could partially explain this result. This is especially clear because the exception, Washington, DC, has a CBD that is smaller than would otherwise be expected because of the height restriction within the city. Thus, policy forces the metropolitan area to have larger employment centers outside the city limits, and the regression results are consistent with this explanation of decentralized employment.

One reason that the size distribution of employment centers is of interest is that it can be used to predict the number and size distribution of geographical areas where there is dense employment but not yet sufficient total employment to exceed the threshold. The data for the forty-eight metropolitan areas do not make it possible to investigate this question, but in previous work (Anderson and Bogart 2001) I have looked in detail at four metropolitan areas: Cleveland, Indianapolis, Portland, and St. Louis. The total employment in 1990 in the regions served by the metropolitan planning organizations (which can differ from the census-defined metropolitan statistical area) was 627,358 in Indianapolis; 984,967 in Cleveland; 1,100,811 in St. Louis; and 992,185 in Portland. Employment centers were identified using the Giuliano-Small methodology of contiguous areas that exceed a minimum employment density (in this case, 5,000 employees per square mile) and a minimum total employment (in this case, 10,000 employees). This approach yielded nine employment centers in Cleveland, eleven in Indianapolis, eleven in Portland, and ten in St. Louis. Unlike McMillen and Smith, I included the CBD in the set of employment centers.

Table 4-8 reports the results of estimating the rank-size regression equation for these four cities. The results are similar to those in Table 4-7, despite the differences in the methodology used to identify employment centers. The coefficients on employment tend to be smaller in absolute value than those in Table 4-7, which is consistent with the idea that the absence of the CBD makes the employment centers seem more decentralized than they would be with the CBD included.

Let us refer to areas with employment density greater than 5,000 per square mile but with less than 10,000 total employees as *proto-centers*. (It is also possible that a geographical area has an employment greater than 10,000 but a density less than 5,000 per square mile. For example, large shopping malls often anchor such an area. Including these types of proto-centers in the analysis could alter the results.) If there is indeed regularity in the size distribution, then the parameters estimated using the employment centers with more than 10,000 employees should be helpful in predicting the number and distribution of proto-centers.

Table 4-9 presents summary evidence on the proto-centers in the various metropolitan areas. With the exception of the smaller proto-centers in Indianapolis, the regression in Table 4-8 is a reasonably good predictor of the number of proto-centers at various employment levels. This is further evidence of systematic structure in the intrametropolitan distribution of employment. It is especially notable that Portland, famous (or notorious)

Table 4-8. *Rank-Size Rule Regressions II*

Metropolitan area	Intercept	ln(Employment)	Adjusted R²	Rank-size rule
Cleveland	9.51	−0.81	0.87	Yes
	(1.08)	(0.11)		
Indianapolis	12.42	−1.09	0.95	Yes
	(0.80)	(0.08)		
Portland	9.29	−0.76	0.95	No
	(0.55)	(0.05)		
St. Louis	9.22	−0.75	0.98	No
	(0.33)	(0.03)		

Note: Standard errors in parentheses. The variable "rank-size rule" is "yes" if we do not reject the hypothesis that the coefficient on ln(Employment) equals −1 at the 95 percent significance level.

as the prime example of urban-growth controls, does not appear to be systematically different from the three midwestern cities in this list.

The rank-size rule has been widely accepted in the research literature as a restriction on acceptable models of aggregate metropolitan growth. The results reported here suggest that a similar criterion should be applied to models of metropolitan structure and the growth of employment centers within metropolitan areas. We should be looking for analytical descriptions of the metropolitan area that are consistent with systematic variation in size among employment centers. On this standard, most descriptions of metropolitan structure are sorely lacking.

Why Might the Rank-Size Rule Hold for Employment Centers?

Employment centers require a fine balance. They need to be big enough and dense enough to have an individual identity. At the same time

Table 4-9. *Size Distribution of Proto-Centers*

Metropolitan area	≥10,000 (Predicted/ Actual)	≥8,000 (Predicted/ Actual)	≥6,000 (Predicted/ Actual)	≥4,000 (Predicted/ Actual)	≥2,000 (Predicted/ Actual)
Cleveland	8/9	9/12	12/15	16/19	29/31
Indianapolis	11/11	14/12	19/16	29/18	62/23
Portland	10/11	12/11	15/16	20/21	34/35
St. Louis	10/10	12/10	15/13	20/18	34/28

Note: The number of centers with the given employment is predicted using the regression coefficients reported in Table 4-8.

they need to be integrated into the overall pattern of activities within a metropolitan area. It is especially interesting to find whether this balancing results in the rank-size rule. An extreme monocentric structure satisfies the rank-size rule trivially, while a completely decentralized pattern of production does not resemble the rank-size rule at all. Why does this statistical regularity hold, and is it likely to hold in the future?

One reason to expect differences in the size of employment centers is that different goods and services are produced at different scales. If the pattern of efficient scales happens to fit the rank-size rule, then complete specialization of centers is consistent with the size distribution we see. However, centers are not completely specialized, nor are there any *a priori* expectations that efficient sizes are distributed according to the rank-size rule, so a complete explanation must go beyond this simple technological explanation.

A second reason to expect differences is land-use controls. In other words, the centers grow as large as possible, but they are constrained by land-use regulation and the constraints lead to the observed distributions of sizes. It would be miraculous, though, for the zoning bodies in local governments across the United States to have created conditions that required the rank-size rule to obtain throughout the country.

A third reason to expect systematic variation is that different goods and services have different market areas. This is the fundamental insight of central place theory, which was introduced in Chapter 3. Central place theory within a metropolitan area has a subtle difference with central place theory applied to the relation between metropolitan areas. In particular, it is not necessarily the case that there is a simple monotonic relation between the market area and the size of the employment center. Regional shopping malls, for example, draw customers from throughout the region (hence the name), but do not necessarily locate downtown. Similarly, major hospitals and other health services can serve the entire metropolitan area while being located in – and probably anchoring – one of the smaller "suburban " employment centers.

There has been a surge of interest in developing models of urban growth that yield Zipf's law for city sizes. The interested reader who would like to explore the features of the various models in detail is directed to the exhaustive survey of the literature in the chapter by Xavier Gabaix and Yannis Ioannides (2004). In general, the most promising approaches combine a focus on employment centers with recognition of the more general intrametropolitan trading relationships. An early and still insightful statement of this eclectic view is developed and applied to urban growth and the pattern of trade among European cities by the historians Paul Hohenberg and Lynn Lees (1985).

One important theoretical issue has to do with the CBD. Any model of the evolution of the size distribution of employment centers must account for the persistent advantage of the CBD. The extent to which city size distributions are stable has also been the subject of recent study, with the consensus being that there is considerable stability and the coefficients of the rank-size rule regression move in predictable ways. This stability for subcenters is an open question. The results presented in this chapter are for one point in time. It is possible, for example, that the rank-size rule for employment centers is an artifact of the transition from the monocentric structure of the early twentieth century to the trading place structure of the twenty-first century.

CHARACTERIZING COMMUTING TO METROPOLITAN EMPLOYMENT CENTERS

[A] man who earns $5.00 an hour would consider the time cost of a half-hour trip to be $2.50. This rate of time cost equals the accrual of interest (at 5 per cent per annum) on an investment of about $880,000. So, calculated on that basis, human freight carries a time cost equivalent to that of a commodity worth at least $300 an ounce – perhaps not "more precious than rubies," but somewhere in the range between gold and diamonds.

Edgar M. Hoover (1968, 242)

We are familiar with the ideas of importing and exporting goods and services from one country to another. However, it might seem puzzling to think about how imports and exports occur within a metropolitan area. After all, there is no customs barrier, no currency conversion, and no passport required when transporting products from one suburb to another. How, then, can we describe these activities as importing and exporting?

When we say that a good or service is exported from an area, all that we mean is that the area produces more of the good than it wishes to consume. The excess is sold to others, in other words exported. Similarly, an import occurs when an economy consumes more than it produces. These definitions of imports and exports apply whether the economy in question is a country, a metropolitan area, a part of a metropolitan area, or even an individual. At the individual level, I export economics lectures and import plumbing services. I also produce some goods and services for my own consumption, for example, when I cook dinner for myself.

When we talk about employment centers within a metropolitan area trading with each other, much of the trade will occur using cars and trucks. My morning commute represents an export of labor services from York Township, where I live, and an import of labor services by Spring Garden Township, where my college office is located. The telephone, e-mail, and fax machine also make it possible to export and import services without anyone leaving their office. The phone call from a manufacturing company in Euclid (a suburb of Cleveland) to its lawyer in downtown Cleveland represents an export of legal services from downtown and an import of legal services to Euclid.

In this section we move from a consideration of employment centers during working hours (a static picture) to a study of how they change during rush hour (a dynamic picture). We will explicitly look at the pattern of trade in labor services represented by commuters traveling to the type of employment centers studied in this chapter, and we will use these data to begin to calculate a balance-of-trade analysis for all of the trading places of the metropolitan area.

Data on Intrametropolitan Trade

Although there is a widespread recognition that population distribution within metropolitan areas is dynamic rather than static, there is not widespread agreement on how to measure the flows. One of the most important flows is the movement of people from their place of residence to their place of employment. I will examine this flow in detail for a five-county region in Northeast Ohio (Cleveland and surrounding area) using a household travel survey compiled in 1994. The survey was compiled by the metropolitan planning organization for the region, the Northeast Ohio Area Coordinating Agency (NOACA). About 1,600 households were chosen, using a stratified sampling technique, to represent all of the households in the region. Each household was asked to keep detailed records of its travel during a particular day and to report that information to NOACA. The data were aggregated by TAZ and expanded to cover all households by using the sampling weights. In the interest of full disclosure, I should report that my family was one of the randomly chosen households, allowing me to fulfill a lifelong dream to be a part of my own data.

The U.S. Census Bureau collects information on commuting every ten years and publishes the Census Transportation Planning Program (CTPP). The CTPP is where TAZs are defined by each metropolitan planning organization, and because it is linked to the full rich data in the census, the CTPP is a likely source for study. The RAND Corporation performed a study (Sleeper et al. 2004) for the Pittsburgh area using census data from 2000 that echoes the approach we will use here and in Chapter 8. People who get tired of looking at Cleveland data analyzed by me are encouraged to look at Pittsburgh data analyzed by someone else. Don't look for differences in the conclusions, though, because the pattern of intrametropolitan trade is similar in both places.

Local Monocentricity in a Trading Place Metropolitan Area

> The functional core of the city is made up of those interdependent economic activities that secure the material reproduction of urban life at the outset. These activities are also the basis of formation of pools of workers who are housed in residential districts located within ready access of employment places.
>
> Allen Scott (1988, 217)

Economists are often accused of not paying attention to the insights of other social scientists. I plead somewhat guilty, but not totally. Allen Scott is an influential geographer whose work anticipates my approach in some ways. His emphasis on the way that the division of labor leads naturally to specialized and interdependent areas within a city is consistent with the trading place approach that I advocate. He finds that residential patterns in Los Angeles, New York, and Orange County (California) have been shaped by commuting. By now, you know the drill – if it's happening in Los Angeles, I'll look to see if it's happening in Cleveland.

In keeping with the emphasis to this point on employment centers, I'll begin by looking at commuting patterns to employment centers in the Cleveland area. Given that there are nine employment centers and 1,003 TAZs in the five counties, it is imperative to find some way of parsimoniously characterizing the trading patterns of labor services.

By analogy with the LQ, we can construct a *commuting quotient* (CQ) that measures the extent to which a TAZ is primarily exporting labor to a particular employment center. In addition, we will be able to investigate whether CQs vary systematically. This will give insight into the structure of the polycentric part of the metropolitan area (less than 50 percent of total employment is in the employment centers) in preparation for a more general look at the overall pattern of intrametropolitan trade in labor services.

Let: c_i = total workers from TAZ i
        c_j = total workers in employment center j
        c_{ij} = workers who travel from i to j
        c = total workers in metropolitan area
Then define the CQ as

$$CQ_{ij} = (c_{ij}/c_j)/(c_i/c)$$

Once we have identified the CQ for each TAZ and employment center combination, we are left with the question of how to succinctly describe the results. Table 4-10 presents two ways of characterizing CQs.

The employment centers are listed in declining order of total employment, beginning with downtown Cleveland. Clearly, the CBD remains quite large relative to other employment centers. The third column of

Table 4-10. *Commuting Quotient Analysis for Employment Centers in Northeast Ohio*

Center	Total employment	Number of TAZ with CQ >1.25	Adjusted R^2	Intercept	Average time	Elasticity at mean
1	155,924	479	0.56	2.527 (0.045)	−0.042 (0.001)	−1.17
2	41,991	453	0.38	2.450 (0.067)	−0.042 (0.002)	−1.16
3	19,082	443	0.20	2.266 (0.102)	−0.036 (0.003)	−1.32
4	18,197	447	0.08	1.969 (0.123)	−0.030 (0.004)	−0.98
5	14,650	463	0.14	2.089 (0.104)	−0.037 (0.003)	−1.08
6	13,779	463	0.38	8.264 (0.339)	−0.155 (0.007)	−3.88
7	13,455	449	0.23	3.609 (0.197)	−0.064 (0.004)	−2.85
8	12,468	481	0.03	2.213 (0.213)	−0.020 (0.004)	−0.78
9	12,152	428	0.13	3.047 (0.207)	−0.052 (0.005)	−2.07

Note: See text for definitions of variables. The elasticity is that of the CQ with respect to average time from the TAZ to the employment center. There are 1,003 TAZs in the data.

Table 4-10 counts the number of TAZs for which the CQ is greater than 1.25, in other words the TAZs that send 25 percent or more commuters to an employment center than would be the case if the trade were proportional to the employment center's share of total employment. Although the total employment varies considerably among centers, we find a very narrow range of TAZs identified as closely related. The minimum number is 428 and the maximum is 481 out of 1,003 TAZs in the region. This result suggests that each employment center – including the CBD – has a sphere of influence that encompasses only a fraction of the metropolitan area. Thus, the economically relevant area to consider is smaller than the entire metropolitan area. A count alone, though, does not indicate how this sphere of influence is determined.

The remainder of Table 4-10 reports a regression of CQ on an intercept and the average time from a TAZ to the employment center. It is necessary to calculate an average time because each employment center consists of multiple TAZs. I do not include distance for two reasons. First, the data do not include inter-TAZ distances. Second, and more important, the time it takes to travel from place to place is a more important determinant of commuting than the distance.

I calculated the elasticity at the mean to investigate whether accessibility as measured by time was an important determinant of the trade pattern described by the CQs. Elasticity measures the responsiveness of one thing (in this case the number of commuters) with respect to another thing (in this case time). An elasticity of -1 implies that a 1 percent increase in the average time would lead to a 1 percent decrease in the CQ. Most of the estimated elasticities cluster near -1. The median is -1.17, and the three extreme outliers (centers number 6, 7, and 9) are near the boundaries of the region. The monocentric model seems like a very good description of individual behavior near centers, even as it seems inadequate as a description of the overall metropolitan structure. This local monocentricity is well illustrated by the results for the CBD. Not only is the explanatory power of the regression highest for the CBD, but the estimated elasticity of the CQ with respect to time is the median among the nine centers. It is not true that the monocentric city model no longer holds. It is just necessary to recognize that the monocentric city model is an appropriate description only for behavior near an employment center.

An important question is whether these results also describe the rest of the metropolitan areas in the United States. Unfortunately, much of the research literature continues to focus on an inappropriate geographical scope for the monocentric city model and therefore does not produce sufficient insight into this question. An especially interesting issue is whether the elasticity of the CQ with respect to average time is invariant across metropolitan areas. This might be one of the empirical facts that any theory needs to explain, but we need more research to confirm whether this result holds more generally.

Trade among Trading Places: Gravity Model Analysis

The pattern of trade between residences and employment centers is interesting but accounts for less than half of the total employment in the metropolitan area. Thus, we need to do a more general analysis to include all of the diffused employment along with the concentrated employment of the centers. A standard empirical approach to measuring international trade is the gravity model introduced in Chapter 3. The gravity model predicts that the total amount of trade between two places will be inversely related to the costs of trade and directly related to the overall size of the places. In our context, the trade is the number of commuting trips from one place to another. The costs of trade will be measured as the time between TAZs, and the overall size will be measured by the total number of commuting trips.

Table 4-11. *Gravity Model Analysis of InterTAZ Commuting in Northeast Ohio*

	OLS	Elasticity (OLS)	Tobit	Elasticity (Tobit)
Intercept	1.802		−46.002	
	(0.042)		(0.240)	
Time	−0.143	−1.40	−1.341	−43.11
	(0.001)		(0.007)	
Origin trips (thousands)	1.986	0.95	11.032	11.07
	(0.014)		(0.057)	
Destination trips	1.444	0.85	6.855	6.87
(thousands)	(0.008)		(0.033)	
Adjusted R²	0.14		0.14	
(pseudo R² for Tobit)				

Note: Dependent variable is the number of commuting trips from one TAZ to another. Standard errors in parentheses. Elasticities calculated at the means. OLS regressions do not include observations where the origin and destination TAZ are the same or where there are no trips between the two TAZs.

Table 4-11 presents the results of estimating a gravity model regression explaining the total volume of inter-TAZ trips. The first regressions are estimated using ordinary least squares (OLS), which only includes the TAZs that had some trips between them. As expected, the amount of trade is negatively related to the costs of trade (time) and positively related to the size of both the origin and destination of the commuting trip. To understand the relative impact, I again calculate elasticities. The OLS regression implies that a 1 percent increase in commuting time (an increase of 0.3 minutes, or 18 seconds, at the mean time of 29.7 minutes) will reduce the number of trips by about 1.4 percent, holding all else equal. An increase in the size of the origin or destination of 1 percent will increase the number of trips by slightly less than 1 percent, holding all else equal. This makes sense, as most TAZs have more than one trading partner.

There are more than 1 million possible trading combinations (1,003 TAZs squared). The OLS approach omits the more than 600,000 combinations where there is no trade or in which the origin and destination TAZ are the same (and thus the time is reported as zero). A more general approach that accounts for this substantial concentration of zero trade is the so-called *Tobit regression model.* The remainder of Table 4-11 reports the results of estimating a Tobit regression for the intrametropolitan trips. The main impact of including the remainder of the possible trading partners is to increase the measured impact of the gravity model determinants on the volume of trade. In other words, there is a substantial

Table 4-12. *Intrametropolitan Trade in Northeast Ohio, 1994*

Variable	Net importers (37)	Net exporters (105)
Exported workers	2,061/6,286	3,497/6,096
Imported workers	5,729/14,946	1,124/3,044
Workers who stay	680/5,636	362/1,362
Percent of total workers exported	29.3/28.3%	66.3/69.4%
Percent of total workers imported	60.8/61.9%	22.8/21.1%
Percent of total workers who stay	5.9/9.8%	8.3/9.5%
Employment-to-population ratio	73/133.4%	23/22.7%

Source: All data from NOACA household survey except for the employment-to-population ratio from U.S. Census Bureau (1990).
Note: Each column includes the median for the municipalities followed by the mean (median/mean). "Workers who stay" live and work within the same municipality. Net importers are municipalities with more workers commuting in than commuting out; net exporters are municipalities with more workers commuting out than commuting in. There are 872,618 total exports (=total imports) and 351,522 total workers who stay.

portion of the metropolitan area that is essentially irrelevant to any given source of commuters or destination for commuters.

Extending the analysis from employment centers to the entire metropolitan area changes some of the estimated parameters but does not change the fundamental conclusion. The monocentric city model is an excellent local approximation for the relations between parts of the metropolitan area.

MUNICIPALITIES AS SMALL COUNTRIES

Although we have focused on employment centers to this point, the travel diary data can be used to consider intrametropolitan trade much more generally. This is vital, because otherwise we are omitting the majority of employment from our study. For example, the data can be used to calculate the current account of municipalities (exports minus imports) in labor services. This is especially straightforward because every TAZ is completely within a municipal boundary. For the current discussion, we will assume that trade is measured simply as the number of commuting trips. In Chapter 8, I present an approach to imputing a dollar value to each trip and use this approach to extend the analysis to simulate the impact of regional tax-base sharing.

There are 142 municipalities in the five-county NOACA region. Table 4-12 presents summary information regarding intrametropolitan trade. There are more than 1.2 million commuting trips identified. More than 70 percent of these trips involve trade between municipalities, with the remainder involving a commuting trip that begins and ends in the same municipality. Only about one-quarter of the municipalities (37 out of 142) are identified as net importers of labor. Nineteen of the net importers have at least 10,000 commuters entering from other municipalities; twenty-six of the net exporters send at least 10,000 workers to other municipalities; and five municipalities have 10,000 commutes that begin and end within the municipality. A statistic that illustrates the interconnectedness of the modern metropolitan area is that the five municipalities that have 10,000 intramunicipal commutes both export more than 10,000 workers and import more than 10,000 workers. In fact, there are thirteen municipalities that both import and export at least 10,000 workers. At the other extreme, there is only one municipality that is found to only export labor; even so-called bedroom suburbs turn out to be homes for employment.

If the household travel diaries identify a municipality as a net importer or exporter of labor, we would expect these results to be consistent with census data on total employment relative to total population. Table 4-12 includes summary statistics on the employment-to-population ratio calculated by the census. Not only are the means very different for municipalities identified as importers or exporters, but there is very little overlap in the total distribution of employment-to-population ratios. The twenty-fifth percentile employment-to-population ratio among the net importers is 0.61, which is almost double the seventy-fifth percentile among the net exporters. In fact, there are only two (of 105) of the net exporters that have an employment-to-population ratio greater than 0.61, while the minimum employment-to-population ratio among the importers (0.25) is larger than the median (0.23) among the exporters.

To conclude this discussion and connect it to the earlier analysis of employment centers, I calculated the import and export figures for the employment centers in the Cleveland area. The median import percentage is 88.4 percent, which indicates the extent to which the employment centers draw workers into a dense agglomeration. Only two of the nine employment centers have an import percentage less than 82 percent, and three of them (including downtown Cleveland) import more than 95 percent of their workers. Employment centers play an important role in the metropolitan area, but as we have seen, they are only one end of a continuum of trading places.

STRUCTURE AND SPECIALIZATION, NOT SPRAWL

Both the aggregate data from metropolitan areas throughout the United States and the detailed data from a few metropolitan areas tell a similar story. There are substantial regularities in metropolitan structure.

These include systematic variation in both the size of employment centers and their specialization. The results justify the analytical approach that I will use in the remainder of the book. The remaining chapters explore important policy questions in more depth using the analytical framework developed in the past three chapters. Specifically, we will explore the impact of various public policies on the efficiency of intrametropolitan trade, focusing on identifying policies that are flexible enough to adapt to changing conditions across the country at a point in time and changing conditions within a metropolitan area over time. Having concluded this chapter with a look at employment as it has diffused throughout the metropolitan area, we return in the next chapter to the role of the CBD in a trading place metropolitan area and evaluate the impact of policies whose goal is to generate economic growth downtown.

5 DOWNTOWN: A PLACE TO WORK, A PLACE TO VISIT, A PLACE TO LIVE

The functions that continue to gather in what may be called central districts or hubs of the urban nebulae are offices, laboratories, and all the activities related to the various forms of entertainment. As in Roman times, the arena and the forum, in their modern versions, occupy an increasing share of the hubs. Entertainment and offices are related one to another, thriving on proximity. They create a large market for white-collar labor. All these trends started at an earlier time and they have already developed on a great scale in Megalopolis. The forces bringing about this evolution are rooted in a deep transformation of modern modes of life and habitat.

Jean Gottman (1961, 776–7)

I T IS COMMONLY BELIEVED THAT THE EFFECT OF NEW TRANSPORTA-
tion infrastructure, such as the interstate highway system, is to suck residents and jobs out of central cities and downtowns. While the decentralization of jobs and residents has been well documented, the logic in this argument about highways is incomplete. The impact of any new transportation (or communications) system should be to increase movement in both directions between the points that it connects and therefore to encourage trade between those points. With greater trade should come greater specialization in the production of the goods and services that each location in the metropolitan area does best.

To stretch the trade analogy further: the interstate highway system is similar to the development of large, fast ocean-going vessels that permitted Britain to specialize in textile production at the start of the Industrial Revolution, trading manufactured goods for grain and timber from America. This simple idea is the economic doctrine of comparative advantage, and it applies within metropolitan areas as well as between nations.

What is the comparative advantage of downtown with respect to the metropolitan region? How does this advantage help the downtown to prosper?

Three comparative advantages are inherent and unique to any city's downtown:

- The downtown is centrally located with respect to the metropolitan area. This immediately implies a role for downtown as a gathering place for civic activities, including cultural, social, and sporting events.
- The downtown has a longer history of major development than other parts of the metropolitan area. It therefore has an interesting architectural heritage and a scale of activity that provide visitors with a unique urban experience.
- The downtown is very high density, therefore it enables people to engage in face-to-face interactions with lots of other people in a relatively short amount of time.

The first two explain why the downtown is the logical place to locate the visitors' industry – an industry that will continue to grow as Americans become more affluent, buy more leisure, and retire in greater numbers.

The most important advantage provided by the downtown, however, is probably the opportunity for multiple face-to-face interactions in a tightly circumscribed geographic space. Geographers argue that this makes downtowns the perfect setting for advanced business services, such as law and corporate accounting. In addition, many downtowns are county seats with county and federal courthouses, which provides another reason for law firms to locate there. So it should be no surprise that the downtown has specialized in this kind of work as transportation and communication infrastructure have improved.

In this chapter, we use detailed information from a few CBDs to explore their role as trading places. As already noted, one of the comparative advantages of downtown is as a location for recreation, and the trend of stadium construction as economic development policy is analyzed in that light. An important benefit from downtown recreation is that it helps attract market-rate housing to the downtown. Unfortunately, there are higher costs for construction and renovation of housing downtown, some of which are due to government regulation. Thus, the final section of this chapter will lead naturally to the next chapter, which will focus on planning and regulation.

DOWNTOWN AS A TRADING PLACE

How doth the city sit solitary, that was full of people! How is she become as a widow! She that was great among the nations, and princess among the provinces, how is she become tributary!

Lamentations 1:1

As we saw in Chapter 4, the CBD no longer dominates the employment picture in twenty-first-century metropolitan areas. This has led to a policy discussion only slightly less urgent than the passage from Jeremiah's lamentation for the fall of Jerusalem. But downtown is still special, and downtowns share some common features. The focus on the decreasing dominance of the central city confuses decentralization with decline. Downtown plays an important role in the metropolitan structure and it is crucial to understand the role of downtown in order to better construct policies to encourage success.

National Trends

One way to demonstrate the continuing importance of the CBD is to consider its role as an employment center. In 1982, the U.S. Census Bureau designated a specific geographic area in each metropolitan area as the CBD. As part of a series of studies of the 2000 census sponsored by the Brookings Institution, Edward Glaeser et al. (2001) took advantage of advances in computer-mapping capability to calculate the fraction of metropolitan employment within a three-mile radius of the CBD for the 100 largest metropolitan areas. On average, only 22 percent of people work within that three-mile radius. There is substantial heterogeneity, though, among areas. They identify four categories of metropolitan area:

1. Dense Employment: Thirty-one metropolitan areas have at least 25 percent of employment within a three-mile radius of the CBD, typically with 70 to 80 percent of employment within a ten-mile radius. This category includes familiar cities such as New York, San Francisco, and Boston, but it also takes in places such as Jacksonville, Louisville, New Orleans, and Chattanooga.
2. Centralized Employment: Thirty-five metropolitan areas have between 10 and 25 percent of their employment within the three-mile radius and at least 60 percent within a ten-mile radius. This category includes not only midwestern cities such as Indianapolis, Columbus, and Minneapolis–St. Paul, but also southern and western places such as Denver, Austin, and Albuquerque.
3. Decentralized Employment: This category includes twenty-three metropolitan areas, and the definition is a slight variation on the previous category. Similar to the centralized employment metropolitan areas, these places have between 10 and 25 percent of their employment within the three-mile radius. Unlike them, they have less than 60 percent of employment within a ten-mile radius. Our familiar example of Cleveland is in this category, along with cities including Chicago, Philadelphia, Atlanta, and Seattle.

Table 5-1. *CBD and Employment Center Employment as a Percentage of Metropolitan Employment*

Metropolitan area	Number of centers	CBD Employment as a percentage of metropolitan employment	Center employment as a percentage of metropolitan employment
Cleveland	9	16%	31%
Indianapolis	11	17%	46%
Portland	11	27%	52%
St. Louis	10	20%	42%

4. Extremely Decentralized: The final eleven metropolitan areas have less than 10 percent of their employment within a three-mile radius of the CBD. Yes, Los Angeles is one of them, along with St. Louis, Tampa–St. Petersburg, and Gary, Indiana.

There is a distinct regional pattern to the data. The metropolitan areas in the Northeast are the most centralized, with 28.9 percent of employment within a three-mile radius of the CBD and 66.6 percent of employment within a ten-mile radius. The Midwest and West are next, with similar figures of 21.1 percent and 66.1 percent (Midwest) and 20.1 percent and 65.2 percent (West). The South has the most decentralized metropolitan areas, with only 18.8 percent of employment within a three-mile radius and 63.9 percent within a ten-mile radius.

The area surrounding the CBD is thus still the economic hub of the typical metropolitan area. Is the CBD still important? Some indirect evidence on this question is provided by Edward Glaeser and Matthew Kahn (2004), who use ZIP Code level employment data for 301 metropolitan areas to calculate employment density. The ZIP Code containing the CBD is the densest employment location in 180 of the metropolitan areas, and among the 4 densest in 270 of the metropolitan areas. Yes, the CBD is still important.

Detailed Analysis

Let us return to the four metropolitan areas introduced in Chapter 4, namely Cleveland, Indianapolis, Portland, and St. Louis. Table 5-1 illustrates the extent to which employment is concentrated into identifiable centers in those cities. Only between 31 and 52 percent of the total employment is in centers, reinforcing the point that an exclusive focus on employment centers excludes much of the true economic picture in metropolitan areas.

Downtown is by far the largest employment center in each city, typically representing about one-half of the total employment in centers. The monocentric model is again demonstrated not to be the best depiction of the overall employment distribution. However, we need to recognize that downtowns remain uniquely important trading places.

An important question is the extent to which the downtowns in the metropolitan areas are similar. There are at least two dimensions to this question. First, is there a set of sectors in which downtowns tend to specialize? Second, are downtowns less specialized than other employment centers, as might be expected given that the monocentric city had concentrated employment in all sectors in the CBD? Most observers take as given that the CBD is less specialized than suburban employment centers, but we will take nothing for granted.

To go further into understanding the role of the downtown, we will again use the LQ approach to identify sectoral specialization. Unfortunately, sectoral employment data was unavailable for Portland, so we will only be able to look in detail at the other three metropolitan areas. Although all three cities are mid-sized and midwestern, they fall into three separate categories of centralization of employment. Thus, they provide an opportunity to see if there are observable differences in the CBD among metropolitan areas with different amounts of decentralization of employment. The LQ is calculated relative to metropolitan area employment to highlight the nature of the CBD relative to the rest of the region. If the LQ is greater than 1.25, then the CBD will be said to specialize in that sector.

Table 5-2 presents the results of the LQ analysis. All three of the downtowns specialize in FIRE, communications and public utilities, and public administration. These sectors make intuitive sense. Edwin Mills (1992) argues that ambiguous information is best transmitted using personal interaction, and much of the data that banks, insurance companies, and related firms deal in is ambiguous. Further, these firms all need continuous interaction with law firms, which tend to cluster near government buildings such as courthouses. The downtown concentration of public administration employment in part reflects the role of each city in hosting local, county, state, and federal government buildings. Finally, communication and public utilities infrastructures were originally constructed in the monocentric era. Both the infrastructures and the employment needed to operate and maintain them remain focused on the downtown. The fact that both downtown Cleveland and downtown St. Louis are also found to specialize in transportation services reinforces this point.

The evidence on the second question, the relative specialization of the downtown, is mixed. The downtowns are less specialized than average, but they are not the least specialized among all of the employment centers. Downtown Cleveland has seven sectors that it exports, the most

Table 5-2. *Downtown Trading Place Analysis*

City	Total employment	Export sectors (in descending order of employment)
Cleveland	155,924	Professional services, FIRE, public administration, communication and public utilities, transportation, mining, armed forces (44.6%)
Indianapolis	105,685	FIRE, public administration, communications and public utilities, mining (31.5%)
St. Louis	224,299	Nondurable manufacturing, communications and public utilities, transportation, public administration (38.8%)

Note: "FIRE" stands for "Finance, Insurance, and Real Estate." The percentage in paren-theses at the end of the list of export sectors is the fraction of total employment in the center accounted for by those sectors.
Source: 1990 Census Transportation Planning Package.

of any center in the three metropolitan areas. Downtown Indianapolis and downtown St. Louis both have four export sectors. One center in Indianapolis and three centers in St. Louis have more export sectors than the downtown.

When we look at the fraction of employment accounted for by the export sectors, the hypothesis of less downtown specialization again receives mixed support. Downtown Cleveland has 44.6 percent of its employment in export sectors, the fifth highest ranking in this category among the nine employment centers in the Cleveland metropolitan area. Downtown Indianapolis, at 31.5 percent, ranks seventh out of eleven, and downtown St. Louis, at 38.8 percent, ranks ninth out of ten.

CENTRAL CITY ECONOMIC DEVELOPMENT

> An urban downtown these days is a high-risk entrepreneurial business, and cities are in it whether they like it or not.
>
> Jonathan Barnett (1995, 119)

Persuading policy begins by determining the strengths of an area and then works to build on those strengths. A complete enumeration of attempts to increase economic activity in the CBD and surrounding areas would fill up the rest of this book and more. Instead I will look at two approaches to improving the economic fortunes of the central city through the lens of trading place theory. The first approach is to target economic development incentives toward distressed areas. This approach, while plausible, has been handicapped by the lack of explicit recognition of the role of these areas as trading places. The second approach is to build on the strength provided by a geographically fixed exporter of educational services, known in the vernacular as a college or university.

I am not the first to emphasize that increasing the links between the downtown and the rest of the metropolitan area is vital to improving the economic condition of the area and its inhabitants. The most influential writer on this subject has been Harvard Business school professor Michael Porter, whose 1995 article on the "competitive advantage of the inner city" argued that these seemingly barren areas had important economic strengths. These advantages include their strategic location, substantial demand for products by residents, and large supply of motivated workers. His focus on developing these strengths to better interact with the rest of the metropolitan economy is an outstanding example of persuading policy applied in a trading place framework.

William Cronon (1991, 326) describes the impact of railroad access to Chicago on formerly isolated towns as "a striking reduction in the capital costs of doing business." If a firm must depend solely on local custom to survive, it must be exceedingly well capitalized to get through occasional local downturns. Ongoing relations with a wide market not only helped small-scale entrepreneurs in the rural Midwest in the 1800s, but they will also help central city entrepreneurs in the twenty-first century who need to connect with the rest of the metropolitan area.

Goldilocks Visits the Enterprise Zone

Enterprise zones and their federal counterparts, empowerment zones, have been used throughout the United States. Broadly speaking, enterprise zones consist of a set of geographically targeted incentives to promote two policy goals. First, they are supposed to attract and retain business investment within their boundaries. Second, they are supposed to increase employment among residents of the zones. Unfortunately, they are typically too big to achieve the first goal and too small to achieve the second goal. We will now explore this issue and I will suggest some "just-right" policies that modify the enterprise zone approach.

Like Goldilocks sitting on chairs, we begin by finding that enterprise zones are too big. Enterprise zones are usually larger than a trading place, and they often incorporate more than one trading place within their boundaries. This makes them inefficient for attracting specific types of business investment to specific places. A cynical reading of enterprise zones is that they are a politically palatable way of reducing corporate taxes. A legislator can run for reelection having "provided incentives for redeveloping blighted areas" instead of having "reduced taxes on businesses." In fact, the proliferation of enterprise zones in many states has effectively enacted corporate tax reform at the state level, truly a Papa Bear approach to targeting.

One reason that enterprise zones are too big is that they are often defined based on the characteristics of residents, and the residential areas extend beyond the employment center. Ironically, incentives aimed at improving labor market outcomes for the residents use too small a region. Not all jobs will be in close proximity to residents. This problem is reinforced by the geographically restricted nature of enterprise zone labor market incentives, as distressed areas are typically not large generators of new employment opportunities. This feature of enterprise zones creates incentives to reinforce labor market autarky separating residents from the rest of the metropolitan area, therefore expanding the underlying cause of the economic problem.

Enterprise zones have been handicapped by their attempt to accomplish two goals using one policy tool, forcing Goldilocks to straddle two uncomfortable situations. Unlike the statistician in the joke, she takes no comfort in being fine on average. Just-right business incentives would be based on trading places, such as employment centers, rather than on residential boundaries that imperfectly reflect the spatial pattern of production. An example of this approach in Pennsylvania will be seen a little later in the chapter. Just-right employment policy would use employment subsidies that are targeted by residence but that are mobile across the entire range of employment locations. Daniel Immergluck and Timothy Hilton (1996) proposed just such a policy and illustrated its impact on Chicago, and their approach can serve as a model to researchers (and, dare I say, state legislators) elsewhere.

Colleges and Universities as Economic Development Engines

Colleges and universities matter. This is not only the immodest and self-serving statement of a person who works in higher education, but also the result of considerable analysis by hardheaded researchers. Michael Porter of the Harvard Business school not only asserted that inner cities had competitive advantages, he founded an organization (Initiative for a Competitive Inner City) devoted to identifying and developing these advantages in various places. In 2002, the organization collaborated with CEOs for Cities on a major study of the current and potential role of institutes of higher education in economic development.

No one doubts the vital role played by colleges and universities in undertaking original research and in educating people in order to add productivity to existing firms. What is less visible, though, is the sheer scale of this sector of the economy. The study found that there were more than 1,900 colleges and universities located in core urban areas in 1996. The combined spending of these institutions was $135 billion, more than nine times the direct federal government spending on urban business and job development. Half of this spending was on salaries, and two-thirds of the more than 2 million jobs are not held by faculty.

Not only are colleges and universities large, but they are also growing. Between 1990 and 1999, more than 300,000 jobs were created in this sector. Unlike many growing industries, institutes of higher education tend to be strongly anchored in a particular place. This makes them especially well suited to redeveloping areas that have declined. The University of Pennsylvania, whose investments in West Philadelphia have been nationally celebrated, undertook these activities at least in part as a way to preserve the university as a going concern, as it was losing students because of its unattractive surroundings.

Higher education is an export from inner cities. Most of their revenue comes from student tuition, and even urban open-enrollment universities draw students from the entire metropolitan area, not just their immediate neighborhood. It is easier to retain people in an area than to attract them in the first place. Graduates of inner-city colleges have demonstrated that they have some strong attraction to the area, which makes them a natural target for retention as part of an overall metropolitan development strategy. Some colleges go so far as to operate their own business incubators. The 2002 study found systematic differences between these incubators and those operated by other actors. They were both more urban (67 percent versus 57 percent) and more technology-focused (70 percent versus 25 percent) than the general population, illustrating the possibility of transformation held out by these institutions.

PERSUADING POLICY IN PENNSYLVANIA: KEYSTONE INNOVATION ZONES. The election of the former mayor of Philadelphia as the governor of Pennsylvania in 2002 was inevitably a time for the commonwealth to consider new urban development proposals. While it was easy to predict that there would be proposals, their persuading nature was not so easy to predict. One of the centerpieces of Governor Rendell's approach is the creation of Keystone Innovation Zones (KIZs), which are designed to build from one of the widespread success areas in the Pennsylvania economy. A report from the Brookings Institution (2003) that is otherwise quite critical of the state recognizes that higher education is one of its two key economic assets, along with the health-care sector ("eds and meds").

The KIZ proposals have a similar name to the enterprise zone program in Pennsylvania, known as the Keystone Opportunity Zones (KOZs), but the similarity ends there. Unlike the KOZ, there is no specific set of incentives attached to KIZ designation. Instead, the KIZ approach recognizes that each city and college is different and serves as a targeting mechanism for the appropriate state funds. To qualify, one or more colleges must team with other local partners to identify a geographic area near the college and a set of industry sectors on which to focus. There have been KIZs approved for some well-known institutions in large cities, including Carnegie-Mellon, University of Pittsburgh, and University of Pennsylvania. But there are also other examples that are not as famous but that also build on local strengths, including institutions in Scranton, Wilkes-Barre, Johnstown, and Williamsport.

The requirement for the partners to be identified along with an annual evaluation process by the granting agency means that specific goals must be agreed on. This makes it more likely that the initiative will result in changes that are efficient, because all of the relevant parties are included from the outset.

Pennsylvania's KIZ is a modest program but one that seems destined for success. By recognizing the differences from place to place, and by building on an important regional fixed asset, it can serve as a model of persuading policies for other states to emulate.

PERSUADING POLICY NATIONALLY: COMMUNITY DEVELOPMENT FINANCIAL INSTITUTIONS. To capitalize on the competitive advantage of the inner city requires making it an attractive place for private investors. In the case of residential investment, this translates into mortgage lending by commercial institutions. This is a problematic proposition given the history of depreciating property values in these areas. In the case of business investment, it can be difficult for entrepreneurs to attract capital at terms that make it possible to succeed.

A general type of intermediate step between outright philanthropy and unrestrained free markets has arisen under the rubric of community development financial institutions (CDFIs). These institutions play a vital role in connecting low- and moderate-income areas with the rest of the metropolitan area by connecting individuals and businesses with the national pool of capital.

The federal government has subsidized the efforts of CDFIs in a variety of ways, including creating various tax credits that can be syndicated to for-profit investors in order to raise working capital. CDFIs often have an underpinning of grant support from philanthropic foundations as well. For example, the Cleveland Civic Vision Housing Fund was created in 2000. This fund is organized as a for-profit corporation with two classes of investor. One class of investor receives a market-rate payout, while the other (consisting of foundations) receives a lower rate of return that is only payable after the amounts due the first class have been satisfied. The goal of this fund and the myriad others across the United States is to render itself superfluous as neighborhoods begin to thrive, allowing people and businesses to qualify for loans on standard terms.

While CDFIs are a good idea, they are hardly a new idea. Rosalynn Baxandall and Elizabeth Ewen (2000, 44–6) describe the efforts of the Regional Planning Association of America during the 1920s to create limited dividend companies. These companies specialized in funding housing for low- and moderate-income workers, paid dividends that were capped, and were government-subsidized by being exempt from state and local taxes. It might be frustrating to discover that repeatedly "there is nothing new under the sun," but reiterating the point might help us to approach our work with some appropriate humility.

STADIUM CONSTRUCTION AS A DOWNTOWN DEVELOPMENT TOOL

Stadium construction is occurring in cities throughout the United States as cities compete to attract and retain professional sports teams. Almost without exception, public funds are sought to augment or substitute for private investment. One study (Swindell 1996) found that the typical stadium includes a financing package that is 61 percent public and 39 percent private. Dozens of new stadiums have recently been constructed at a cost of (usually hundreds of) millions of dollars each. This implies a public expenditure of billions of dollars to help construct buildings that are used mainly for the enjoyment of sporting events. Surely, one might think, there are more important things for governments to spend their scarce resources on.

The response to such a criticism is usually that the stadium is not desired as an end in itself, but is instead a means of promoting economic development in a metropolitan area. There are tangible benefits in the form of increased revenues from various taxes, increased employment in businesses that serve the people that visit the stadium, and an increase in the export of visitor services if new people are attracted to your metropolitan area to visit the stadium. There are also intangible benefits associated with the presence of professional sports, including free television coverage (usually positive) of your city, a perception as being "major league," and an increased ability to attract and retain workers for whom the presence of professional sports is important.

The typical economic analysis of the effect of a stadium proceeds by evaluating these benefits and comparing them to the costs. There have been several thorough and analytically valid exercises of this sort. Dean Baim (1994) carefully calculates the benefits and costs accruing to cities from fifteen stadium projects. A volume edited by Roger Noll and Andrew Zimbalist (1997) includes another set of case studies along with a conceptual overview of how to measure costs and benefits correctly. Every serious analyst finds that public finance of stadiums fails a benefit-cost test when only the tangible financial benefits are considered.

In this section, I will address two questions. First, should stadiums receive public financing? In other words, what is the economic benefit from a stadium? Second, should stadiums be located downtown? The questions are familiar but I will use an unfamiliar approach to them, albeit one that follows naturally from the trading place analysis we have been doing. I will begin by using an indirect approach to estimate the impact of stadiums. This approach involves calculating the "office space equivalent" to a stadium. I will then go on to analyze why one can argue both for a significant economic impact of stadiums and why that impact is maximized by the choice of a downtown location. The example of recently constructed stadiums in Cleveland is used to illustrate the analysis, but the approach is applicable to any city.

What Is a Stadium?

Consider the following situation. During a short time period, several thousand people arrive at and enter a structure. They remain in the structure for a few hours, perhaps purchasing a meal while there. They all leave at about the same time and go home. What is this structure? Wrong – it's an office building. And this idea gives us an approach to estimating the impact of a stadium.

What are the external economic development impacts of an office building? They're similar to those provided by a stadium, without the TV coverage. So what I'd like us to do is to think about the "office equivalent" of a sports stadium. In other words, if the stadium were an office building, how big would it be?

An example will suffice to show the basic idea. Jacobs Field in Cleveland is the home of the Cleveland Indians. Suppose that the attendance at an Indians game is approximately 42,000 per night, which is the capacity of the stadium. There are about ninety home games per year, including exhibition games.

There is a rule of thumb in commercial real estate that it takes 250 square feet of office space for each employee (Garreau 1991, 119). Thus, if you employ 300 people then you will require 75,000 square feet of office space. Pursuing the metaphor, Jacobs Field attracts 42,000 people to the "office" each time that the Indians play. That implies a space equivalent of 10.5 million square feet, or approximately one-half of the total nongovernmental commercial office space in downtown Cleveland at the time of its construction (20.9 million square feet available as of June 1996, with about 16.3 million square feet occupied).

Of course, there is an important difference between Jacobs Field and the other office buildings. Jacobs Field is only occupied on about ninety days, while the other buildings are occupied year-round. If we subtract weekends, then we can estimate that a typical office building is open 260 days per year. Assuming that the impact is proportional to the number of days that people actually go to the office, we should reduce our estimate of the impact of Jacobs Field from 10.5 million square feet to 3.63 million square feet to account for the reduced number of days that Jacobs Field is open.

How big is 3.63 million square feet? It is a little more than 17 percent of the entire stock of downtown commercial office space around the time that the stadium was constructed. An alternative is to compare Jacobs Field with other landmarks. The heart of downtown Cleveland is Public Square, bordered on three sides by office buildings. These buildings – Terminal Tower, the BP Building, and Society Tower – have a combined 3.2 million square feet of space. Thus, Jacobs Field is the equivalent of the entire Public Square area and more.

Given that Jacobs Field ranks as a massive commercial development, was it worth its price? Ignoring financial complications, we can approximate the construction cost of Jacobs Field at $180 million in 1994 (*USA Today*, September 6, 1996). The construction cost of the BP Building alone was about $200 million in the early 1980s, making Jacobs Field a comparative bargain even before taking inflation into account.

Jacobs Field was not constructed as an isolated project, but as part of a combined project known as "Gateway." The Gateway project includes Gund Arena, home of the Cleveland Cavaliers basketball team and the Cleveland Lumberjacks hockey team. Gund Arena also hosts events ranging from ice skating to rock concerts. All told, 1.8 million people attended events in Gund Arena in its first full year of operation (1995). The capacity of the arena is 21,000, so if we assume that it sold out every event then the arena was open on eighty-six days. The office equivalent of Gund Arena at capacity is 5.25 million square feet, which after adjusting for the number of days open yields 1.74 million square feet net office space. The construction costs for Gund Arena were $192 million in 1994, including $37 million for parking. Adding Gund Arena to Jacobs Field means that the Gateway project as a whole yielded the equivalent of 5.37 million square feet of office space to downtown Cleveland – a 25 percent increase in the amount of space – at a cost of approximately $400 million. This total cost includes both private and public sources and thus overstates the public cost.

Finally, we should consider the implications of the football stadium in Cleveland. This stadium seats approximately 73,000 people and cost approximately $300 million to build. At capacity, then, we would estimate the office-space equivalent to be 1.8 million square feet (73,000 people × 250 square feet/person). Football-only stadiums have far fewer dates than baseball stadiums or arenas. There are only limited alternative uses. A study by Economics Research Associates (2004, 21) for Arlington, Texas, anticipates thirty-five events in addition to Dallas Cowboys games, ranging from a college football bowl game to high school football and "other" (seven events). This exaggerates the alternative uses for the Cleveland stadium and perhaps for the stadium in Texas. Suppose the football stadium can be used for thirteen dates per year. The net office equivalent is 5 percent of 1.8 million square feet, or 900,000 square feet of office space. In other words, the stadium cost 50 percent more than Jacobs Field while yielding only 25 percent of the office space. This is not as strong an investment as the Gateway project, all else being equal.

This discussion has used the situation in Cleveland for illustration, but similar calculations can be made for other stadiums in other cities. There are two important components to calculating the office space equivalent of a stadium: the number of dates the stadium is open and the average attendance. If either of those components changes, then the calculated impact of the stadium will change. For example, when the Indians returned in the late 1990s and early 2000s to their poor performance of the 1960s, 1970s, and 1980s, attendance at Jacobs Field declined from its capacity of 42,000 per game to as low as 21,000 per game. In that case, we calculate the impact of Jacobs Field as being only 1.81 million square feet rather than the 3.63 million square feet under the conditions of full attendance. If you build it and they don't come, it doesn't help your economy.

Why Should a Stadium Be Downtown?

The short answer is that it's a massive office building. The slightly longer answer is that there are three characteristics of the downtown of most (all) cities that make locating a stadium there optimal from a perspective of economic development impact. In other words, if a stadium is going to have a significant impact on a local economy, it's going to do so from a downtown location. The three characteristics of downtown that make it attractive are its accessibility to the entire metropolitan area, its existing transportation infrastructure including parking, and the potential for agglomeration economies of scale with the "other" large office buildings located there. I should point out that my thesis is not that only cities with deteriorating CBDs should locate stadiums there. My argument is that regardless of whether the CBD is declining or thriving, the proper location for a stadium, assuming that it is worth constructing in the first place, is downtown.

The first argument for putting a stadium downtown is the fact that the CBD is likely to be the place that minimizes total transportation cost for the entire metropolitan area. This is true both because the central city of a metropolitan area typically contains a large fraction of the metropolitan population and because of the roughly symmetric distribution of population around central cities. There is a caveat, though. Suppose only a relatively small fraction of the population attends events at the stadium. In that case, the transportation-cost-minimizing location would be close to that group of people. The existence of luxury boxes, corporate loges, and club seats at modern stadiums suggests a distinctly upper-income flavor to the crowd. Because most of the people sitting in club seats will be suburban dwellers, wouldn't it make more sense to locate the stadium in the suburbs? Possibly, but only if there is a strong asymmetry to suburban development. In other words, if all the suburbs are located to the east of the city, then moving the stadium east might reduce travel cost. If they are evenly distributed to the east and to the west, then reduced travel time to eastern residents would be offset by increased time for western residents.

The second argument for a downtown location is the existence of a transportation infrastructure, including parking, designed to deal with rush-hour commuting. There are approximately 155,000 people working in downtown Cleveland, as we saw earlier in this chapter. Most of them drive to work and arrive within a relatively small time window. A transportation system that can handle 155,000 people arriving en masse should be able to handle 42,000 people arriving at and departing from a baseball game. The fact that the streets, rail lines, and parking garages would otherwise be fully occupied only during working hours during weekdays means that there is excess capacity downtown on weekends and evenings. Stadiums have peak hours that do not coincide with the peak hours for office buildings, and therefore they provide an opportunity to more efficiently use the existing infrastructure.

The third argument for locating stadiums downtown is the possibility of agglomeration economies of scale with other attractions and offices. These spillover effects are the main justification for public involvement in stadium finance. For example, the presence of a sports stadium can reduce the entertainment budget for a professional services firm, in that it only has to walk its clients down the street as opposed to transporting them someplace else. More prosaically, downtown security is enhanced by the presence of activity in the downtown outside of working hours during the work week. Of course, nearby restaurants and bars are also better off. One benefit of the move to an upper-income clientele at sporting events is that the types of restaurants that they frequent will be similar to the types of restaurants that they frequent during the work week. A downtown stadium that helps to expand the downtown restaurant market that appeals to downtown workers can also help to attract service firms – renters of commercial office space – to the downtown. This leveraging of the stadium is a positive externality that the stadium owner could not necessarily capture and is therefore an argument for transfers from beneficiaries to the owner of the stadium.

Objections and Caveats

The arguments to this point have been generally favorable to the modern practice of large-scale public finance of downtown stadiums. Let us now turn to some of the restrictions of the analysis. Given that the thrust of the argument is that stadiums are economic equivalents to commercial office space, we will be particularly interested in exploring the limits to that comparison.

STADIUM ATTENDEES DON'T PRODUCE ANYTHING. Perhaps the most obvious objection to my comparison of stadium attendees to office workers is the observation that stadium attendees are consumers of services while office workers are producers of services. Note, though, that stadiums and office buildings have very similar external economic impacts. The offices export services to the rest of the metropolitan area and to other metropolitan areas. The office workers provide external benefits by eating at downtown restaurants, shopping at downtown stores, and walking on downtown streets. These external benefits come not in their capacity as producers of services, but in their capacity as people who happen to be downtown. It is true that people who attend sporting events do not produce the services within the stadium ("the wave" that entertains people in the stands and TV viewers is perhaps a counterexample), but they produce external economic impacts in exactly the same way that office workers do.

ON THE NONLINEARITY OF OPERATING DATES. When calculating the office space equivalent of a stadium, I assumed that a stadium that was open for eighty days per year was equivalent to two stadiums that were each open for forty days per year. In the case of a combined baseball stadium/arena project, such as Gateway, such an argument is perhaps reasonable. After all, if the stadium is open for ninety days and the arena for eighty-six days, as I estimated previously, then you have 176 out of 260 work days covered. Further, the stadium and the arena have different seasons, the stadium attracting commuters from April to October (baseball season) and the arena from October to May (basketball and hockey season). Restaurants that depend on a regular flow of customers can therefore locate near Gateway, especially if there is a related strengthening of the downtown lunch crowd.

If we attempt to extend this reasoning to a football-only stadium, though, then the argument is more strained. In the example considered earlier, the stadium would only be open for business on thirteen days.

While thirteen is unquestionably 5 percent of 260, one might question how much of an impact thirteen days would actually have. Consider an office building that is 95 percent vacant. Does it have more or less impact on the local economy than a stadium that is empty 95 percent of the time but filled to capacity on the remaining 5 percent of the days?

PUBLIC VERSUS PRIVATE FINANCE. Even if we are convinced that the right way to think of a stadium is as a massive office development, it does not immediately follow that it should be publicly financed. The argument for public financing in this analysis proceeds with some slight changes from the traditional economic impact story, though. The crux of the argument is that there are positive externalities that result from stadium development that the developer of the stadium is unable to capture. As a result, stadiums will be underprovided in the absence of subsidies.

There are externalities of two types that result from stadium construction. The first are what I call "direct" externalities. For example, there is the increased patronage of restaurants that surround the stadium, the increased public safety resulting from the presence of people on downtown streets after working hours and on weekends, and the increased congestion (a negative externality) as people travel to and from the stadium. These externalities are familiar to connoisseurs of economic impact studies.

The second type of externalities resulting from stadium construction is "indirect" externalities. These include the familiar list: positive image of the city generated by television coverage, the civic unity and pride provided by professional sports, the benefit to local nonprofit organizations of athletes' involvement in fundraising, and other intangible benefits. However, there is a less familiar type of externality that is implied by the analysis here, the benefits to downtown commercial office space users from the presence of a stadium. If the service-providing firms that are located downtown find it easier to attract and retain employees or to entertain clients as a result of a downtown stadium, then their costs of doing business fall. This is a classic agglomeration economy of scale. The strength of this argument is bolstered by the willingness of firms to pay large sums of money for corporate suites, even in a time of expense reductions and less favorable income tax treatment of entertainment expenses. Of course, to the extent that the rentals of luxury suites reflect the positive economic effect of the stadium on the firms, there is less reason for government intervention because the externality has already been internalized.

"PUSHPINS VERSUS POETRY." The utilitarians argued that redistributing income from the rich, who had a low marginal utility of income, to the poor, who had a high marginal utility of income, would improve societal welfare. An argument used to rebut the utilitarians was that not all activities are of equal merit. In the early 1800s, this argument took the form of invidious comparisons between the game of pushpins, a way the lower classes spent their leisure time, with the reading and writing of poetry, a way the upper classes spent their leisure time. Surely, it was argued, the appreciation of poetry was a greater contribution to happiness than participation in a meaningless game.

The application of this debate to modern society is immediate. Why should we fritter away resources on an admittedly popular set of activities when more worthy activities, such as ballet and opera, go begging? Consider the case of the performing arts in downtown Cleveland. A long-term major renovation of five historic theaters in downtown Cleveland, the so-called Playhouse Square development, has led to more than 2 million visitors per year to the theaters. We could develop an office space equivalent of theaters as we did for stadiums. In fact, arts organizations always remind funders and politicians about the economic development aspects of their activities as well as the cultural dimension.

Suppose that there are two alternative developments with equivalent economic development impacts, a baseball stadium and a theater. If there are only sufficient resources to construct one of the two developments, which should be built? This is the pushpins versus poetry question brought up to date, but with a twist. Because of the tilt of professional sports attendance toward richer people, it is now a question of the relative worth of the leisure activities of different groups of high-income people. And the extent to which both sporting events and theatrical events are extensions of the weekday office, with corporate seats to entertain clients, complicates the question.

A related question, and arguably a more important one, is the tradeoff between activities that have immediate impacts and those that don't pay off for a long time. In most cities, this question can usually be phrased in terms of development projects versus school funding. Without going into the detailed question of whether more money would improve the schools or even whether the money devoted to subsidizing a stadium would be available for schools, I will only observe that there is a clear bias in the political process against activities that do not pay off until after the next election, much less after a ten- to twenty-year period as children receive a better education.

Why Build Stadiums? Enjoyment, Not Financial Benefit

There is by now an extensive literature that details not only that the economic impact claims of stadium proponents are exaggerated, but also that stadiums might detract from local economic performance. Noll and Zimbalist (1997, 497–8) provide a systematic deconstruction of how an asserted economic impact of $760,000 is more accurately described as $22,200. The general inflationary procedure includes three steps. First, count all people at the game, not just the ones who came to town specifically to attend the game. Second, count all the revenue, not just the local value added. Third, use a multiplier that is larger than justifiable for the impact on the regional economy of an added amount of spending brought in from outside the region.

Heywood Sanders (2005) performs an even harsher analysis of convention centers. Unlike professional sports, where the league limits the number of teams, there is not a central body restricting the number of centers. This makes any financial benefits even more likely to be competed away.

For an example of how economic impact might be exaggerated, return to the case of Arlington, Texas, and a new stadium for the Dallas Cowboys. (This is especially painful to write as a lifelong fan of the Cowboys.) The study assumes that all of the impact of the stadium would be new to Tarrant County, while at the same time noting that the proximity to Dallas makes it likely that some of the impact will "leak" out of the county. Why not make the obvious point that Irving, current home of the team, is in Dallas County but close to Tarrant County, so that there should already be some economic impact in Tarrant County from having the team in the region?

Suppose, for the sake of argument, that there is no net financial benefit to a metropolitan area. Is it possible that there are still reasons to support the use of public funds to construct a stadium? Clearly, that's a rhetorical question. But it gets at the distinction between financial benefits and economic benefits that confuses many people. There are benefits that are real despite not having any financial measure. For example, if I am very thirsty and willing to pay you $2 for a drink of water, but you give it to me for free, does that mean that the drink has no value? No, it has a value of $2, even though no money has changed hands. This difference between the amount that a person is willing to pay and the amount that they actually pay is called *consumer surplus*. It is very likely that a local sports team generates consumer surplus. The willingness of people to wait in line for tickets, purchase paraphernalia, and spend time analyzing the local team's prospects are evidence of the value that they place over and above any metropolitan employment impact.

There is an important potential inefficiency in the case of professional sports in that people can benefit from the team without paying for the service. For example, a person can be an avid baseball fan but not attend a single game. A less extreme situation would be someone who attends an occasional game but mostly listens to games on the radio and discusses the events the next day at work. If this type of situation is typical, then a simple calculation of the dollars exchanged for the sports team will underestimate the benefits that people in the metropolitan area derive from its presence.

The question, then, is whether the consumer surplus from the presence of a local sports team exceeds the cost. Consider a simple, but representative, example. A metropolitan area spends $400 million to build a baseball stadium, and receives no net financial benefits. The annual costs of debt service and depreciation for the stadium can be estimated at about 10 percent of the total, or $40 million per year. If 2 million people live in the metropolitan area, then all that is necessary is for each person to get $20 of consumer surplus each year from the baseball team. This is an interesting number precisely because it is relatively small. Unfortunately, there have not yet been systematic studies of the magnitude of the public consumption benefits from professional sports. The issue of the range of consumption benefits available in a metropolitan area leads naturally to the final topic of this chapter: downtown as a residential location.

LIVING FOR THE CITY

> The crucial difference between cities and suburbs, then, is that they are often home for different kinds of people. If one is to understand their behavior, these differences are much more important than whether they reside inside or outside the city limits. Inner-city residential areas are home to the rich, the poor, and the nonwhite, as well as the unmarried and the childless middle class. Their ways of life differ from those of suburbanites and people in the outer city, but because they are *not* young working or lower or upper middle class families.
>
> Herbert Gans (1967, 288–9)

Once we free ourselves from the monocentric city model, the idea of the CBD as a place to live emerges naturally. Like any other location, it will be more attractive to some people than to others. An influential vein of analysis has focused on both the type of person that is attracted to live downtown and on the impact on the metropolitan area of attracting downtown residents.

The Creative Class Moves In

The most prominent example of analysis emphasizing the heterogeneity in tastes among groups is the "creative class" hypothesis of Richard Florida. In a series of articles and books, Professor Florida has linked metropolitan economic success with attracting members of the creative class, people who are "primarily paid to create and have considerably more autonomy and flexibility than the other two classes" (2002, 8). The creative class, according to Florida, is divided into the supercreative core, who "produce new forms or designs that are readily transferable and widely useful" (69), and the creative professionals, who "engage in creative problem solving, drawing on complex bodies of knowledge to solve specific problems" (69). He estimates that the creative class numbers about 38 million, or 30 percent of the workforce, and that it has grown substantially over the past few decades.

Florida asserts that members of the creative class are drawn to cities and the organic street-level culture that is found there. In addition to a natural affinity to other creative individuals, the flexible time schedule of the creative class requires a cultural setting that accommodates them. If not "the city that never sleeps," this group at least requires activities that don't have specific beginning and ending times. This is a problem for the standard economic development approach of stadium or cultural center construction, as the baseball game and the symphony will begin and end regardless of whether the computer programmer has finished the software design. On the other hand, more flexible cultural ameni-ties, such as restaurants or clubs, are conducive to creative-class behavior. They are also often related to colleges, which provide both the education necessary for membership in the creative class and the introduction to a specific area. Clearly, the college and university–based approach to eco-nomic development discussed earlier is amenable to a creative-class view of the world.

The increased role and numerical prominence of the creative class bode well for cities, asserts Florida. The CBD stands to benefit as it provides high levels of amenities, sometimes as the result of consumption-oriented economic development and sometimes organic to the area. One attraction to people who work long and irregular hours is the prospect of a short commute, as long as the person's job is in the CBD. The downside of the downtown includes expensive living space and low-quality public schools. Hence, the creative-class household that includes children or wants a big yard will not join in the return to the city. Rather, Florida's analysis applies to a subset of creative-class workers, including highly paid professionals, families without children (either because they haven't had them, they've already raised them and are now empty nesters, or because they are non-traditional households), and people with a strong distaste for commuting. So even the most avant-garde city still needs boring suburbs for some of its inhabitants. As Florida says (234), "Members of the Creative Class come in all shapes, sizes, colors, and lifestyles; and to be truly successful, cities and regions have to offer something for them all."

Amenities and Power Couples

Urban economists have tended to focus on the production advantages of cities, such as agglomeration economies of scale, and the consump-tion disadvantages, such as congestion and other negative externalities. The creative-class approach of Florida is a specific example of a broader view that appreciates that dense residential settlement can come with consumption advantages as well as disadvantages. This point is developed most generally in an article by Edward Glaeser, Jed Kolko, and Albert Saiz (2001). Because the transport costs for many goods and services have fallen, the relative cost of personal access to amenities has increased. Telecommuting is the most extreme version of this phenomenon. If you can work from anywhere, then all that matters for your location decision is how you spend the time that you are *not* working. This is a radical change from traditional household location choice.

We expect people to cluster in places with attractive features. For the creative class, this could mean a location near the CBD. For nature lovers, it could mean a place with a particular configuration of features (warm or cold, mountains or ocean). One piece of evidence introduced by Glaeser, Kolko, et al. is the increase in commuting trips that begin in the central city and conclude elsewhere in the metropolitan area. In 1960, 12.1 percent of commuters traveled from residences in the city to workplaces outside the city, while in 1990 24.3 percent of workers did so. This reflects the decentralization of employment, but it also illustrates a willingness of people to pay high housing costs while undertaking a longer commute. The inference is that these people receive consumption advantages from urban residence that outweigh the costs.

For highly educated people, whether creative class or otherwise, there is an attraction to large cities that goes beyond the possibility of amenities outside of work. This attraction is vital not only to the development of cities, but in fact to the continuation of the species. The increase in dual-career couples and the requirement that people live in the same metropolitan area where they work combines to give an advantage to larger cities in attracting educated workers. Dora Costa and Matt Kahn (2000) provide evidence that power couples, in which both husband and wife are college graduates, have become increasingly concentrated in large cities. Because of this concentration, large cities get an advantage in both innovation and adaptation of inventions and thus serve as a magnet for highly educated people who are single as well. In addition to their statistical analysis, the lives of Costa and Kahn (a married couple) illustrate the colocation problem, as he left Columbia University in New York to join Tufts University in Boston, and she is a professor at MIT.

Hotels as Housing

Purchasing a house is a form of investment under uncertainty. From our earlier analysis, we know that people will wait to make investments until the benefits seem to outweigh the costs by a substantial amount. For suburban residents contemplating a move downtown, the level of uncertainty is very large. Will they be isolated pioneers living in a deteriorating area, or will they be trendsetters riding the wave of amenity-driven redevelopment? This is not an academic question, as they are being asked to risk substantial amounts of time and money on the outcome.

For someone to be willing to purchase a housing unit downtown, he or she has to be willing to spend the night downtown. This is not only a necessary condition, but it suggests a prescription for helping reduce the uncertainty facing a potential resident. Instead of moving permanently downtown, why not consider moving downtown temporarily, even overnight? Visit the shops, have dinner in the nearby restaurants, go to a game or show, and then stay in a hotel. This is a direct link between the visitor-driven function of the downtown trading place and its residents. By reducing the size of the step that a person needs to take, hotel development can increase residential development.

There is a further benefit from a substantial hotel population. Many retail activities, such as pharmacies or grocery stores, need a minimum amount of traffic to thrive. Hotel visitors can help to support these retail activities, which in turn contribute to the needed amenities to make downtown living attractive.

DECLARING VICTORY: WHEN CAN A LOCAL GOVERNMENT STOP SUBSIDIZING ACTIVITY?

As suburban trading places grow to resemble downtown, there has also been some movement in the opposite direction, as downtowns look to add residents. For example, downtown Minneapolis went from 10,100 households and 17,700 residents in 1990 to 13,600 households and 23,500 residents in 2005, and this was considered a success. Interestingly, the growth there was ascribed to demographic changes (fewer families with children) and increased amenities. This story is compatible with the earlier theoretical discussion about sources of growth for downtown residents.

What follows is a case study of Cleveland's efforts in the mid-1990s to encourage market-rate housing downtown. As with the other situations in which I focus on Cleveland, the themes are general, although the circumstances in which those themes have developed are unique.

Similar to many cities in the United States, Cleveland, Ohio, has been aggressively using tax abatement and other public subsidies to encourage the development of downtown market-rate rental housing (as distinct from low-income public housing). This policy has been successful, in that 1,470 new units were added to the downtown between 1994 and 1998. This is especially impressive in that new rental unit construction in Cuyahoga County (where Cleveland is located) has steadily declined since the 1970s and did not exceed 500 units per year during the time period

Table 5-3. *Rents in Selected Locations 1990–1999*

City or neighborhood	Median gross rent, 1990	Median gross rent, 1999	Percent change 1990–1999
Cleveland Heights	$489	$625	27.8%
Lakewood	$409	$555	26.3%
Shaker Heights	$591	$730	23.5%
Downtown Cleveland	$388	$770	98.5%

Note: Downtown Cleveland in this table is defined as census tract 1078, which included two large market-rate apartment developments in 1990. The rents have not been adjusted for inflation.

Source: 1990 rent from Census of Population and Housing. 1999 rent calculated from data provided by Cuyahoga Metropolitan Housing Authority.

considered. As a result, the city government faces the question of whether to continue the subsidies or remove them. This is a question that arises not only in the context of housing, but also for other activities, such as stadiums, hotels, shopping centers, and office buildings.

In the case of downtown housing, the objective of the local government is to help generate a self-sustaining market. In other words, the demand for downtown housing should be high enough that rental revenue covers both the capital and operating costs of the housing plus a normal rate of return. One way of measuring success is by counting the number of units constructed or renovated. This is important because there are some nonlinear impacts of housing on downtown amenities. For example, a minimum local population would be needed to support a grocery store, which could then make downtown even more attractive as a place to live.

A second way of measuring success is by comparing the price that people are willing to pay to live downtown to the price that they are willing to pay in other locations in the metropolitan area. An increase in the attractiveness of downtown over time should be reflected by an increase in downtown rents relative to suburban rents.

In fact, downtown apartment rents increased relative to suburban rents over the period from 1990 to 1999. Rents increased by 98 percent in the downtown compared to an increase of between 24 and 28 percent in inner-ring suburbs (see Table 5-3). These changes did not occur by themselves. Direct public subsidies, including tax abatement, city loans, and federal and state tax credits, totaled $50 million over that time. These subsidies represented 28 percent of the cost of construction or renovation of downtown rental units. There has also been a variety of indirect subsidies in the form of public amenities. For example, a new baseball stadium and arena opened in 1994, an extension to the local trolley line opened in 1996, and a new football stadium opened in 1999. A new federal courthouse and other government office buildings have also been built, adding to the available jobs downtown, which in turn adds to the attractiveness of living downtown to be close to work.

Subsidies for private activities are generally justified because of positive externalities. In the case of downtown housing, there are at least four externalities to consider. First, there is a positive externality in that activity outside of daytime business hours adds to the safety of downtown streets. Second, there is a positive externality in that a sufficient mass of people who are middle class will generate sufficient demand to support grocery stores and other retail activity, which will also benefit the residents of low-income public housing in the area. Third, there is a positive externality in that people who live and work downtown may be able to walk to work, therefore reducing congestion. Fourth, because downtown is the face that a metropolitan area presents to the world, a lively residential life will improve the overall perception of Northeast Ohio as a place to live and do business. Each of these externalities is implicitly or explicitly behind the decision of local government officials to subsidize downtown apartments.

Our primary tool for assessing current market conditions is a comparison of rents between downtown and other locations. Observed rent is assumed to be a function of the characteristics of the apartment and its neighborhood. This is known as *hedonic analysis*, and it is the standard approach used by economists to characterize housing markets. One characteristic is the location of the apartment, whether downtown, in another part of Cleveland, or in a suburb. The analysis included two Cleveland neighborhoods and fourteen suburbs.

The work relied on data collected by the Cuyahoga Metropolitan Housing Authority (CMHA). As part of its mission, the CMHA maintains a rich set of data on the characteristics and market rents of apartments in Cuyahoga County. The data include multiple observations from some apartment buildings at a point in time (where there are different types of apartments in the building) as well as multiple observations of some apartment buildings at different times. In addition to the rent, the data include the census tract and municipality where the building is located. The type of apartment (high-rise, garden, house), number of bedrooms, whether some utilities (heat, oven, electric, refrigerator) were present, and whether the utilities were included in the rent or billed separately were also included in the data. In addition, the data include the date that the apartment building was observed and the total number of units in the building. There were 382 observations used, where each observation was a building/number of bedrooms/date combination. For some buildings, there were multiple observations either because the building included both one-bedroom and two-bedroom units or because the rents were observed in different years (e.g., 1995 and 1998).

The data were analyzed using a linear regression analysis, in which the monthly rent is described as a function of the characteristics of the apartment. The adjusted R^2 was 0.64. In other words, the model explained 64 percent of the variance in rent across apartment buildings in the county. We compared one community to another by examining the premium over a baseline community. We chose Lakewood, a suburb that borders Cleveland and contains a large number of rental units, as the baseline community.

Based on the complete analysis of regional rental differences, there are two principal conclusions:

- First, Downtown Cleveland commands a substantial rent premium relative to our baseline community of Lakewood. The result suggests that an apartment located downtown will rent for $314 per month more than an identical apartment located in Lakewood. The estimate of $314 represents a 55 percent increase over the mean rent in the data of $572 per month. This is a large difference.
- Second, the premium commanded by downtown is larger than that commanded by most of the other suburbs. Downtown Cleveland and Westlake (an edge city) were comparable in their rental premium, while downtown housing rented at a discount relative to Beachwood (another edge city).

Trading place analysis gives us a natural hypothesis to test against these empirical results. In theory, downtown should have a substantial advantage over suburban locations. Downtown is closest to all of the prime amenities for entertainment and recreation and is no more than fifteen minutes farther than the nondowntown locations from parks and recreation, affording the downtown resident the best of both worlds. It is ten to fifteen minutes from virtually all of the suburbs, suggesting that downtown can also be a primary site for reverse commuting.

With all of those amenities working in favor of downtown, we would expect to see substantial premiums for downtown housing relative to all of the communities in the region. The lack of such a premium relative to Westlake and Beachwood suggests that additional action is necessary to continue downtown development if that is desired by the city. It also indicates that disamenities, such as a perception of less public safety downtown, outweigh some of the amenities.

Cleveland thrives when developers determine they can make more money building in the city than in a different metropolitan or national location. Like a renter, the developer also faces an array of considerations, all of them looking at competition in the marketplace. They boil down to the developer's long-term view of downtown.

A developer's view is essentially a comparison of costs and benefits. The costs include not only the direct expenses, but also the opportunity costs involved. For example, if projects are delayed because of difficulty in obtaining permits, then the developer's carrying cost of the investment is higher. The developer must also predict the future rents in the downtown, which can be difficult because the level of rents might depend on the actions of other developers. The clearest example of this interaction is when several developers are bidding for a relatively fixed supply of labor, which can increase the construction and renovation costs for all of them. There can also be demand-side interactions, if demand for downtown apartments increases as a critical mass of apartments is reached, for example.

These considerations are weighed against the many alternatives faced by each developer. The developer looks at alternatives in the region, and many of the larger developers look at alternatives across the country. There are many specific elements of the risk taken by the developer: the project could cost more to develop than expected, it could lease up more slowly than expected, or the ultimate rents could prove lower than anticipated. Tax abatement is especially meaningful in the early phases of a project when it has high operating costs (including taxes and interest expenses) relative to the rental income it produces.

Public investment (tax abatement and other subsidies) in downtown housing represents an effort to lower the risk that a developer faces in making the choice to generate housing downtown versus the many other locations available to that developer. That risk is lowered by the supply of public funds that lower the amount of capital needed to build the project or to operate it.

The federal government has been the primary source of subsidy for downtown housing. Low-income housing tax credits and historic tax credits are part of virtually every housing development during this period in downtown, and Cleveland is a typical city in this respect. Local property tax abatement has been the largest operating subsidy for the rental market.

The quantity of downtown housing brought on line since 1994 has been impressive, but it has required substantial public investment. All but one of the new units developed in downtown Cleveland have used tax abatement plus a combination of other public investments including federal tax credits and specialized loan and investments pools. Not counting tax abatement, these specialized investments have averaged 28 percent of the total cost of the projects (Table 5-4).

To complete our understanding of the environment facing developers we compared the environment for development of apartments in suburbs with downtown information. A combination of lenders, owners, developers, and architects were interviewed to gain a better perspective on the relationship of tax abatement to development decisions. This part of the study was based on interviews, not on a review of a large number of

Table 5-4. *Public Investment in Downtown Cleveland Construction,*
1994–1998

Project	Total cost (millions)	Units	Public investment (millions)	Public percent of total cost	Cost per unit ($)
Nautica	8.0	56	2.6	32%	142,857
Grand Arcade	10.2	90	2.5	24%	113,333
425 Lakeside	7.7	56	3.3	43%	137,500
Perry Payne	9.4	93	3.4	36%	101,075
Worthington	14.0	53	5.0	36%	264,151
Buckeye	3.4	36	0.8	24%	94,444
Crittendon Court	18.0	209	3.4	19%	86,124
National Terminals	26.0	250	6.4	25%	104,000
Water Street	10.0	100	6.1	61%	100,000
Pointe (Gateway)	7.0	42	1.6	23%	166,667
Kirkham	1.3	6	0.0	0%	208,333
Windsor Block	5.2	52	1.3	24%	100,000
Otis Terminals	37.0	249	8.1	22%	148,594
1001 Huron	8.0	70	3.0	37%	114,286
Osborne	8.0	67	2.3	29%	119,403
Marshall Building	7.0	41	0.9	14%	170,732
Total	180.2	1470	50.7	28%	122,585

Source: Department of Community Development, City of Cleveland.

private financial statements because of the confidentiality of such
statements. However, taken as a group they represented a consistent
feedback.

   It costs more to build rental units downtown. Interviews suggest that
garden apartments with three-story walk-ups represent the limited development occurring in the rest of the county. A downtown product must be
built to a higher-quality level to command the higher downtown rents.
There is not much downtown-style high-rise construction occurring anywhere else in Cuyahoga County, which limits complete comparability
between suburban development and most downtown developments. In
addition, the heterogeneity of the downtown rental housing stock relative to the relatively newly constructed and homogeneous suburban rental
housing stock makes direct comparisons a bit difficult.

   The most recent 1,470 units downtown have been built at an estimated
cost of $122,585/unit (Table 5-4). Based on interviews, apartment units
elsewhere in Cuyahoga County have sold at prices ranging from $30,000
to $50,000/unit. One new development in one suburb (in 1999) was in
the $50,000 to $65,000/unit range. Assessed valuations per unit in the
county averaged almost $57,000 over the period of this study.

These findings suggest that downtown developments continue to face up to double the costs in the suburbs. Hence, rents need to be higher downtown to cover these higher costs. These results are similar to those found in Philadelphia by The Reinvestment Fund and the Metropolitan Philadelphia Policy Center (2001). They detail how identical homes cost $74,000 to construct in the suburbs but cost $116,000 to build in the city.

Most of the interviewees concluded that downtown projects also have higher operating costs that can include waste-hauling elevators and on-site security. Heating and utilities for larger units with loft-style ceilings can also be higher.

The downtown of the central city in a metropolitan area is the most attractive setting for housing people who prefer apartments, work downtown, and consume downtown amenities. Thus, downtown apartments should command a rent premium over comparable apartments in other parts of the metropolitan area. If they do not, and construction and operating costs are higher downtown than elsewhere, then public subsidies will be needed to persuade developers to construct, renovate, and operate rental housing.

This extended case study has illustrated the challenges for developers of one form of residential housing in one setting. In Chapter 6, we turn to the more general question of the interaction between developers, land-use regulations, and metropolitan structure. After all, every export from a trading place results because the landowner decided to do something with the property and made that decision under a set of government regulations.

6 HOW ZONING MATTERS

Z ONING, AND PLANNING MORE BROADLY, CONSTITUTES THE RORS-
chach test for observers of metropolitan areas. It is blamed for caus-
ing a host of problems and hailed as the solution to those problems. In
such an environment, this chapter will not try to be definitive. In fact,
much of my contribution will be to provide another way of viewing zoning, one that flows directly from the analysis of trading places. Specifically,
we will see how zoning operates as a trade barrier and as an inducement
to trade. Zoning also has similarities to taxation, and this metaphor is
explored. We'll begin, though, in the traditional way, by considering how
zoning operates as one way to control externalities.

EXTERNALITIES

> Southern California doesn't know whether to bustle or just strangle itself on
> the spot. Not enough roads for the number of people. Fairlanes, Inc. is laying
> new ones all the time. Have to bulldoze lots of neighborhoods to do it, but
> those seventies and eighties developments exist to be bulldozed, right? No
> sidewalks, no schools, no nothing. Don't have their own police force – no
> immigration control – undesirables can walk right in without being frisked
> or even harassed. Now a Burbclave, that's the place to live. A city-state with
> its own constitution, a border, laws, cops, everything.
>
> Neal Stephenson (1992, 6)

Externalities are rampant in urban areas. This can be good, because of the
increased productivity created by agglomeration economies of scale. It is
also bad, as the intense interaction of people creates conflict. The fundamental justification for zoning is as a way to control negative externalities.
Note that I say control, not prevent, and this language is intentional. Efficiency requires that costs be balanced against benefits, not that costs be
eliminated. Because of the prominent role played by externalities in the

next two chapters, it's worth pausing for a moment to introduce two broad classes of response to them.

Controlling Externalities with Quantity Regulation

In the case of an activity generating negative externalities, unconstrained individual decisions will tend to overproduce the activity because people do not face the full costs. Consider the case of a restaurant deciding whether to serve alcoholic beverages. This decision imposes costs on the surrounding neighborhood in the form of potential drunk driving and other inappropriate behavior, especially around closing time. Financially, these costs can appear as higher property taxes to fund additional police to enforce order. Most municipal governments in the United States have responded by requiring a license before an establishment can serve alcohol and by limiting the number of licenses given. Intuitively, a balance is struck between the desire to allow residents (and others) to enjoy alcohol and the desire to limit negative externalities. In many cases, the license is geographically restricted to regulate not only the quantity but also the location of establishments serving alcohol.

Another familiar case of quantity regulation of externalities is a dress code for a school or workplace. Each of us makes choices about what to wear without necessarily taking into account the impact of these choices on others. Invidious comparisons between people have led to problems in many schools, including the extreme case of children being killed or injured because of their clothing. A school uniform removes this issue and can have the additional academic benefit of reducing distractions caused by loud or skimpy clothes.

Early zoning reflected this approach to controlling negative externalities. Land uses were ranked from those generating the fewest negative externalities (single-family houses) to those generating the most (e.g., slaughterhouses). To put it in concrete terms, suppose that each land use was assigned a number, with higher numbers being less desirable because the activity generated greater negative externalities. If an area was zoned at four, then any land use with a score of four or lower could locate there. In fact, it was theoretically possible to build single-family homes in an area zoned to allow slaughterhouses.

The most common zoning these days is more prescriptive but keeps the same underlying rationale. It's no longer permissible to develop a parcel of land for a use other than that for which it is zoned, even if the alternate use would generate fewer negative externalities. One of the main criticisms of quantity regulation is that it requires a vast amount of information to implement accurately. The modern approach to zoning requires not only understanding what the extent of various externalities is, but also on what their optimal spatial arrangement should be.

Controlling Externalities with Prices

An alternate approach to controlling negative externalities is to make individuals face the full cost of their actions. This is known as *internalizing* the externality, and it is typically accomplished by using prices as a way to inform people about costs.

One of the difficulties in measuring and responding to externalities is that by definition they apply to people outside of a decision. Thus, there is not necessarily any incentive for the parties to an agreement to either measure the extent to which their decision affects others or to include those others in making the decision. We should not mistake difficulties in measurement with nonexistence, though. In some cases, there is clear evidence both of the existence of an externality and in markets responding to it.

Prices can be used in conjunction with quantity regulation. Recall the example of a liquor license. If the license is sold to the highest bidder, then we have combined quantity and price. One inefficiency that can result is when the license is transferable among individuals or firms. In that case, the revenue goes not to the municipal government acting as an agent for its residents, but to the previous owner.

A familiar example of an externality that can be quantified and for which a market for amelioration has been developed is the case of anchor stores in shopping malls. Consumers shop in malls to save on the costs of finding what they need or on the basis of comparison shopping and also to be able to combine several shopping trips into one. Because consumers are attracted to malls, stores in turn pay for the privilege of locating there. Some stores, especially so-called anchor stores, are the most attractive to customers and thus create a positive externality in the form of increased traffic to other stores.

If a mall developer does not adjust rent to reflect the positive externality provided by an anchor store, then the mall is relatively less attractive to the store. Peter Pashigian and Eric Gould (1998) compare the rents paid by anchor stores to those paid by other stores in order to estimate the size of the externality. They find that anchor stores pay lower rents and that these rents are lower in larger malls and for more attractive anchor stores. They supplement this indirect evidence with direct evidence on the sales per square foot by non-anchor stores in malls, and they find that the increase in sales by these other stores varies directly with the rent subsidy to anchor stores.

Mall developers do not rely solely on prices, though, but also on a form of control directly analogous to zoning. Some stores are unable to obtain mall locations because they are undesirable. For example, it is the rare mall (if one exists) that includes a strip club or pornography dealer, even if municipal ordinances would allow them to operate such establishments. Presumably, the negative externalities of these activities outweigh the potential gain in rent to the developer from allowing such stores to rent space.

HOW ZONING IS LIKE A TAX

Local land-use controls restrict the amount of factors of production (land, labor, capital) that can be used in various activities. As such, they are quotas on the import of factors of production. An alternative arrangement would be to impose a tariff on the import of factors of production, but this is unconstitutional. Zoning is similar in some ways to factor taxes (taxes on land, labor, or capital) in its impact on factor prices, local production, and intrametropolitan trade. (One immediately obvious difference is that taxes yield revenue for the local government. In most of the analysis, though, I will not focus on this difference.)

There are several interesting complications in the analysis. First, zoning is typically a discontinuous constraint on land use. Under a regime that sets a maximum floor-area ratio (FAR), any FAR that is less than the limit is unconstrained. By contrast, the most common factor taxes are more continuous. For example, an increase in property value will increase the property tax, all else being equal. Second, imposing a constraint in one municipality will affect behavior in other municipalities. Their actions will affect land values and trade patterns throughout the metropolitan area, not only in the municipality making the land-use decision. Third, zoning is not permanent, but is subject to change. Thus, we need to consider the dynamic process by which land-use decisions are made, noting that the existing zoning regulations are only the starting point for future negotiations.

Both zoning and factor taxes affect the way in which land is used. Zoning and related land-use restrictions (such as subdivision regulations and building codes) limit the extent to which land can be used to produce certain goods and services. As a result, it can have an influence on the pattern of intrametropolitan trade. For example, forbidding an activity within a suburb that the suburb would otherwise have exported does not necessarily mean that the activity doesn't occur, only that the residents of the suburb will now have to import the activity from another suburb. Just because your town doesn't allow Wal-Mart to locate there doesn't mean that there will be no Wal-Mart in the region; it only means that your residents may be shopping at Wal-Mart in another town. It is possible, in addition, that changing the pattern of intrametropolitan trade will change the pattern of trade between the metropolitan area and other metropolitan areas.

In fact, widespread exclusionary zoning developed as a response to the new possibilities for intrametropolitan trade created by cars and trucks. Because business activities became more footloose as a result of trucks, zoning developed as a way for homeowners to avoid the risk of an undesirable business locating nearby. The widespread use of private automobiles created similar concerns about undesirable homeowners locating nearby.

Intensive Zoning and Extensive Zoning

Zoning and related land-use regulation have two effects on production of traded goods within a region. The first effect of zoning is to alter the factor intensity of production. I call this effect *intensive zoning* because it operates at the intensive margin of production, the intensity with which a particular parcel of land is used. If we simplify and assume that capital and land are the only factors of production, this effect is modeled as a reduction in the capital-land ratio. Alternatively, it could be modeled as a reduction in the labor-land ratio. Regardless, intensive zoning lowers the density with which land can be used to produce goods and services.

The second effect of zoning is to allocate a maximum amount of land for use in production of a good. I call this effect *extensive zoning* because it affects the extensive margin of production, which is whether a particular parcel of land is used at all. Extensive zoning that is a binding constraint represents a maximum production level for the good. This observation makes one result immediate: if extensive zoning is binding on a good or service that would be exported from the municipality in the absence of zoning, then it is possible for that good to be imported in the presence of zoning.

Most analyses only include one of the two types of zoning. An interesting example is William Fischel's book (1985), which remains an important benchmark in zoning analysis. His definition of zoning as the division of land into areas in which some activities are permitted and others prohibited is clearly based on extensive zoning. But his formal analysis of zoning uses the idea of trading property rights to the intensity of land development, an intensive zoning concept. Less formal analyses, such as that of Anthony Downs (1994), implicitly recognize that there are two effects and that they are connected. Downs argues that restrictive suburban zoning (e.g., minimum lot size restrictions, which are a form of intensive zoning) leads to conversion of agricultural land to urban land use (a change in land use at the extensive margin).

It is true that zoning and factor taxes are substitutes in the sense that one can achieve similar results using either policy. However, they are also complements in the sense that the use of one can influence both the efficiency and the political desirability of the other. This is most clear in the Hamilton extension to the Tiebout model (introduced in Chapter 3).

Intensive zoning leads to a reduction in the capital-land ratio in the production of traded goods. This is also the effect that a tax on capital would have. If the tax was imposed only on capital used in the production of one product, for example, office services (a *partial factor tax* in the language of public finance economists), then the capital-land ratio (height of the buildings) in office services would decrease, all else being equal. If the tax were imposed on all capital, there would be a decrease in the capital-land ratio in all goods.

Differences between Zoning and Taxes

There are three differences between the effects of imposing a tax on capital and the effects of intensive zoning. The first difference is that intensive zoning can have differential effects on different goods, whereas a general tax on capital would not. However, if the capital tax was imposed as a series of separate partial factor taxes, then the effects of intensive zoning on both goods could be replicated.

The second difference between a tax on capital and zoning is more substantial. A tax on capital does not impose an upper limit on the production of the capital-intensive good, as does zoning. Suppose there is a partial factor tax on office service production. This might reduce the desired density of employment to the point that the profit-maximizing employment pattern would be to have no office employment in the suburb, perhaps because only retail and manufacturing activity is the highest and best use for the land. Under a tax regime, such an outcome is possible. However, if some land is zoned for office activity rather than retail or industrial activity, then zoning will have a different impact from the tax, as the retail and industrial users will be unable to convert the land from office use. (Of course, this would provide landowners with an incentive to lobby for either a zoning variance or a reclassification of their property.)

The third difference is that zoning is a discontinuous constraint on development that only affects sectors or projects where the landowner wishes to exceed the allowable density (in the case of intensive zoning). Factor taxes, on the other hand, alter the optimal mix of factors even in cases where zoning is not binding. The relative efficiency cost of the two policies will depend on the extent to which zoning imposes large constraints on a few sectors as opposed to structure and land taxes imposing marginal adjustments on all sectors.

While zoning is therefore not equivalent to a tax on capital, it does have similar effects. This implies that some of the same principles can be applied to the general equilibrium effects of zoning as apply to the general equilibrium analysis of taxation. In particular, it is likely that even if the municipality is small relative to the rest of the metropolitan area, its zoning could nevertheless have an impact on other municipalities. David Bradford (1978) and Paul Courant and Daniel Rubinfeld (1978) illustrate this possibility using tax policy. The logic of their analysis is that the local taxation of capital (in their papers through a tax, in our situation through zoning) will lead to the migration of capital elsewhere, which will in turn lower the overall return to capital in other places as its supply increases. Hence, capital owners everywhere bear some of the burden of the restriction on the use of capital in one area.

ZONING AND TRADE

In Chapter 4, we saw evidence that parts of metropolitan areas specialized in production. If employment centers are specialized, then it must be the case that they export their goods and services to other employment centers and import goods and services from other employment centers. It makes no sense, in such a world, to think that we can study the economy of a suburb in isolation. Rather, each suburb is part of a system of interactions, and the economic theory of trade is vital to understanding the modern metropolitan area.

Gordon Hanson (1998) empirically tests modern theories of trade using data from counties in the United States. He finds that the economic spillovers resulting from a change in activity in one county are concentrated in nearby counties, which accords with the approach taken here of considering a metropolitan area in isolation.

Zoning reduces the quantity and types of goods and services that are produced in a municipality. However, if the residents (households or firms) of the municipality demand those goods and services, then they must be obtained elsewhere. Thus, zoning is not only a barrier to trade but also an encouragement to trade. Most intrametropolitan trade is facilitated by automobile use, whether it is trade in labor services (i.e, commuting) or trade in other goods and services.

This dimension of zoning again emphasizes the fact that it is inappropriate to restrict the analysis of zoning purely to the municipality that is implementing the zoning. Rather, the institution of restrictive zoning in one place inevitably spills over into the remainder of the municipality. To repeat our earlier example, consider a town that does not allow for big box retail development. As a result of that decision, the town is simultaneously deciding that the roads linking its residents to the eventual location of the retail activity will be more congested.

Advocates of smart growth understand that zoning can be a spur to trade as well as a trade barrier. Their advocacy of mixed-use, walkable communities is directly targeted at reducing certain types of trade. Their mercantilist aspirations, though, run afoul of the economics of retail trade, the demographics of two-worker households, and the psychology of individual autonomy.

Retail trade has evolved over the past century in the direction of larger stores carrying a wider variety of products. The modern grocery store contains more than 10,000 products and serves a population of tens of thousands. It is impractical for that many people to live within walking distance of the grocery store. A study by Randall Bartlett (2003) found that almost no retail activity could survive based on walking distance demand alone unless the population density was a multiple of the densest urban settlement currently observed in the United States. Even stores located in pedestrian-friendly developments will depend on sales to non-residents for much of their viability, so that *pedestrian friendly* should not be interpreted to mean *automobile unfriendly*.

It is difficult to match the characteristics of one's employment with the characteristics of one's residence, but this is necessary for walkable neighborhoods to succeed. (There is some evidence, in fact, that most people *prefer* to live about twenty minutes from work, which further undermines the case for autarkic walking neighborhoods.) Difficult becomes impossible when a household must match two jobs with a residence. We had better hope that any transfers of one spouse are matched by that of the other spouse. Otherwise, someone needs to drive.

For the sake of argument, suppose that there are exactly the number of jobs so that all of the employees could live within walking distance. People are not identical. Even people that have similar professions have very different personal preferences. Thus, even if it were theoretically possible for all of the employees to live within walking distance, it is unlikely they would want to. We would have to ignore fifty years of research validating the Tiebout model and assume that all of them will find the same combination of local government activities desirable just because they happen to work at the same place. The Garden City ideal of Ebenezer Howard was a product of its time, which included company towns built by large employers. This time has passed, but the vision is still implicit in the approach advocated by many planners.

ANALYZING THE IMPACT OF ZONING

A thorough analysis of zoning must include the impact of zoning on location decisions of firms and households and on the intrametropolitan trade among municipalities. A thorough analysis of zoning must also include the explicit land-use regulation and integrate it with local taxes, as in the Hamilton-Tiebout framework. Even these minimal requirements lead to a complicated model, and the further desirability of an explicitly dynamic framework makes it almost impossible to design a model that adequately captures the rich local government environment.

In this section I present, with all due modesty, an analysis of zoning that includes more than one jurisdiction and that includes taxes on land and structures. The zoning analysis is then embedded in a standard tool of economic analysis, the Hecksher-Ohlin-Vanek model of trade, applied in this case to trade among municipalities within a metropolitan area.

Much of the analysis to this point has been at a relatively aggregate level, such as an entire employment center or other trading place. The overall structure results from a multitude of individual decisions about how to develop land and where to locate a household or business. Each of these decisions is affected by local taxes and local land-use regulation, and the decisions in turn affect local taxes and government services. In other words, it's complicated to analyze the effect of zoning on land use because there are many things happening simultaneously.

There is a big difference between something being difficult and something being impossible. Analyzing zoning systematically is difficult, but not impossible. The key is to start with one decision maker – a developer with a piece of land – and then work our way up to a metropolitan area full of trading places built by developers.

One Developer, One Parcel

I'm an economist, so I'm going to assume that the developer wants to make as large a profit as possible. (This is not only the party line of the profession, it's also the impression I get from speaking with developers.) Profits are the difference between the price at which land's services can be sold and the cost of producing those services. One cost is local property taxes.

To simplify, suppose that the developer's only decision is the FAR, or the density of development. The value of the development depends on the density, but also on the general characteristics of the location not under the control of the developer (amenities). Examples of amenities include the view from the piece of property, access to water, or having a fashionable ZIP Code or an excellent local public school system. The higher the FAR or the level of amenities, the higher the value. Of course, the higher the density, the higher the cost. Increasing density on a given amount of land means eventually building higher. This requires installing an elevator, reinforcing lower levels to accept the greater weight of the structure, and more sophisticated construction equipment.

Under these conditions, a developer will choose a FAR where the additional revenue from a slightly higher density, such as adding a story to the building, is just offset by the extra cost. Even this highly stylized setting lets us say three things about the impact of zoning and property taxes.

First, zoning only matters if it imposes a FAR that is lower than that which would be chosen by the developer. If the developer wants to build at a FAR of 0.8, and it is illegal to build at a FAR greater than 1.0, then the rule hasn't affected the outcome. On the other hand, if the maximum FAR is 0.6, then the developer will be constrained.

Second, local taxes distort the developer's decision, as they reduce revenue without changing cost (alternatively increase costs without changing revenue). This point is complicated by the possibility that the local taxes might be used to provide local government services that are valued because they either increase revenue or reduce costs. The direct effect of taxes, though, is to reduce the FAR chosen.

Third, it is theoretically possible to choose a property tax rate such that the FAR chosen by the developer is precisely that desired from a zoning ordinance. After all, if the taxes reduce the desired FAR, then there is a tax rate at which the developer's choice of FAR is low enough to make the zoning constraint no longer binding. A developer that wishes to develop at a FAR of 0.8 in the absence of taxes is constrained by a maximum FAR of 0.6. If the FAR chosen when the tax rate is 2 percent is 0.6, then a tax rate of 2 percent or more makes the zoning constraint redundant.

Multiple Locations

The logic that we've developed to look at one isolated decision can be applied more generally. To begin with, consider that amenities will vary from place to place. Because people and firms are willing to pay more for amenities, these differences will be reflected in the price of land. This process, known as *capitalization*, is a widespread phenomenon and is frequently used by economists to infer the value of amenities.

For development to occur in each location, it must be equally profitable to develop there. In the absence of zoning, there is a level of development that will be chosen. Suppose that zoning exists and that it is binding. Then the intensity of development will be reduced, as the FAR is lower than it would otherwise be. This in turn will lower profits (if profits were higher at the lower FAR, then developers would have developed at that density even in the absence of zoning). If zoning is restrictive enough, the land value in the high-amenity location could actually be lower than that in the low-amenity location. This immediately raises a question: why would a town want to reduce the value of land by implementing restrictive zoning?

Most analysis by economists of municipal government decision making assumes that the goal is to maximize land value. Because of capitalization, decisions that make a town more attractive will be reflected in higher values. If a town increases the density allowed for a particular location, then the value of that location increases. However, there is a negative externality in the form of increased congestion for other locations. This increased congestion lowers the value of those locations. Because of this negative externality, the FAR chosen by the developer concerned with a single location might not be efficient from the standpoint of the municipality as a whole.

While zoning can mitigate the negative impact of congestion, it is not infallible. Zoning can also be inefficient because it can reduce development beyond the point at which there are agglomeration economies of scale. A density restriction can prevent a critical mass of related activities from developing in a commercial area. Restrictions on the range of permitted activities can prevent an attractive location from reaching its full potential. In fact, this last criticism is at the heart of the New Urbanism movement and is well articulated in popular works such as the books by James Kunstler (1993, 1996). In turn, the changed pattern of production in a specific trading place will alter its pattern of exports and imports with the rest of the metropolitan area. It is even conceivable that zoning, by altering local production, could alter the trade of the metropolitan area with the rest of the world if land use is so restrictive that export industries choose an alternative location.

What difference do taxes make? Again, they will reduce the value of land, all else (especially how the tax money is spent) being held equal. If a town is trying to maximize land value, then the direct effect of taxes is to increase the desired restrictiveness of zoning, because the net after-tax value of increased FAR is lower, while the induced costs, such as congestion, are not affected. This result will vary, though, depending on how the tax revenue is used. For example, if the taxes are used to alleviate congestion, then the desired FAR will not decrease as much. In Chapter 7, we will explore the issue of congestion and responses to it.

Zoning, Taxes, and Trade

We are now able to return to our trading places and consider the effect of zoning on intrametropolitan trade. The formal analysis of this relationship is still being developed, but the underlying ideas are clear enough. Let's continue with our simple example and add a bit more to it.

Suppose that there is a given amount of commercial space and residences to be developed within a metropolitan area. There are multiple locations that are available, some of which have constraints on either the type of development (residential, office, industrial, retail) or the density (in our simple example). As we saw in the previous section, the impact of these restrictions is to alter the pattern of development, which in turn will affect the pattern of trade. A property tax will also affect development decisions, only it will influence all types of development, while zoning only matters if it is a binding constraint.

If every municipality is maximizing land value, why don't we just observe one activity, the one with the maximum land value, throughout the metropolitan area? There are several answers. First, places have different amenities, which make them differentially attractive to different uses. Second, there is a need for a wide variety of activities, and so the demand for any given use will only account for a subset of the total land. After all, if there are all houses and no offices, then people won't be able to go to work to earn money to pay for their house. Third, individual preferences can vary, which can lead to restrictions and taxes that vary from place to place.

The result is that the pattern of trade will depend on the pattern of production. (This is the basic principle of central place theory). Towns with higher FAR will export goods and services produced at high density to towns with low FAR. For example, a person might live in a bedroom suburb, commute to work as a banker in an office in the CBD, and shop at a regional mall on the outskirts of the metropolitan area. This represents an export of labor services from the bedroom suburb that is used to produce exportable financial services in the CBD. The proceeds from the banker's work are used in turn to import retail services from the municipality containing the mall.

One of the workhorse models used by economists to analyze international trade is the Heckscher-Ohlin-Vanek model. In this model, countries trade goods and services when it is less costly to do so than for factors of production to migrate from place to place. The approach that we have developed in this chapter is a version of this model applied to trading places. One factor of production, land, is clearly immobile among places. Labor, on the other hand, is highly mobile, depending on the transport infrastructure (roads, bus routes, streetcar lines) in the metropolitan area. Capital is an intermediate case. Theoretically, one can construct buildings anywhere. In practice, though, zoning constrains both the type of capital that can be deployed in a given place and the amount of capital (density). Thus, zoning is a trade barrier, and the pattern of trade reflects the distribution of land, labor, and capital across the metropolitan area.

TOWARD A DYNAMIC MODEL

MASTER PLANNING: In theory, that enterprise which all design professionals and a great number of citizens believe an Edge City never has enough of. In practice, that attribute of a development in which so many rigid controls are put in place, to defeat every imaginable future problem, that any possibility of life, spontaneity, or flexible response to unanticipated events is eliminated.

Joel Garreau (1991, 453)

The analysis we have developed to this point is complex, but it is only a static analysis. Land use and land-use regulation vary over time. In this section, I discuss how to extend the analysis to address topics in dynamic zoning.

Changing Circumstances and Local Support for Infill Development

The decisions made today about zoning and taxes affect the land-use decisions made today. Those decisions, in turn, influence who will have the opportunity to make land-use decisions in the future. An important line of research has considered how the metropolitan economic structure and the local political situation coevolve. Mark Baldassare and Georjeanna Wilson (1996) examine the changing support for growth controls in Orange County as the municipalities change. They found that support increased over the time that they study, 1982 to 1993, but that the determinants of support vary over time, making it difficult to see a consistent political coalition in favor of growth limits. One consistent finding is that people want to limit growth in their own community but not in the region as a whole. Intuitively, it seems, people understand that a land-use regime that is too strict can have negative effects on the metropolitan economy. They don't seem to understand that in equilibrium with the type of preferences described by Baldassare and Wilson, every community is limiting growth, which is a de facto regional growth policy. Yes, there can be externalities that reach beyond the municipal level.

The survey results from Southern California are consistent with a study by Richard Peiser (1989) asking whether greater density results from zoning regimes that are relatively flexible or inflexible. While the answer seems obvious, Peiser's insight was that infill development in the future might mitigate the sprawl that results in the short run from a zoning regime that is flexible. He compared land use in Dallas, Texas, Montgomery County, Maryland, and Fairfax County, Virginia, three rapidly growing areas with varying approaches to planning. The more flexible approaches found in Fairfax County and Dallas permit rezoning for higher density over time, whereas the more rigid approach in Montgomery County does not. Peiser found that the density when the study areas were built out was higher in the flexibly zoned places, although it was often lower in the initial stages of development for these places. He emphasizes that these changes in density are a natural result of developers making investment decisions under uncertainty. Because it is very difficult to convert from one density to another, it makes sense to develop at low density first and to reserve some land for high-density development later if land prices increase enough to justify it. This reserved land, which could be thought of as the future density strategic reserve, instead is criticized in its undeveloped state as sprawl and criticized on its development as lost open space.

The Homevoter Hypothesis

William Fischel (2001) has argued that exclusionary zoning is often driven by the uncertainties that homeowners face when new developments enter their town. The analysis to this point has been of a world that is static and in which outcomes are certain, so it does not allow us to directly address that question. We can, however, speculate on what an extension would look like.

Dean Gatzlaff and Marc Smith (1993) anticipated Fischel's argument and provided a formal model, albeit one lacking the rich institutional detail found in Fischel's book. Their basic point is that risk-averse households are more sensitive to unanticipated costs than unanticipated benefits. Thus, even if the estimated mean impact of a development is accurate, it could be rational for households to oppose growth. They advocate using marginal cost pricing instead of using quantity controls to increase efficiency. This argument is a specific case of a more general result, to which I now turn.

Zoning is a restriction on the quantity produced of a good, whereas a tax on capital affects the price of the good. Because it imposes a maximum capital-land ratio in production, zoning is also similar to a maximum land price. There is a well-known (to economists, anyway) result first published by Martin Weitzman (1974) that quantity controls are preferred to price controls in controlling the impact of negative externalities if and only if the benefits function has greater curvature than the cost function near the optimum. An interesting question is whether the theoretical justification of Weitzman is applicable to the practice of zoning in the United States.

The three main situations where quantity controls are to be preferred are as follows. The first situation is where the cost curve is very flat, which would render prices almost useless as a control instrument. This doesn't seem to be the case with most land development.

The second situation is where there is a "kink" in the benefits curve, for example, a point at which a situation suddenly goes from being tolerable to intolerable. (Weitzman's example is a river that becomes too polluted for swimming.) This situation seems likely to occur in some cases, particularly in congested urban areas.

The third situation is when a high degree of coordination is required. This situation is compelling only to the extent that developers are unable to act at a large enough scale to internalize coordination problems. William Fischel (1994) provides an interesting case study of the ability of developers to allocate land use optimally. He found that Foster City, California, a town of about 30,000 residents, had some areas where houses and apartments were mixed and other areas where they were separated. This pattern reflected decisions made by the initial developer, T. Jack Foster, who took into account potential externalities from the various land uses and allocated land to maximize his profit. The conclusion is that developers are able in some situations to act at a large enough scale.

One explanation for the prevalence of quantity controls, whether or not they are more efficient than price controls, is that quantities are more easily observed than prices, so that zoning is easier to administer. Edward Glaeser and Andrei Shleifer (2001) provide a theoretical analysis of the use of quantity regulation that relies on the relative cost of enforcing quantity and price controls. Their insight is that quantity controls might be less costly to enforce if private individuals must identify violations. This situation is applicable to zoning, as violations are often first noticed by a neighbor who then notifies the local government (or in the case of community associations, the board).

A second, and quite plausible, explanation is that quantity controls are legal and price controls are not. A local regulation imposing a maximum land value would almost certainly be viewed as a taking, while local zoning laws that effectively impose a maximum land value have been upheld as long as there is some justification for them based on public welfare. Similarly, local tariffs on trade in products produced by capital in various uses would almost certainly run afoul of the commerce clause of the U.S. Constitution. Classified property taxes, in which different tax rates are levied on land used in different ways, are a step in the direction of a price control.

Quantity controls might be relatively inefficient, but from the point of view of a town's residents they are better than nothing. In his 2001 book, Dr. Fischel prescribes a policy of an "equity insurance market" in which residents are insured against negative impacts from a new development. This approach can be thought of as a form of price control. The premium for the equity insurance is a price facing a prospective developer, and such an approach might be more efficient than exclusionary zoning. Formal theoretical and empirical analysis of this topic is still in its infancy, but it is a promising area with the prospect of influencing public policy.

The formation of homeowners' associations that have control over a wide range of activities can be interpreted as an example of an institution developed to reduce uncertainty. A question, to which we will return in Chapter 8, is the extent to which one can look at those institutions as benign and voluntary. After all, if one does not like the decisions of the homeowners' association, one can always choose to live elsewhere, in a privatized version of the Tiebout model. However, the existence of substantial transaction costs to relocation implies that market discipline alone might be insufficient, and legal restrictions might need to be placed on homeowners' associations.

Public expenditures on roads, stadiums, and so forth are nontariff barriers (or encouragements) to trade in the same way that zoning is.

To this point, we have neglected the expenditure side of the public sector because the discussion was already lengthy and unwieldy. The analysis of local public expenditures as trade policy takes on added relevance and urgency in a world of free trade in educational services – how else could one describe the proliferation of charter schools, public school choice, and vouchers? Further, the role of private entities, such as homeowners' associations, in providing substitutes for the local public sector is also likely to influence public support for both zoning and taxes.

John Wilson (1987) demonstrates how the Tiebout model of differences in public spending across municipalities implies a reason for trade in other goods and services. His analysis relies on the observation that different goods and services are produced using different combinations of capital, labor, and land. Public education, for example, uses a large amount of labor but little land, while public parks use a lot of land but not as much labor. If a municipality has devoted a large amount of land to parks, it has less available for producing other goods and services, which it will then have to import. Even if municipalities were identical in their initial attributes, the operation of the Tiebout mechanism would lead them to differentiate as residents adopt different local tax, spending, and regulatory patterns.

DOES ZONING HAVE A MAJOR IMPACT ON URBAN STRUCTURE?

It is said that the Village of Euclid is a mere suburb of the City of Cleveland; that the industrial development of that city has now reached and in some degree extended into the village and, in the obvious course of things, will soon absorb the entire area for industrial enterprises; that the effect of the ordinance is to divert this natural development elsewhere with the consequent loss of increased values to the owners of the lands within the village borders. But the village, though physically a suburb of Cleveland, is politically a separate municipality, with powers of its own and authority to govern itself as it sees fit within the limits of the organic law of its creation and the State and Federal Constitutions. Its governing authorities, presumably representing a majority of its inhabitants and voicing their will, have determined, not that industrial development shall cease at its boundaries, but that the course of such development shall proceed within definitely fixed lines. If it be a proper exercise of the police power to relegate industrial establishments to localities separated from residential sections, it is not easy to find a sufficient reason for denying the power because the effect of its exercise is to divert an industrial flow from the course which it would follow to the injury of the residential public if left alone, to another course where such injury will be obviated. It is not meant by this, however, to exclude the possibility

of cases where the general public interest would so far outweigh the interest
of the municipality that the municipality would not be allowed to stand in
the way.

Euclid v. Ambler (1926, 389–90)

The use of zoning has been unquestionably constitutional since the 1926
decision of the U.S. Supreme Court excerpted in the preceding text.
The Court thought that the impact of zoning could be to change the
entire course of development for a municipality and, by extension, of the
metropolitan area of which the municipality was a part.

There was no explicit dissenting opinion written for the *Euclid* case in
the U.S. Supreme Court. This leaves us with the prior decision (*Ambler
Realty Co. v. Village of Euclid, OH, et al.*, 1924) as the only basis for
counterfactual analysis. Suppose that the U.S. Supreme Court had upheld
the lower court's opinion – would anything substantive have changed?

The key feature of the *Ambler v. Euclid* (1924) ruling was the requirement that local governments compensate landowners for the lost economic value of their land due to the constraint on its use imposed by
zoning. The prediction of most commentators is that zoning would be
less widespread and less restrictive if this policy was used. In addition,
the inference is that zoning would be more efficient because of the greater
restraint with which it was applied by governments.

There are two approaches to critically examining this conclusion. The
first approach is a theoretical one based on the path-breaking analysis of
Ronald Coase (1960). The second approach is more empirical and relies
on an analysis of the genesis of popular support for zoning and the early
experience in applying zoning.

Coase points out that if transaction costs are low and there are no
endowment effects, then the efficient outcome will be achieved regardless
of how property rights are assigned. The only difference is in who will be
compensating whom, so there is a difference in the distribution of benefits
but not in the total surplus available to be divided. William Fischel (1985)
applies this analysis to the determination of the restrictiveness of zoning.
The difference between the 1924 and 1926 rulings, then, can be described
as merely a reassignment of property rights with no impact on efficiency.

Fischel (1985, ch. 7) does point out that there are still reasons to think
that the *Euclid* case did reduce efficiency. First, there remain substantial
transaction costs in zoning, particularly because developers are restricted
in their ability to pay cash directly to residents to alter zoning, instead of
being forced to rely on in-kind compensation.

Second, it is possible that the price at which someone is willing to sell
a right is considerably higher than the price that he or she would pay to
purchase it. Thus, the almost complete license given residents under *Euclid*
has substantially increased the degree of restrictiveness relative to a regime

in which the property rights to control land use were more concentrated with landowners and developers. Because of the desire of homeowners to reduce the uncertain impact of mobile industry (and mobile low-income residents) on their homes, which constitute a substantial fraction of their wealth, a reallocation of the property rights would nevertheless have led to a substantial degree of restriction. Losing the right to restrict land use except through contracts could in theory have led to even greater restrictiveness, as explicit contracts with a range of individuals might have been more difficult to negotiate and renegotiate than altering zoning legislation has proved to be.

In addition to the theoretical argument that the impact of *Euclid* might be overstated or even misconstrued, there is evidence that is suggestive as to the likely impact of a different adjudication of the case. This evidence is from a variety of sources, but it consistently indicates that homeowners are willing to pay for exclusion and developers are creative at finding ways to provide it.

An alternative form of restriction is to use contracts between the developer and homeowners to dictate the type of structure and resident that are acceptable. These contracts are most useful in the case of newly developed "greenfields," where the developer stands to benefit from carefully arranging land use to maximize the value of the land. For example, the same upheaval in urban structure that led to the advent of zoning also led to the creation of relatively elaborate deed restrictions. William Worley (1990) provides a list of deed restrictions in Roland Park, Maryland, and Armour Hills, Missouri, to illustrate the approach of the influential developer J. C. Nichols.

Developers, in fact, favored the creation of zoning laws, rather than opposing them as an imposition from an external source. Marc Weiss (1987) describes the major developers' view of zoning. Although they were not generally in favor of government regulation, zoning offered a chance to solve the negative externality of poorly planned subdivisions caused by unscrupulous small developers that reduced the profitability of more professional developers. Fischel (2001) argues that you can interpret the evidence in Weiss as proving that developers were unable to accomplish their land-use objectives without government assistance in the form of zoning. And homeowners showed themselves willing to pay a premium for housing in restricted communities, a phenomenon that continues to the present.

The underlying argument is that regulations are only effective in constraining choices to the extent that people cannot find a way of accomplishing what they want. An instructive epilogue to this section is to note that the parcel of land in question in the *Euclid* case, while initially zoned for residential use, was eventually incorporated into a Fisher Body plant.

Zoning and Property Values

> The Improvement of the place is best measur'd by the advance of Value upon every man's Lot.
>
> Witold Rybczynski (1995, 73, quoting William Penn)

Zoning is a direct way to control externalities. If it is successful in reducing negative externalities, it should make the properties that were formerly affected by the negative externalities more attractive. As a result, the property values should go up.

George Washington Plunkitt (in Riordon, 1905 [1963], 61–2) provides an illustration of this concept from the turn of the twentieth century when discussing his support for relocating gashouses from his district in Manhattan to Astoria in Queens. "I needn't explain how they're nuisances. They're worse than open sewers." As a result, he goes on to say, removing them would be very valuable. "I know the value of every foot of ground in my district, and I calculated long ago that if them gashouses was removed, surroundin' property would go up 100 percent." Zoning often attempts to maintain high property values by preventing the negative externality in the first place.

Edward Glaeser and Joseph Gyourko (2005) use land values to analyze whether zoning is a binding constraint. If it doesn't matter, then land should be equally valued on the intensive margin (adding more housing to a given parcel) and the extensive margin (building a new house on a parcel). For example, the price of a half-acre of land can be calculated in two ways. First, compare the price of a house on a half-acre with its construction cost, and the difference is an estimate of land value. Second, compare the price of a house on a half-acre of land with the price of a house on an acre of land. Glaeser and Gyourko find that these values diverge, particularly in growing areas. One inference is that zoning is being used by homevoters, who exercise monopoly control over land use in a municipality, to increase the value of their houses by restricting development rather than as a response to externalities.

Although zoning can increase property values by preventing negative externalities, it can also reduce property values by restricting the use of the property. If my property values are reduced by a land-use control, then I am likely to oppose it. Presumably, if the total gains exceed the total losses, then the winners could compensate the losers, making the regulation unanimously supported. In 2004, Oregon put this theory into practice by passing Measure 37, a ballot initiative that requires compensation to landowners if their property value is lowered by regulation. (Essentially, this is the outcome in the 1924 *Ambler v. Euclid* case discussed earlier.) It could be argued that Measure 37 is asymmetric, in that there is no parallel requirement for landowners to compensate the government in return for regulation that increases property values. However, property taxes depend on assessed value, which in turn is related to market value, so there is a mechanism already in place for some payment. (Although for the same reason, reduced property taxes provide some compensation to those who are constrained by regulation.)

What is ironic about Measure 37 is that it was passed in Oregon, a state that has been among the most aggressive in land-use control since the early 1970s. As of this writing, it is too early to tell whether this initiative is an anomaly or the leading edge of a national change in land-use regulation. It is certainly a timely reminder of the point first made in Chapter 2 that people are not passive inhabitants of a world designed by planners, but rather they are active participants in shaping the world. This is true even of people who have been attracted to live in a state famous for its strong approach to planning.

Zoning and Loans

Another way that zoning might matter is that it affects the terms of loans that property owners can obtain. Essentially, the restrictiveness of zoning places limits on how easy it is to redeploy a particular parcel from one use to another. The easier it is to change the use, the more valuable the parcel is if the lender is forced to repossess it. All that one needs to do is assemble evidence on whether zoning restrictiveness is related to loan terms in the way that theory predicts. Efraim Benmelech, Mark Garmaise, and Tobias Moskowitz (2004) perform exactly this test. They find, using data on commercial property from Chicago, that properties with less restrictive zoning receive larger loans with longer maturities and lower interest rates, all else being equal.

There is an efficiency tradeoff implied by this finding. Financial market efficiency is being bought at the potential cost of negative externalities. This is possibly evidence that commercial zoning is being used beyond the point where it is controlling externalities, at least for the areas studied in the article. However, one of the characteristics of the property included in the analysis was its value, which might arguably be higher because of effective zoning. If this were the case, then excluding the value from the analysis should tend to make restrictive zoning appear more favorable. The authors find exactly the opposite result, solidifying the evidence that zoning is too restrictive in this case.

Zoning, Housing Supply, and Urban Structure

There are two dramatically different situations with the respect to the impact of land-use regulation on housing markets and by extension to commercial land markets as well. Put most simply, on the one hand, regulations only reduce the amount of construction if someone wants to build on the land. In many metropolitan areas, there are substantial regions where the cost of constructing housing is higher than the price the housing would command in the market. Thus, no developer interested in making a profit would want to operate, and land-use regulations have no effect. However, if construction costs are lower than the price of housing, then developers will want to build, and land-use regulations potentially have a substantial effect on both the level and location of activity. It is not sufficient to assert a given impact of zoning on land use. One must first identify the nature of the market before predicting a particular relationship between regulation and outcome.

To understand the relation between zoning and housing supply, one must compare construction costs to house prices. Edward Glaeser, Joseph Gyourko, and Raven Saks (2004) use data for 102 metropolitan areas in the census years from 1950 to 2000. They find that almost all of the variation in price across metropolitan areas before 1980 is due to differences in construction costs. After 1980, though, a few metropolitan areas (especially in California) have seen large and growing disparities between cost and price. This is a sign that developers are restricted from supplying new houses, especially as there has been a simultaneous drop in new construction in these places relative to the pattern in previous decades.

Because zoning affects how developers are able to respond to the demand for housing, it can influence the future of a metropolitan area. The logic is straightforward, and Glaeser et al. (2005) formally develop it in another paper. People who work in cities need to live somewhere. If an area booms, and it is difficult to build new housing, then the effect of the boom is to increase housing prices. On the other hand, if it is relatively easy to build new housing, then the effect of the boom is to increase population. Even a casual comparison of the trajectories of housing prices and population in various parts of the country will indicate the applicability of this insight, and in-depth analysis in this case is consistent with casual observation.

ALTERNATIVES TO ZONING

Zoning assigns the right to develop a parcel of property in a particular way to the municipality or other local government. This can help to prevent negative externalities, as discussed earlier, but it can also be inefficient as it can prevent activities that would be desired by those directly affected. For example, a neighborhood might not mind if a piano teacher used his or her house to give lessons, even if the area is not zoned for commercial use. However, if this nonconforming use is permitted, and the precedent is used to allow another use that is not desired, then the neighbors are worse off.

Even worse is a situation where the nonconforming use is opposed by those in other neighborhoods who are completely unaffected. The scholarly research on externalities finds that they have a very small radius of impact. Thus, most zoning decisions in a municipality of even relatively small size will be made by those who are not directly affected.

Several approaches are possible to avoid the problems of inflexible or absentee control through zoning ordinances. One of the most common is transferable development rights (TDRs), in which a developer can obtain the right to develop differently from what is allowed by the zoning law by compensating the municipality in some way. For example, a developer might be permitted to construct houses at a greater density than the one-acre minimum lot size at one location if he or she creates a park at another location. Various states have also experimented with wetlands banking, in which developers are allowed to build in ways that affect wetlands as long as they contribute to offsetting that impact elsewhere. This can be mutually beneficial in that the developer makes more money, the municipality gets to control where development occurs, and a critical mass of ecologically sustainable wetlands can be built up.

While they respect the market mechanism, TDRs are usually mediated through a government and related to modifying existing zoning ordinances. Thus, they are probably better thought of as market modifications of zoning rather than as pure alternatives. Trading rights to develop is a natural part of a trading place metropolitan area, but it is not trivial to set up a successful market. William Fulton et al. (2004) look systematically at both the broad challenges of TDRs and several case studies including Montgomery County, Maryland, the New Jersey Pinelands, and Boulder, Colorado. They conclude that the successful programs contain several common elements. These include a balance between demand and supply, low administrative costs, and strong community support, none of which is particularly surprising. The most interesting element is the presence of a land bank or other clearinghouse to help stabilize the market over time, because otherwise the illiquidity can make transactions too rare and costly to keep the market viable.

An alternative to standard or *Euclidean* (named after *Euclid v. Ambler*) zoning that has been proposed by New Urbanists is code-based or performance zoning. Euclidean zoning permits specified land uses, implicitly as a way to reduce or prevent negative externalities. Performance zoning allows any land use that meets certain standards, which can include congestion, pollution, or aesthetic considerations. Returning to the example of the piano teacher, he or she would be allowed to operate the business under a performance zoning regime as long as the induced traffic and parking needs did not exceed the performance limits. The strength of performance zoning is that it allows people to determine over time whether a particular use of a location makes sense, subject to certain constraints, rather than dictating in advance the presence or absence of certain activities. Standard zoning has a difficult time distinguishing between a piano teacher and a saloon. After all, both are commercial activities that involve serving people who come to a place and stay for a while. A performance zoning rule about parking, though, distinguishes between them without difficulty (except when the teacher wants to have a recital and the cars spill out of the driveway and onto the street).

The world evolves in ways that are difficult to predict, and people respond to changes in ways that are hard to imagine in advance. Rather than trying to anticipate every possible outcome and require or forbid it, these alternative approaches to zoning are more flexible in terms of the details while arguably more firm in terms of their principles. After all, it is possible to engage in commercial activity in a variety of ways, some of which inflict greater negative externalities or proffer greater positive externalities than do others. By specifying which behaviors and outcomes are unacceptable but leaving the rest to human creativity, they represent a persuading approach that contrasts with the crusading approach of zoning.

WHAT HOUSTON SUGGESTS ABOUT ZONING

Houston, Texas, is famous as the only major city in the United States to lack zoning. This makes Houston a likely place to look for evidence on whether zoning is effective. Bernard Siegan (1972) conducted the most influential study of Houston. He found that there are not major differences between land-use practices there and those found in cities with zoning. This outcome, while surprising on its surface, is explained by three factors. First, there is a natural separation of uses that is impelled by economic forces rather than forced by zoning. While it is theoretically possible for an oil refinery to locate next to a housing development, it is unlikely that profit-maximizing real-estate developers will allow this to happen. Second, there are widespread private covenants that accomplish many of the same goals as zoning. These covenants are even more effective because the city government has chosen to assist in enforcing them. Third, where there are specific land-use problems, the city government has adopted ordinances that specifically address the problem.

Ironically, the mixed uses found by Siegan in Houston, particularly small retail such as convenience stores within walking distance of residential areas, are one of the main policy goals of the New Urbanist movement. However, rather than take the lesson of Houston at face value and abandon zoning in favor of private contracts enforced by the municipal government, planners and architects have focused instead on writing smarter zoning codes.

The citizens of Houston have consistently rejected zoning. There have been referenda in 1948, 1962, and 1993. In the most recent referendum, the margin of victory was 53 percent opposed to 47 percent in favor, with low-income and minority neighborhoods voting no by a larger margin than the city as a whole. What seems surprising, given these results, is that other cities have not moved in the direction of Houston. One explanation is that politicians have little incentive to reduce their control over land use, so that new restrictions are more likely to be introduced rather than the opposite. However, this runs the risk of an eventual backlash such as Measure 37.

EMINENT DOMAIN AND DEVELOPMENT

> And they covet fields, and take them by violence; and houses, and take them away: so they oppress a man and his house, even a man and his heritage.
>
> Micah 2:2

One challenge in urban redevelopment is land assembly. Developers need to acquire sufficient property to allow them to have a significant impact, or else the negative externalities from surrounding properties could overwhelm the good resulting from the project. This can lead to the so-called holdup problem, in which one or a few landowners charge an exorbitant amount for the final parcels assembled for a major project. Local governments have undertaken to assist developers in a variety of ways, including tax abatement, expedited permitting processes, and land acquisition through condemnation.

Zoning is fundamentally a defensive weapon in the battle to create and shape trading places. Restricting land use to a particular purpose can prevent it from being developed in other ways but does not in itself guarantee that the land will be developed at all. Eminent domain permits governments to take the offensive, so long as they are acquiring land for a public purpose and so long as they compensate the landowner. The Fifth Amendment to the U.S. Constitution states, "nor shall private property be taken for public use without just compensation." The classic use of eminent domain is to acquire property for various forms of public infrastructure, such as roads or parks. Roads are crucial for building trading relationships and parks represent an important amenity for a place.

The definition of *public use* has not been universally agreed on. One reason is that once we deal with the public domain we are in the realm of politics, and outcomes will reflect influence. This can be seen even in the case of roads, a relatively uncontroversial application of the power of eminent domain. One example from the career of Robert Moses is notorious.

The route of the Northern State Parkway in Long Island included an eleven-mile curve around the property of some wealthy landowners while cutting directly through some farms. The freeway has created wonderful opportunities for trade throughout the region, but the costs of doing so were borne unevenly. Robert Caro, biographer of Moses, summarizes the result (1974, 301–2): "a commuter who lived anywhere east of Dix Hills and who used the parkway to get to his job in New York City was condemned to drive, every day of his working life, twenty-two extra and unnecessary miles. He had to drive 110 unnecessary miles per week, 5,500 per year – all because of Moses' 'compromise.' By the 1960's there were about 21,500 such commuters, and the cost to them alone of Moses' accommodations totaled tens of millions of wasted hours of human lives." However, if the wealthy landowners were able to block construction of the freeway, then the commuters would have had even more trouble, or else the places where they lived would not have been developed, which would have meant reduced property values for the owners of that land.

The role of politics looms even larger when eminent domain is used to assemble land for private developers. The zenith (or nadir) of this approach was seen in Poletown, Michigan. Detroit condemned land in a neighborhood to build a new headquarters for General Motors. Even though there was no evidence of urban blight, the Michigan Supreme Court upheld the condemnations because it considered economic development to be a public purpose (*Poletown Neighborhood Council v. Detroit* 1981). This case led to the widespread use of eminent domain to assist developers with land assembly. Because condemnation is fundamentally political, though, a countervailing force developed emphasizing the importance of private property rights. One manifestation of this political evolution was the Michigan Supreme Court overturning its earlier *Poletown* decision in *County of Wayne v. Hathcock* (2004).

Recently, the U.S. Supreme Court heard an eminent domain case for the first time in more than fifty years. In *Kelo v. New London* (2005), the question was posed whether condemning property for economic development represented a genuine public purpose. The Court held that it was, although it emphasized that this power was limited, and recognized that individual states might place restrictions on the use of eminent domain. The controversial nature of eminent domain is illustrated by the five to four vote on the case, so we can expect ongoing debate on specific applications of this general government power. Some state governments had already limited the extent to which eminent domain can be justified by economic development before the decision, and others are currently considering such limits.

7 LOVE THE DENSITY, HATE THE CONGESTION

Humphrey tells them about a trip he and Sandy and some others took to Disneyland. "We had been in the line for Mr. Toad's Wild Ride for about forty-five minutes when [Sandy] went nuts. You could see it happen – we were all standing there just waiting, you know, hanging out and moving with the line, and suddenly his eyes bug out past his nose and he gets that happy look he gets when he's got an idea.... So he says real slow, 'You know, guys, this ride only lasts about two minutes. Two minutes at the most. And we'll have been in line for it an hour. That's a thirty-to-one ratio of wait to ride. And the ride is just a fast trackcar going through holograms in the dark. I wonder... do you think... could it be... that this is the *worst* ratio in Disneyland?... I wonder, I just wonder,... which one of us can rack up the *worst* ratio for the whole day?'... So we call it Negative Disneyland and agree to add points for stupidest rides combined with the worst ratios."

The four in back can't believe it. "You've got to be kidding."

"No, no! It's the only way to go there! Because with Sandy's idea we weren't fighting the situation anymore, you know? We were running around finding the longest lines we could, stepping through our paces like we were on the ride itself, and timing everything on our watches, and every time we turned another corner in the line we'd see Sandy standing there up ahead of us towering over the kids, eyes bugged out and grinning his grin, just digging these monster delays to get on Dumbo the Elephant, Storybook Canal, Casey Junior, the Submarine...."

Kim Stanley Robinson (1988, 139–40)

IT TAKES EITHER GENIUS OR A WARPED SENSE OF HUMOR TO APPRE-ciate waiting in line, whether at Disneyland or at your favorite local intersection to make a left turn. It takes an economist to analyze why there is a line at all and whether there is anything to be done to improve the situation. Lines and other forms of congestion are a fundamental feature of urban life. They represent a negative externality, just as was the case with house maintenance and other design features that we saw in the previous chapter. Congestion, similar to other negative externalities, represents a challenge to both the residents of urban areas and to policy makers. The challenge is especially difficult because congestion is a byproduct of density, and density leads to positive externalities. The agglomeration economies of scale that lower production costs and the varied street scene of a vibrant urban district both require density to exist.

COMMUTING: HOW BAD IS IT?

Before we enumerate and evaluate the alternative approaches to controlling congestion, it makes sense to explore its origin and the size of the problem. In order to keep the discussion manageable, we will continue to focus on individual decisions and how those decisions affect trade within a metropolitan area.

On Minimizing Congestion: A Mickey Mouse Analysis

People do not like to travel. They especially do not like to travel in congested conditions. Why then is the garden suburbs ideal, now recast as the walking city of the smart-growth movement, not universally embraced? One answer can be found by traveling to Orlando, Florida. For most people, this travel will be on a crowded airplane. Once you get there, you'll drive on a crowded road to a variety of destinations, each of which will be congested. People seek out this congestion from their homes around the world because there is something there that they are seeking. In economist's terms, the benefits of being at Disney World outweigh the costs of travel and congestion.

What is true in this admittedly extreme situation also applies on a more mundane level. People are not trying to minimize commuting distance; they are weighing the cost of the commute against the benefits they achieve by it. These benefits include not only the job waiting at the end of the inbound commute, but the various benefits associated with residing where they do at the source of the inbound commute.

Not only an economist's tautology about costs and benefits is occurring here. People are not minimizing commuting *distance* because they are more concerned with commuting *time*. In a world of parking lots connected by highways, a person can cover a great deal of distance in the same amount of time that a person of a different era could walk from home to market. Is one choice more appropriate than the other? The answer to that question will vary from person to person. The answer is likely to be correlated with whether the person thinks it is acceptable for people to choose to travel in crowded conditions to a congested location such as Disney World.

Congestion's Effect on Trade

> If one judges this situation realistically, it is apparent that the era of the
> commuter suburb's explosive growth will be rather brief – in terms of human
> time and social institutions, comparable to the flash of a meteor against the
> long darkness of a winter night.... When the day comes that the time spent
> commuting cancels out the value of making the trip, then the spread of
> suburbia will stop and a return to vertical city living will be necessary to
> accommodate the growing hordes of humanity.
>
> Edward Higbee (1960, 114)

Zoning was shown in the previous chapter to be a trade barrier in its
impact on the pattern of trade among the trading places of a metropolitan
area. Now comes another type of tax imposed on trade by your fellow
citizens, this time in their role as drivers rather than their role as voters.
Congestion, similar to zoning, is a tariff.

The equivalence of congestion to a tax on trade is not as subtle as was
the case with zoning. In the absence of congestion, one can get from home
to office in, say, twenty-three minutes. During rush hour, when the roads
are full of other people, suppose it takes thirty-two minutes. That is nine
minutes added to the price of transporting labor to the office. This extra
nine minutes must be compensated for somehow – whether in the form
of higher wages to the worker, which in turn lead to higher prices for the
consumer or lower profits to the shareholder, or more simply in the form
of lower net benefits of holding the job. If I have to allocate an extra nine
minutes every morning to work instead of leisure and my pay does not
increase commensurately, then my hourly wage has decreased.

Thinking of congestion as an additional cost to trade helps us to clearly
see the alternative ways to address it. One way is to reduce congestion
by helping trade occur in different ways, such as people walking instead
of driving. Julius Caesar, in his Law on Municipalities promulgated in
44 BC, advocated reducing Rome's congestion by making it illegal to
"drive a wagon along the streets of Rome or along those streets in the
suburbs where there is continuous housing after sunrise or before the
tenth hour of the day." A modern Caesar might forbid trucks in the CBD
during rush hour. Alternatively, manufacturers have moved themselves
out of the CBD to avoid the traffic congestion, which can be especially
costly in terms of idle time for plants using a just-in-time inventory
system.

There are a variety of other approaches. One is to reduce congestion by
increasing the capacity of the road, allowing a greater volume of trade to
occur. Another is to reduce congestion by reducing traffic whose benefit
does not exceed the cost it imposes on others; this is the approach of
congestion tolls. In every case, though, the emphasis is not on reducing
congestion for its own sake, but rather maximizing the net benefits from

trade. In particular, it might be efficient for there to be congestion, just as it can be efficient for other forms of taxation to exist.

Cars versus Mass Transit: A Time Capsule

The question as to whether people can be induced to leave cars for street-cars and subways has a long and distinguished history. In 1957, the editors of *Fortune* magazine compiled a collection of essays in an attempt to document the problem of sprawl and to suggest policies to combat it. One of the essays, "The City and the Car," by Francis Bello, documents the difference in commuting time for cars and mass transit. Remember, now, that Mr. Bello was writing before massive employment decentralization, so that the commutes were largely from the suburb to the CBD. Thus, the comparison favors mass transit relative to the situation today for two reasons. First, the route is served by mass transit, which is not always the case today. Second, the scale of congestion in a monocentric city's CBD exceeds much of what we see today.

Bello reported results from the twenty-five largest cities in the United States. Starting from the busiest corner in the CBD, a motorist could typically travel between sixteen and twenty-four miles per hour outbound, or between eight and twelve miles in a thirty-minute commute. On the most heavily used transit line, the commuter could cover on average only 6.5 miles in thirty minutes. And this does not take into account the time spent waiting at the station for the bus, subway, streetcar, or train. This huge time advantage for the car is magnified in a world of decentralized employment. The findings illustrate clearly why automobile use has continued to increase since 1957.

Shorter Commutes Thanks to Sprawl?!

> The only effective cure for urban congestion is to so relate industrial and business zones to residential areas that a large part of their personnel can either walk or cycle to work, or use a public bus, or take a railroad train. By pushing all forms of traffic onto high speed motor ways, we burden them with a load guaranteed to slow down peak traffic to a crawl; and if we try to correct this by multiplying motor ways, we only add to the total urban wreckage by flinging the parts of the city ever farther away in a formless mass of thinly spread semi-urban tissue.
>
> Lewis Mumford (1961, 508)

A recurring theme in the anti-sprawl literature is the longer commutes necessitated by the evolution in urban form. However, much of the evidence for this theme is anecdotal rather than statistical. The availability of high-quality data on commuting allows researchers to understand the relation between urban structure and travel.

It might seem obvious that decentralization of employment and households will inevitably worsen the commute. However, there are some countervailing forces. First, if the residence is closer to the new location of the job than the old location (e.g., the CBD), then the distance commuted will drop. In the extreme case of perfect jobs-housing balance, people will walk to work. Second, a longer distance commuted can be a shorter time commuted if the roads are less congested. The CBD is typically the busiest part of the metropolitan area, so at least one effect of decentralizing employment is to move commuters away from congested downtown streets and onto less congested suburban streets (making them more congested, in turn).

Although the relation between spatial structure and commuting is of critical importance to evaluating the changes we have observed, it has not been the subject of a large research literature. One exception is a study by Randall Crane and David Chatman (2003) that uses detailed data on individuals who participated in the American Housing Survey (collected every two years by the U.S. Census Bureau) between 1985 and 1997. They include observations on more than 185,000 people in more than 42,000 housing units when deriving their conclusions. The data are not perfect, because they only include commuting distance, not commuting time. Nevertheless, it is hard to find such extensive information for so large a sample over so long a time.

The average commute increased from 10.7 miles in 1985 to 11.3 miles in 1997. Men, with an average commute of 12 miles, travel farther than women, whose commute averages only 9.7 miles. Homeowners, who are less flexible in adjusting their housing location, commute farther than renters (12.4 miles versus 9.8 miles). The key question is whether the commute has lengthened due to employment decentralization.

When Crane and Chatman perform a regression analysis to understand the impact of various characteristics on the distance commuted, they find that rising incomes and an increase in the fraction of two-worker households are the main factors explaining the longer commutes. The effect of employment decentralization considering these other factors was actually to reduce the distance traveled. In other words, commutes would be even longer without the ongoing decentralization of employment. With all due respect to the late Mr. Mumford, there seems to be an alternative cure to urban congestion that also reduces commutes – decentralize.

Turning from distance to time, we find that commuting times have not changed substantially over the past few decades. In a series of papers, civil engineer David Levinson and coauthors have documented this finding and explored various explanations for it (Levinson and Wu, 2005; Levinson 1997; Levinson and Kumar 1994). In Washington, DC, for example, the average commute for a person driving alone went from 33.5 minutes in

1957 to 32.5 minutes in 1968 to 32.5 minutes in 1988. This is not a substantial increase in time.

Suppose that people are trying to reduce their commute time. In that case, recent movers should have shorter commutes, as they will have chosen a residence with full knowledge of their current employment. Long-term residents should have longer commutes on average because some of them will have changed firms or had their firm change locations. In fact, there is not an observable difference between the two groups in the time spent commuting.

There seems to be a comfort zone for most people with respect to commuting. People tend to prefer commutes of at least fifteen minutes but less than forty-five minutes, although there is considerable variation in the distribution of commutes between those two times. In a study of sixty-eight metropolitan areas, Levinson and Wu (2005) find that longer commute times are correlated to higher congestion, higher density, and geography. Once again, the main impact of density is to increase commuting time. The heading of this section is not entirely facetious; rather, it is arguably a concise way of summarizing the research.

Gains and Losses from Changing Commuting Patterns

No one enjoys being stuck in traffic. But we must never lose sight of the fact that much of the time is spent by choice. It is also instructive to compare the time lost to congestion with the time gained by driving relative to alternative commuting modes. The U.S. Census Bureau did not collect data on travel time until 1980. In 1980, the average one-way commute was twenty-two minutes, while in 2000, it was twenty-six minutes. Thus, the average worker added eight minutes per day to his or her round-trip commute, or 1,920 minutes in a 240-day working year. This is thirty-two hours (four work days) that are no longer available for whatever purpose the person chooses.

The increase in average commute over the past twenty years suggests that a problem exists. However, there is an alternative comparison that should be made as well. Suppose that a substantial number of people switched from driving to riding buses or other forms of mass transit. The average travel time in 2000 for workers who drove alone was twenty-four minutes, while the average for transit riders was forty-eight minutes. The average person who chooses to drive instead of using transit enjoys a savings of twenty-four minutes each way, or forty-eight minutes per day. This is six times the size of the increase in the average commute and represents 192 hours over the course of a 240-day work year. Some people will choose to spend some of their 192 hours driving, and some of that driving will be done in congested conditions. (According to the 2005 Texas Transportation Institute report, Los Angeles travelers incurred ninety-three hours of delay per year in 2003, but no other metropolitan area had an average per-traveler delay of more than seventy-two hours.) But is that a decline in the quality of life relative to spending those 192 hours at the bus stop or the train station?

While the dominance of driving alone has not changed, there have been some minor shifts in the relative importance of other modes of commuting. The combined number of people walking to work and working at home has exceeded the number using transit since the census began collecting this information in 1960. Walking to work declined from 10.4 percent of the commutes in 1960 to only 2.9 percent in 2000. Transit has also fallen substantially as a percentage of total commuting trips, from 12.6 percent in 1960 to 4.7 percent in 2000. Work at home, with 3.3 percent in 2000 relative to 7.5 percent in 1960, is also lower, but it has increased from a low of 2.3 percent in 1970.

The overall numbers are misleading with respect to the relative importance of mass transit, as most of the total is contributed by a few metropolitan areas such as New York and Chicago. They are also misleading about overall travel patterns, as commutes account for fewer than one-fifth of all personal trips. Despite decades of rhetoric about commutes getting worse, people continue to choose to drive.

CONTROLLING CONGESTION

So people will choose to drive, and this decision will cause congestion. In fact, some of the congestion is likely to be efficient. To review, the efficient level of a negative externality is greater than zero if there are benefits from the activity that generates the externality. Urban land is scarce, so it should be used intensively. Until we learn to stack cars vertically as we stack desks in a skyscraper, the only way to use roads intensively is to cram a lot of cars onto them.

Infrastructure Orthodontia

It is a commonplace to opine that roads are too crowded. A natural inference is that the supply of roads is insufficient. Thus, by building new roads or widening existing roads, congestion will disappear (or at least recede to more tolerable levels). I refer to these activities as *infrastructure orthodontia* because of the obvious similarities to the impact of braces on one's smile. Like regular orthodontia, infrastructure orthodontia can be unsettling. The main topic of conversation at my twentieth high school reunion in 2001 in Manassas, Virginia, which has undergone considerable treatment, was that my classmates and I were having a hard time finding the houses where we had grown up. Unfortunately, infrastructure orthodontia does not have the same lasting effect on roads as orthodontia has on teeth, with any smiles due to road construction tending to disappear quickly.

Why doesn't highway construction eliminate congestion? The answer is found in what Anthony Downs (1992) named the "triple convergence" of modal choice, travel route choice, and travel schedule choice. In short, with roads as with fields of dreams, if you build it they will come.

Congestion is a negative externality, so any solution begins with an analysis of individual decisions. From a person's point of view, what matters is getting from point A (e.g., my house) to point B (e.g., my office). How will I get there? The first choice is the mode, or vehicle. One possibility, which has dominated in the United States for the past fifty years, is to drive by myself. Other familiar modes include the carpool, bus, subway, bicycle, or even walking. In general, modal choice will depend on the relative speed and convenience of the alternatives, and this leads to the first reason for the triple convergence. The immediate impact of newly constructed or improved roads is to increase the desirability of the car relative to other modes, increasing the number of drivers on the road.

The second choice for the commuter (or traveler, more generally) is the route of travel. This choice can be compared to choosing a checkout line in the grocery store. If one seems empty or faster, then people will choose it until it is roughly as crowded as the others. A new road is similar to a newly opened checkout line. It will draw traffic from the alternatives, but the end result will be to have a balanced amount of time stuck in traffic among the choices. One reason for optimism, in this example, is that the average time spent waiting will go down, as the same number of cars (grocery carts) are distributed over more routes (checkout lines). However, the induced changes in modal choice will result in more total cars, so it is not even guaranteed that the average congestion will decline.

The depressing conclusion of the previous paragraph is accentuated by the third convergence, travel schedule. If I expect that the road will be congested at 8:30 A.M., I might leave home at 8:00 A.M., even if I'd rather be sleeping later. New road capacity could inspire me to hit the snooze button on my alarm and leave at my preferred time. So we not only see additional cars added as people move from alternative modes, but we see cars that formerly avoided peak-hour travel.

Does the triple convergence imply that road improvement is always a bad idea? No, it only means that we must temper our expectations. Again, this comes from recognizing that people adjust their behavior to circumstances. Unfortunately, people don't always adjust their behavior in the way that some of us would prefer. Consider the following headline from the November 29, 2000, issue of the satirical newspaper

The Onion: "98% of U.S. Commuters Favor Public Transportation for Others." Building mass transit in the hope that other people will use it, reducing congestion for the favored remainder who continue to drive, is an excellent approach for satire but is not recommended as public policy. When we build roads, people will drive up to the point it is no longer convenient for them, without necessarily taking into account the impact on us.

Remember that the triple convergence represents people making choices that make them happier than before. After all, they could continue to travel by an alternate mode, on an alternate route, or at an alternate time, but they have chosen to change. While this is bad because it increases the negative externality of congestion, it is good because the consumer surplus for the triple convergers increases. If I am now able to have breakfast with my family because I don't have to leave for work as early as I did before the road was constructed, then that is worth something to me.

It is also important to recognize that increased capacity is an effective way of ameliorating congestion. Every year, the Texas Transportation Institute publishes a study of congestion in U.S. metropolitan areas. The most recent report (Schrank and Lomax 2005) found by looking at trends from 1982 to 2003 that residents of metropolitan areas in which road construction kept up with traffic growth were able to maintain constant travel times. However, only four of the eighty-five metropolitan areas were in this situation, while fifty-three of the eighty-five had traffic growth that increased at least 30 percent faster than the growth in road capacity. Even though the net result is a substantial increase in congestion, the road network in 2003 accommodated about twice as much travel as it did in 1982.

Direct Approaches

A direct approach to controlling congestion is any policy that has an impact on the decision by a person to drive on a congested road. The general idea is to internalize the externality as economists like to state oxymoronically. In other words, a policy should cause the person to consider the costs they are imposing on others when they decide to drive.

The most straightforward congestion relief policy is to charge a price for driving on the road. This price, theoretically, can vary by time of day, road, and even type of vehicle to more accurately reflect the negative externality imposed. A tractor trailer on a downtown street at 8:30 A.M. imposes a much larger congestion cost than a small car on a suburban street at 11:00 P.M., and the drivers should face different tolls.

The theory of congestion tolls is more than forty years old, and there have been various experimental implementations of tolls around the world. There have been two principal difficulties, neither of which is technological. The first is a concern with privacy, as a technology that can identify your car's location at various points during the day is a technology that can be used for malign purposes as well as for controlling congestion. The second is political, as people object to paying twice for the road (once for building it and again for driving on it). This represents the failure of economists (actually, the failure of politicians, but I'm being nice) to adequately educate the public about what a congestion toll is designed to accomplish. Regardless of the road capacity and how it is financed, a congestion toll will be necessary so that people are confronted with the full cost of their choice to drive.

As noted, one source of political difficulty with congestion tolls is the idea that people are being forced to pay twice for the road, once through taxes that fund construction and again through congestion tolls. However, two different things are being purchased, not one. By building a road, you have created an opportunity to travel from place to place. But you haven't compensated everyone else for the inconvenience you impose by traveling and slowing them down, which is what the congestion toll accounts for. The experience of congestion tolling in London suggests that this message can be heard, but the message is spreading even more slowly than traffic travels at rush hour. Marlon Boarnet and Saksith Chalermpong (2001) demonstrate that the construction of toll roads in Orange County, California, increased house values in areas with the best access to the roads. In other words, not only were people willing to pay the tolls, but they were also willing to pay a premium to live close to the opportunity to pay tolls. Such a finding in proverbially car-crazy California illustrates that tolls are potentially popular even in America.

Another type of direct policy is to institute lanes that are reserved for certain types of vehicles. One type of reserved lane is solely for the use of buses and other forms of transit. By removing the buses from the regular flow of traffic, there are benefits on both sides. The bus gets a (presumably) uncongested lane for driving, which can help offset not only the reduced amenity value of a bus relative to a car but also the necessity of the bus to stop and start more frequently.

The other type of familiar reserved lane is for cars with several passengers, so-called high-occupancy vehicle (HOV) lanes. Recall the analogy between choosing a travel route and choosing a checkout line in a grocery store. An HOV lane is similar to the express line at the supermarket, only instead of being restricted based on a maximum number of shopping items it's restricted based on a minimum number of passengers. Toll lanes, vilified as "Lexus lanes," are similar to HOV lanes but subject to charge. They are perhaps more appropriately called "daycare lanes" because the cost of a few dollars to avoid draconian penalties for late pick up of kids from childcare can be well worth it.

Indirect Approaches

Having failed to eliminate congestion using policies that focus on congestion, clever people have designed policies that aim to eliminate congestion by focusing on something else. The general idea of these policies is
to increase the cost of driving, in the hope that this increased cost will
cause people to stop using their cars. The general criticism of the policies
is that they are inefficient because they do not distinguish between car use
in congested and uncongested situations.

The largest and most ubiquitous indirect approach is the tax on gasoline. Cars do not move without fuel, so taxing fuel should reduce the
reliance that people place on cars. This is true, but the empirical results
in reducing congestion are not promising. After all, taxes in Europe are a
multiple of those in the United States and car use has continued to grow
in Europe. Gas taxes are also arguably regressive, as the price of gas is the
same for expensive cars and for inexpensive cars. For congestion control,
it makes no sense to charge the same congestion toll (in the form of a gas
tax) for using a CBD road at rush hour and a country road on a summer
evening. The gasoline tax does have the potentially desirable feature of
automatically varying by type of car. For example, a car that gets twelve
miles per gallon will pay twice as much gasoline tax per mile as a car that
gets twenty-four miles per gallon. To the extent that cars that get better
gas mileage also cause less congestion, this feature enhances the efficiency
of the policy.

The level of gasoline taxes required to account for congestion is higher
than politically feasible, at least under current conditions in the United
States. If congestion externalities are estimated to average $0.10 per mile,
a reasonable figure, and a typical car gets twenty-two miles per gallon,
than a tax of $2.20 per gallon is needed. A letter I received (anonymous,
signed "A Lot of Concerned Citizens") in response to an opinion piece I
wrote on this topic (Bogart 1997) illustrates the popular reaction to this
analysis. "The thing you suggest in this article is the most ridiculous thing
I have ever heard . . . you must be nuts. You certainly aren't thinking of
others and how they will manage to get around." My response is that
those others, as they get around without facing the full costs of doing so,
are making it harder for everyone. But I can make those responses safely
because I'm not running for elective office.

The next level of cleverness for increasing the cost of car use is to
increase its *relative* cost by subsidizing mass transit. This is even cleverer as
the subsidies are financed by the taxes collected from car users through the
gas tax. (My aforementioned opinion piece emphasized that the efficient
use of gas tax funds is to reduce congestion, for example, by building
roads, given that people are willing to pay for it.) The problem here is
that the level of transit subsidy needed for people to get out of their cars

is too high to be politically feasible. More precisely, people would need to be paid a considerable amount of money to ride transit, making this approach not only politically infeasible but also budgetarily intractable.

Another clever idea has been a recurring visitor in this book: the use of land-use planning to satisfy people's needs without requiring them to drive. This vision, which dates (at least) to Ebenezer Howard, has already been criticized. If you didn't believe me then, you're unlikely to change your mind now. If your mind is still open, then read a book by two urban planners (Boarnet and Crane 2001) that thoroughly analyzes the connections between land-use planning and travel patterns.

A fertile area of study in recent years has been parking. The idea here is so simple that it's brilliant. When someone arrives someplace, they need to do something with their car. This means that rather than try to charge the car while it's in motion, we could wait until it comes to rest. In addition, a considerable amount of congestion in urban areas consists of cars looking for parking spaces. Donald Shoup (2004) suggests that if the price of parking were raised, it would directly generate revenue and indirectly reduce congestion as some of the cruisers (or parked cars) would decide that the benefits of driving no longer exceed the total cost of the trip. Some companies make the costs of parking clear to their employees by offering a cash payment in lieu of free parking, which should encourage some people to commute using some mode other than private automobile. As an economist, I'm all in favor of charging prices that reflect costs, especially when externalities are present. On that score, the new attention to parking is welcome. It doesn't affect traffic that is just passing through, though, so it can't be considered a panacea.

TRAVEL FORECASTS AND REDUCING CONGESTION

Why wait until congestion appears to build capacity? Why not build roads, bridges, and rail capacity that can handle the entire load when an area is completely developed? After all, if we know the zoning plan, then we can calculate the total number and type of businesses and house-holds that will inhabit an area. Then it should be straightforward to deter-mine the total trip requirements and therefore the capacity. This approach has the additional benefit of avoiding high congestion costs during future construction by building in advance of the heavy demand. Alas, it is not so simple.

In 2005, the *Journal of the American Planning Association* published an article that was critical of the efforts of planners to forecast travel (Flyvbjerg, Holm, and Buhl 2005). The authors examined evidence from 210 projects (27 rail and 183 road) in fourteen countries and concluded that the forecasts were inaccurate. For roads, about half of the projects had actual travel that deviated by at least 20 percent from the forecast. The inaccuracies were not systematic, with 21.3 percent of the predictions exceeding actual travel by at least 20 percent and 28.4 percent of the predictions falling short of actual travel by at least 20 percent. The largest causes of uncertainty were the number of trips, which is predicted by combining historical data on traffic (e.g., those used in Chapter 4 to study commuting) with demographic information and the pattern of local development, which is predicted from local land-use plans. In other words, road predictions were inaccurate because prediction is difficult and because plans change.

Rail predictions are less accurate than road predictions but more systematic in their inaccuracy. Ninety percent of the predictions were overestimates, with the average difference between prediction and observed travel being 106 percent. Using the 20 percent criterion applied to road projects, the authors found that 84 percent of the predictions were at least that inaccurate, with *all* of the inaccuracy being overestimates rather than underestimates. Similar to traffic forecasts for roads, the largest source of uncertainty is in the demand for travel. This is especially difficult to forecast for rail because people are switching from other modes, typically cars. The second largest source of uncertainty is forecasts that are deliberately slanted. This result, while both shocking and controversial, is consistent with the asymmetric nature of the differences between forecast and observed travel. The authors interpret these results as evidence that planners are playing a biased role in the political process, which combines with unequal government policy (favoring rail over roads in some places) to lead to an inefficient amount of rail construction.

This is not a new result. A study by Donald Pickrell (1992) of eight transit systems built in the 1970s and 1980s found systematically optimistic forecasts of ridership, construction costs, and operating costs. Pickrell considers this evidence of inefficient financing rather than poor planning. The problem is that the main source of money is the federal government, which provides few incentives to local planners to forecast the benefits and costs accurately. Regardless of whether the source is poor financial incentives or some other reason, the net result is a bias by planners toward rail transit.

Planners have not accepted the Flyvbjerg et al. (2005) conclusions uncritically. One response is that the study only observed travel in the first year after the project was completed, which is likely to be lower for rail than for roads because of the need for people to change their travel mode. Another criticism is that forecasts can be made more accurate only by increasing their expense, and the benefit of a more accurate forecast is not worth the cost. This seems reasonable in the case of roads, but it doesn't really address the systematic inaccuracies observed for rail projects.

Planning requirements can be biased toward cars even if forecasts aren't. Parking requirements are often set by calculating a maximum need for parking under peak conditions (e.g., the week before Christmas at a shopping mall) and interpreting this amount as a required minimum. Some cities have been taking a creative approach toward a more reasonable parking forecast (Governor's Office of Smart Growth n.d.). For example, both San Diego and Seattle have reduced their parking requirements for certain projects, and Portland, Oregon, has even imposed a parking *maximum* instead of a minimum. Montgomery County, Maryland, has taken an approach reminiscent of the discussion in Chapter 5 about adapting infrastructure developed for the weekday rush hour for evening and weekend stadium use. Rather than just adding all of the parking requirements of neighboring businesses, the county first checks whether the peak times coincide. If they do not, then the required parking can be reduced relative to a simple sum of the peak parking needs of the businesses.

Regardless of the precise extent of inaccuracy or its causes, we can comfortably conclude that forecasting travel is difficult and that the accuracy of the forecasts is highly variable. The theory of investment under uncertainty tells us that a higher variance in future outcomes implies that we should wait longer to invest, all else being equal. Thus, it is inefficient to build too far ahead of demand, which argues that some of the congestion we observe is efficient. Forecast uncertainty thus adds another reason that it is inefficient to eliminate congestion to our previous conclusion that scarce urban land should be used intensively. Because the triple convergence explained that congestion is difficult to eliminate, even if we so desired, it is reassuring to conclude that we don't want to eliminate congestion. Flexibility again shows its value. The quicker we can respond to actual demand for travel, the better off we will be, and this benefit is multiplied when we are waiting to be sure that our forecasts of future travel are accurate.

MUNICIPAL WASTE

> Thou shalt have a place also without the camp, whither thou shalt go forth abroad: And thou shalt have a paddle upon thy weapon; and it shall be, when thou wilt ease thyself abroad, thou shalt dig therewith, and shalt turn back and cover that which cometh from thee.
>
> Deuteronomy 23:12–13

Roads are not the only component of urban infrastructure. In fact, sewers and water can control growth patterns more effectively than zoning or even roads. Land uses can change, but no one can live without water coming in and sewage going out. Joel Garreau captures this idea during an interview with a developer in the rapidly developing area in Northern Virginia near Washington, DC (1991, 226). "So the controlling thing was sewers?" [says Garreau] "Yeah, not traffic," responds the developer.

Waste is interesting in that, similar to traffic, it can result in negative externalities. Unlike congestion, waste is durable and not only affects trade but is a traded good in its own right.

The question of waste disposal is not a new one, as the verses from Deuteronomy attest. The phenomenal growth of cities from the Industrial Revolution onward, though, has made the question more difficult and more urgent. Even in the early twentieth century, the inhabitants of New York each generated "160 pounds of garbage, 1,231 pounds of ash, and 97 pounds of rubbish annually" (Melosi 2001, 70). The amounts continue to grow, increasing from 2.8 pounds per person per day in 1920 to 4.46 pounds per person per day in 1998. Unlike in biblical times, we are unable to simply dispose of all of this waste in place. Rather, it becomes another commodity to trade, and there are externalities aplenty in this field.

In refuse collection, there are benefits from high density of settlement, because there are economies of scale in collection. In fact, doubling the tons per mile can reduce the average cost per ton by as much as 50 percent. This is a positive externality from dense settlement that is not as glamorous as other agglomeration economies of scale, but it is relevant nevertheless. While there are technological approaches to mimicking density, such as trucks with compaction equipment, none are as effective as density.

Collecting municipal waste creates new negative externalities at the same time it alleviates others. The trucks that are used generate both pollution and congestion. As is so often the case in economic analysis, density creates two effects that move in opposite directions. On the one hand, greater density reduces collection costs. On the other hand, greater density increases the negative effects of congestion and pollution caused by the trucks. These issues, similar to so many, have been recognized for millennia, and people have reached different conclusions about the relative benefits and costs. Remember Caesar's prohibition on wagon traffic in Rome during the day? He specifically makes an exception for "carrying out dung from within the city of Rome or within one mile of the city."

Concurrency

One response to strained municipal services has been to mandate that the services must be in place prior to development occurring. This is known as the *doctrine of concurrency*, and it has been upheld in a series of court decisions dating back to the 1970s (Eric Kelly 1993).

While attractive on its face, concurrency brings with it an ironic drawback: it discourages redevelopment of older urban areas, particularly CBDs. Critics of sprawl often promote these areas for redevelopment because they already have infrastructure, such as roads and sewers, in place, reducing the need to expand those services into previously rural areas. However, the dense nature of these older areas means that the services are under great strain, and if planning standards are applied blindly, then the services will be considered too congested for development without considerable investment. The sewage system developed for the new housing of 1930 is not necessarily up to the code of 2005.

A contentious question in both new development and redevelopment is how to allocate the costs of the infrastructure, because the fixed costs of setting up a system are very large relative to the additional costs imposed by each new unit tied into the system. If the full costs of a new system are imposed, the additional households and firms will not want to participate, which can lead to continued use of inefficient septic systems. It is always tempting to the residents who will not have to pay the development fees to impose as heavy a cost as possible. This can be efficient if it causes the externality to be internalized, and some municipalities impose fees on new developments calculated on this basis. However, it can also be an opportunity for a politically powerful majority to impose large costs on the minority.

Sewage tends to be traded only over relatively short distances. Solid waste, in contrast, is the basis of considerable intermetropolitan and interstate commerce. An interesting feature of this trade is that nonresidents are typically charged a higher price than are residents for disposal. Surely such a trade barrier will outrage an economist. Sorry, not this time. Such a pricing system makes sense for two reasons. First, residents bear the infrastructure costs, including the congestion and other negative externalities imposed by the shipments of waste. Second, the waste generated by municipal residents is more predictable than the amount generated by nonresidents. This greater uncertainty means that capacity is more difficult to determine, with residents facing the unenviable choice between excess unused landfill or incinerator capacity and stressed facilities. It is fair (and efficient) to pass along these higher costs resulting from the uncertainty to nonresidents.

Urban growth boundaries are an extreme form of concurrency, in that they forbid the extension of certain services beyond the boundary. This policy faces a very difficult design problem that is not too different from other capacity planning exercises (e.g., roads or solid waste disposal). First, if the boundary is inflexible, then there are surpluses or shortages depending on the direction of inaccuracy in planners' projections. Second, if the boundary is flexible, then it doesn't really constrain the pattern of development.

Pollution and Property Values

Markets for undesirable features such as pollution or taxes are similar to a game of "Hot Potato." If you can't pass something along, you're stuck with it. This humble metaphor is the essence of capitalization, which we met in Chapter 6. Land doesn't move, so landowners at the time a problem becomes apparent are stuck with it in the form of lower property values.

Pollution has been thoroughly analyzed as a source of variation in property values. It will come as a relief, I suppose, to learn that economists consistently find that pollution is something that people and businesses will pay to avoid. This has been confirmed for sources of pollution ranging from smokestacks (Chay and Greenstone 2005) to leaking underground storage tanks (Simons, Bowen, and Sementelli 1997) to Superfund sites (Kohlhase 1991).

Ironically, pollution can be attractive if someone is looking for relatively inexpensive property. A political controversy exists over the siting of incinerators and other pollution-generating facilities. Companies and government officials have been accused of forcing low-income, and especially minority low-income, neighborhoods to accept these facilities. This accusation has the emotionally loaded term of *environmental racism*. However, there is evidence that in some cases the facilities were in place *before* the low-income households were. Vicki Been (1994) is credited with being the first to carefully explain this possibility and confirm it using data from Houston. Her conclusions, needless to say, have not gone unquestioned, and the topic remains controversial.

The observation that benefits and costs are unevenly distributed is not limited to pollution. In the next chapter, we explore a variety of ways in which the components of metropolitan areas are arguably too varied or too similar. Ultimately, this leads us back to the causes and effects of trade.

8 HOMOGENEITY AND HETEROGENEITY IN LOCAL GOVERNMENT

The franchise and the virus work on the same principle: what thrives in one place will thrive in another. You just have to find a sufficiently virulent business plan, condense it into a three-ring binder – its DNA – xerox it, and embed it in the fertile lining of a well-traveled highway, preferably one with a left-turn lane. Then the growth will expand until it runs up against its property lines.

In olden times, you'd wander down to Mom's Café for a bite to eat and a cup of joe, and you would feel right at home. It worked just fine if you never left your hometown. But if you went to the next town over, everyone would look up and stare at you when you came in the door, and the Blue Plate Special would be something you didn't recognize. If you did enough traveling, you'd never feel at home anywhere.

But when a businessman from New Jersey goes to Dubuque, he knows he can walk into a McDonald's and no one will stare at him. He can order without having to look at the menu, and the food will always taste the same. McDonald's is Home, condensed into a three-ring binder and xeroxed. "No surprises" is the motto of the franchise ghetto, its *Good Housekeeping* seal, subliminally blazoned on every sign and logo that make up the curves and grids of light that outline the Basin.

The people of America, who live in the world's most surprising and terrible country, take comfort in that motto. Follow the loglo outward, to where the growth is enfolded into the valleys and the canyons, and you find the land of the refugees. They have fled from the true America, the America of atomic bombs, scalpings, hip-hop, chaos theory, cement overshoes, snake handlers, spree killers, space walks, buffalo jumps, drive-bys, cruise missiles, Sherman's March, gridlock, motorcycle gangs, and bungee jumping. They have parallel-parked their bimbo boxes in identical computer-designed Burbclave street patterns and secreted themselves in symmetrical sheetrock shitholes with vinyl floors and ill-fitting woodwork and no sidewalks, vast house farms out in the loglo wilderness, a culture medium for a medium culture.

Neal Stephenson (1992, 190–1)

O NE EFFECT OF TRADE IS TO REDUCE DIFFERENCES AMONG PLACES. In 1977, a blockbuster movie, *Smokey and the Bandit*, could be premised on the idea that someone in Georgia could only drink Coors beer if it was smuggled from Texas. Today, this basic plot point, reasonable at the time, seems as implausible as most of the rest of the movie. Neal Stephenson's metaphor about franchises as viruses presents the ambiguity of the spreading homogeneity available to people in the United States. The world for an individual is more inviting, so that people travel and trade more. But the places to which they travel have become more similar.

Homogeneity within metropolitan areas is a cause of and result of government activity. So too with heterogeneity. Throughout this chapter, we will explore the tension between homogeneity and heterogeneity as it is realized in the United States today.

INTRAMETROPOLITAN COMPETITION FOR BUSINESSES

One of the challenges for local governments within metropolitan areas is to attract and retain businesses. This fiscal competition is for high stakes, as the tax revenue and prestige that accrue from being the site of a high-profile business are crucial to local politicians and occasionally their constituents. Similar to so many other phenomena, the modern version recapitulates ancient themes. Wolf Schneider (1963, 181) tells the story of the founding of Munich as resulting from just this type of competition for revenue. In the case of Munich, the attraction was control of the salt trade crossing the Isar River during the Middle Ages. Henry the Lion, Duke of Saxony and Bavaria, burned down the town of Föhring and its bridge over the Isar, which was not in his territory. In its place, he constructed the new town of Munich, which was upstream from Föhring and had the advantage from his point of view of being located in his territory. Today's mayors are unable to destroy each other's towns, but they find other ways to compete in the high-stakes game of business attraction.

This competition among trading places is serious because of the nature of firm-location decisions. Businesses choose a location to maximize profits. Taxes and government spending are secondary factors compared to other determinants of profitability, such as access to markets and labor costs. Typically, government incentives only serve to influence firm location within a metropolitan area. A general conclusion of economic theory is that competition benefits the one being competed for. In the case of municipalities within a metropolitan area, this means that firms can extract substantial benefits as municipalities compete.

Places with natural advantages or places that "win" the game of attracting and retaining firms will have a larger local tax base. This in turn will enable them to provide higher-quality local government services, which will help them continue to improve. We saw this issue from the other side in Chapter 5, as enterprise zones and other policies are designed to offset the disadvantages that some places have. Now we will look more broadly at a systemic way to curb intrametropolitan competition among trading places.

Metropolitan Tax-Base Sharing

> The time is comin' and though I'm no youngster, I may see it, when New York City will break away from the State and become a state itself. It's got to come. The feelin' between this city and the hayseeds that make a livin' by plunderin' it is every bit as bitter as the feelin' between the North and South before the war. And, let me tell you, if there ain't a peaceful separation before long, we may have the horrors of civil war right here in New York State.
>
> William Riordon (1905 [1963], 65)

George Washington Plunkitt, the straight-talking sachem of Tammany Hall, had a strong opinion about the way that tax bases were shared in the New York area. As the preceding quote illustrates, he had a straightforward solution – the secession of the city from the state. The unequal allocation of economic activity throughout metropolitan areas continues to raise difficult questions of public policy.

One approach to this issue of unequal tax bases is to adopt a program that distributes the taxes throughout a region. The most famous example of this approach is found in Minneapolis–St. Paul, Minnesota. In 1971, the state legislature enacted a law designed to reduce intrametropolitan competition in the seven-county metropolitan area. The centerpiece of the legislation is the requirement that every municipality contribute 40 percent of the increase in its commercial and industrial property tax base to a pool that is taxed at a uniform regional tax rate. The revenue from this pool is then distributed in an equalizing manner, that is, the per-capita amount received is higher for places with a lower tax base.

The tax-base sharing pool now distributes more than $400 million per year and includes 32.3 percent of the total commercial and industrial property tax base, up from 6.7 percent when the program started in 1975. Many opponents of urban sprawl, most famously former Minnesota state legislator Myron Orfield (1997), hold it up as a model. Because all municipalities in the metropolitan area benefit whenever any new development occurs, there is more incentive for them to work together to plan efficiently for growth. In turn, this can encourage redevelopment in places where infrastructure already exists. The largest municipality in the region, Minneapolis, transformed from a net beneficiary to a net contributor as it redeveloped.

The incentive provided by tax-base sharing is not always sufficient to eliminate intrametropolitan competition to attract development.

Jonathan Barnett (1995, 141) narrates how Minneapolis built a downtown baseball stadium for the Twins, attracting them from their former home in the suburb of Bloomington. In turn, Bloomington redeveloped the stadium into the Mall of America, using several hundred million dollars to improve the infrastructure and build 13,000 parking spaces in garages.

Another case study is an industrial park in Anoka, a suburb of Minneapolis, as described by Greg LeRoy, Sara Hively, and Katie Tallman (2000). The good news is that the city successfully redeveloped a formerly contaminated site. The bad news is that it attracted firms by offering free land to companies, attracting all of its twenty-nine tenants from elsewhere in the seven-county region. Keeping 60 percent is sometimes more attractive than waiting for your share of 40 percent.

If metropolitan consolidation, of which tax-base sharing is just a single component, is the answer to the problem of urban sprawl, then we should find that metropolitan areas that are consolidated are less sprawling than those that are not. An obvious case study suggests that there is no relation between metropolitan consolidation and perceived urban sprawl. Houston, Texas, has grown from 17.4 square miles in 1910 to 617 square miles in 2000 through annexation. The city of Houston includes more than half of the metropolitan population in its city limits. Further, the state of Texas has passed legislation giving Houston considerable control over activities outside of its city limits. In fact, around 1,289 square miles – twice the current area – is reserved for future annexation by the city. Despite these powers, which far exceed those in most places, observers tend to consider Houston an example of sprawl rather than smart growth.

Metropolitan area tax-base sharing can be supported because it promotes the efficiency of the trading places. If the various suburbs are acting in a Tiebout manner, then government officials will want to promote efficiency to keep their homevoters happy. However, the central city is too big and heterogeneous to be a Tiebout place. Economists often expect that the government of the central city will try to grow beyond the efficient size, as government officials try to increase their power at the expense of others. The way to do this is to increase taxes. However, higher taxes will tend to drive businesses to relocate outside of the central city. If agglomeration economies of scale are lost as a result, then the efficiency of the entire region can fall. This efficiency justification, if valid, adds to equity arguments in favor of suburban support for central cities, including the use by suburban residents of city services (this also raises efficiency issues) and the concentration of low-income households in central cities.

Andrew Haughwout and Robert Inman (2002) formally analyze the possible productivity effects of high central-city taxes taking the Philadelphia region as a model. Using a simulation, they conclude that a transfer from the suburbs to Philadelphia that funds property-tax abatement for business could have a dramatic impact on the regional economy.

A redistribution of $251 million per year (smaller than the Minnesota program) could double land values in the suburbs as productivity benefits are capitalized, according to their calculations. Even if only a part of this benefit could be realized in practice, it seems that any politician would support such a program.

One difference between reality and theory is that their model treats more than 300 municipalities distributed among three states as one unified suburban government. The costs of coordinating all of these individual governments are large, perhaps leading to alternative approaches. An enterprise zone program, for example, is implicitly a reduction in taxes in the central city financed by taxes throughout the state.

Implicit Tax-Base Sharing

No metropolitan area has gone as far as Minneapolis–St. Paul in implementing an explicit system of tax-base sharing. It is nevertheless the case that there are three types of implicit tax-base sharing mechanisms used throughout the United States.

The first type of implicit tax-base sharing is city-county consolidation. Once the city and county are one government, it is automatically true that they share their tax base and impose a uniform system of tax rates. As a result, there is the potential for both the efficiency-enhancing internalization of externalities (and common tax rate) and the equity-enhancing equalization of the per-capita tax base throughout the county. Well-known examples of unified regional governments include Nashville-Davidson County, Tennessee, Indianapolis-Marion County, Indiana, and Jacksonville-Duval County, Florida.

The second type of implicit tax-base sharing, introduced in the previous section, is statewide taxes that fall unevenly on different parts of the metropolitan area. Alternatively, it can be statewide spending that is not evenly distributed. The largest such policy is state finance of public schools, but enterprise zones and other targeted policies have this nature as well. In the other direction, the favorable tax treatment of owner-occupied housing constitutes a subsidy from the (typically rental-dominated) central city to the rest of the metropolitan area.

The third type of implicit tax-base sharing is commuter income or payroll taxes. These local taxes are imposed on people based on their place of work. If people work in a different municipality from their place of residence, we can think of the payroll tax as a grant from their residence to their workplace. Payroll taxes are relatively widespread in the United States, with twelve states allowing their local governments to impose them.

In Chapter 4, we described the flow of commuters across locations in the Cleveland area using data from individual travel diaries. Now we will use that information to infer the magnitude and distribution of implicit tax-base sharing in one county, Cuyahoga, which includes Cleveland.

ESTIMATING PAYROLL TAXES PAID BY COMMUTERS. The methodology for computing the value of taxes paid by commuters is straightforward. Each worker is assumed to make one trip from his or her residence to their workplace, at which time they are paid their annual salary.

The most difficult aspect of this analysis is assigning a salary value to each commuter. The travel diaries do not include any income information. Further, because the data are aggregated from a sample, we could not observe individual incomes for every commuter even if the diaries contained income information. But the 1990 census journey-to-work file includes information on the median income of the population living within each TAZ. Each trip was assigned the value corresponding to the median income of its TAZ of origin. This reflects the greater homogeneity of residences than workplaces, as predicted by the Tiebout model. Both CEOs and clerks work in the same office building, but they usually don't live in the same neighborhood. The RAND study of Allegheny County (Sleeper et al. 2004) independently developed the same approach to imputing the income of commuters.

Conveniently, TAZs are always completely within municipal boundaries so that aggregating the TAZ data to the municipal level was straightforward. The payroll taxes collected by municipal governments in Cuyahoga County are a flat-rate tax of between 1.0 and 2.9 percent of gross wages. To calculate the flows of tax revenues, it is first necessary to determine the incidence of the payroll tax, that is, whose buying power is reduced by the tax. If the incidence of the tax is on the worker, as assumed here, then the tax reduces the buying power at the worker's place of residence. Thus, the gross flow of grants from one municipality to another is simply the payroll tax rate in the destination municipality multiplied by the total incomes of commuters from the source municipality. The taxes paid by residents to other municipalities are exported taxes and the taxes paid by residents of other municipalities are imported taxes. Of course, the total exported taxes in the county equal the imported taxes.

The average municipality generates about 46 percent of its income tax revenue from commuters, while the median generates about 43 percent. This is the first evidence of how significant the implicit intergovernmental transfers are. There is substantial variation, though, among municipalities. The seventy-fifth percentile for this variable is 56 percent, while the twenty-fifth percentile is 32 percent, for an interquartile range of 24 percent.

There is even greater variation among the municipalities in the percentage of their local tax revenue that is exported to other municipalities.

This is in part due to the fact that there is no theoretical reason to expect this variable to be capped at 100 percent. In fact, any suburb that has a relatively low employment-resident ratio, a relatively low tax rate, and allows a tax credit on taxes paid at the workplace could easily have a ratio substantially in excess of 100 percent. These characteristics are a good description of a high-income bedroom suburb. More than 25 percent of the municipalities export more in taxes than they collect from both residents and nonresidents. At the other end of the spectrum, the municipality of Cuyahoga Heights (home of a major steel mill and not many residents) is found to export only about 2 percent of its tax revenue. The city of Cleveland, with a great deal of employment including high-income jobs and a substantial fraction of the low-income residents in the county, has the next lowest export percentage at 12.5 percent. The mean export percentage is 79 percent, which is also the median. The seventy-fifth percentile is 111 percent, and the twenty-fifth percentile is 37 percent, illustrating the wide range of municipal experiences.

To have a benchmark, define the "base case" situation as one in which each town's exported taxes are returned to it. This is not precisely the same thing as repealing the payroll tax and replacing it with an increased income tax on residents for two reasons. First, the tax rates vary from town to town, so that it is possible that the income earned by commuters would be taxed at a different rate in their municipality of residence than in their workplace. Second, it doesn't account for the effect of the tax credits provided by some municipalities to residents who paid taxes at their place of work.

The total amount of money redistributed in 1994 by the actual system is $264.6 million or about $188 per capita. This figure is comparable to the $241 million ($103 per capita) distributed in the Minneapolis–St. Paul fiscal disparities program in 1995.

When we compare the hypothetical base case to the actual system of implicit grants, there is dramatic redistribution, as would be expected from the large size of the program. Of the fifty-six municipalities in the analysis, thirty-nine lose revenue from the actual system relative to the base case, while seventeen gain. The winners from the actual system are relatively large, with the seventeen municipalities that gain possessing a total population of 602,601. This figure is largely due to Cleveland being a winner under the actual system relative to the base case.

One way to describe the total extent of redistribution under the actual system is to compare the ratio of the tax base per capita for the municipality at the seventy-fifth percentile with the tax base per capita for the municipality at the twenty-fifth percentile (the *interquartile ratio*). Under the base case, this ratio is 3.5, while under the actual system of implicit grants the ratio is 4.5. In other words, the actual system reinforces the differences between relatively high-tax-base and low-tax-base municipalities. This is unsurprising given that places that import a high percentage of their municipal income tax base are also likely to have large concentrations of commercial and industrial property. By contrast, the Minneapolis–St. Paul system, which is explicitly equalizing, reduces the ratio of the ninety-fifth percentile to the fifth percentile from 4.8 to 3.6 (Luce 1998).

AN EXPLICIT REVENUE-SHARING SYSTEM. Let us now move to an analysis of a system that explicitly redistributes in a manner similar to the Minnesota system. The contribution of each municipality to the common revenue pool for the redistribution will be 40 percent of its growth in imported payroll taxes between 1989 and 1994. The 40 percent of growth figure is chosen to accord with the Fiscal Disparities program. The years are chosen to correspond with years for which commuting data are available. The U.S. Census of 1990 asked about work location in 1989, while the NOACA survey in 1994 provides us with information about commuting patterns in that year.

The common pool to be redistributed in 1994 would have been $51.4 million or $37 per capita. This compares with $46 million, or $21 per capita, in 1980, the fifth year that the Fiscal Disparities program operated in Minnesota.

The simulated system works as follows. Each municipality contributes 40 percent of the growth in income tax revenue paid by residents of other municipalities. Each municipality then receives an equalizing grant that varies directly with population and inversely with tax base per capita. Because we only have household income information for 1989 (from the census), the 1994 incomes are the 1989 incomes inflated by the Consumer Price Index.

An interesting question is whether 40 percent of growth is the most efficient allocation between the municipality where the person works and the rest of the metropolitan area. There is one tantalizing piece of evidence on this issue. Warren McHone (1990) identifies the source of location rents as access to the intrametropolitan and intermetropolitan transport network. This is a trading place approach to thinking about property values, even though his analysis is restricted to industrial firms. If the main reason for the variation in property values is access to the transport network, then it is reasonable for some of the benefits from increases in property values to flow to the larger area that finances the transport network.

McHone's analysis uses data from the Philadelphia metropolitan area from the years 1978 through 1982. Looking at property taxes only, not local income taxes, he finds that about 40 percent of increased revenue represents site rents while about 60 percent represents compensation for negative externalities. This is an efficiency justification for the 40 percent redistribution rule, because it is also efficient for a local government to

receive compensation for allowing activities that generate negative externalities to locate in their borders. I suspect that the 40 percent rule in
Minnesota was more of a political compromise than a carefully calibrated
calculation on economic efficiency grounds.

If we simulate the revenue-sharing system described previously, we find
that (compared to the actual system) thirty-nine municipalities are better
off. They are the same thirty-nine municipalities that are better off under
the base case than under the actual system. The most prominent loser
from a move away from the current system is Cleveland. This is likely
to create substantial political difficulty in implementing any move to an
explicit metropolitan tax-base sharing system. Under the revenue-sharing
system, the interquartile ratio falls from 4.5 to 3.4. Observe that a system
that only redistributes about 20 percent of the total commuter taxes is
actually more equalizing than the base case that redistributes all of the
commuter taxes. This efficiency in redistribution reflects the explicitly
equalizing nature of the simulated system.

Unlike the situation in Minneapolis–St. Paul, the implicit redistribution system in Cuyahoga County was created by an independently acting
set of local governments, each presumably acting in the best interest of
its residents. Hence, any change that does not yield efficiency gains is
strictly zero-sum redistribution. It could be argued, in fact, that the current system's rewarding of people for living in the same municipality in
which they work offsets some of the underpricing of automobile use.
This is an extremely indirect form of congestion tax, though, and it has
the weakness of not affecting congestion within a municipality or varying
from municipality to municipality. The added local tax imposed when you
work in a municipality that you don't live in is the same whether you are
walking across the street or driving on crowded roads across the county.

REGIONALISM AND GETTING AN EDUCATION

Proponents of regionalism argue that moving toward a more centralized
system of service provision and finance would lead to increases in both
efficiency and equity. They do not choose, however, to use the results of
an ongoing set of experiments in centralization to investigate their claims.
These experiments involve the publicly provided service that is the largest
in terms of expenditure and arguably the most important in determining
the character of a place in the present and future of the country. I refer,
of course, to public schools.

Since the *Serrano* case (1971), eighteen states (and counting) have
joined California in having their public school finance systems found
unconstitutional. The general response has been to reduce the emphasis
in school finance on the local property tax and to increase reliance on

sales and income taxes that are collected at the county or state level. In addition, concerns about quality have been met with an expanding battery of tests from elementary school through high school, and these tests are determined at an increasing level of centralization. Most states now have required proficiency tests, and the federal government has expressed interest in a national curriculum, with the No Child Left Behind requirements as a de facto set of national standards.

These activities represent centralization beyond the wildest dreams of the regionalists. Why, then, are they not trumpeted as the leading edge of regionalism, so that people can understand that the city-county consolidation or metropolitan area tax-base sharing are just mop-up operations in a campaign that is largely concluded? There are two reasons. First, the effects of centralized provision and finance have not led to a clear increase in equity and efficiency. Second, a simultaneous movement has developed to undo much of the impact of the centralization. It would take us too far afield to look at education reform in depth, so we will remain focused on its role in intrametropolitan trade.

No one disputes that the quality of education is related to the resources available to provide the education. Most school finance lawsuits in recent years have focused on the adequacy of the finance capacity of schools. However, even large changes in funding have not always led to improved outcomes. One possible explanation is that the money is ill spent by greedy or misguided educational administrators and their political overseers. Perhaps, but a more general and compelling explanation might begin with the difficulty of substituting some traded goods and services for untraded goods and services. The untraded service in this case is the nature and extent of parental involvement in education, with the traded services being provided by the school in the form of teachers, counselors, and other workers. Keeping with our theme of homogeneity and heterogeneity, we can observe that charter schools, home schools, and private schools have increased the scope of choice in education even while public schools have been made more homogeneous as the result of state and federal government action.

Understanding Schools as Part of a Trading Place Economy

The most important local government service is the public school system. It is not only the largest in financial terms but it is also vital to the present attractiveness of a location and the future success of the town, region, and even the nation. It is straightforward to analyze schools as part of the trading place economy.

Begin with the most familiar situation, the classic neighborhood school. This is a nontraded service, produced locally and consumed locally. The quality of the service depends on the purchased inputs, including teachers, books, and equipment. It also depends on nonpurchased inputs such as the extent of parental involvement and the safety of the neighborhood. For a neighborhood school to be successful, it must provide a service that combines the advantages of large scale (relative to home schooling) and small scale (relative to a large regional school). While the school services are not tradable, they affect the market for tradable goods, such as houses, and tradable services, such as labor, as people attempt to locate near high-quality schools. Even if the educational services are produced efficiently, there is no guarantee of equity. In fact, the dominant role of nonpurchased inputs along with the important role of purchased inputs financed in a decentralized manner combine to create a very unequal situation.

Another approach to public school provision is the regional school, which serves an area beyond walking distance. This is an export of educational services from one part of the district to the remainder of the district, although it is still a service produced and consumed entirely within one school district. Again, the structure's efficiency depends on the extent of economies of scale in production. The advantages of larger scale are that a wider range of services can be provided and that the fixed costs of providing services can be spread over more people. The disadvantages include the greater transportation costs: both for the children to attend school and for the parents whose involvement is important to the quality of the education.

Some public school districts include the option of magnet schools (so-called because they attract students) with a particular curricular emphasis such as science or the arts. These are exporters of a specialized set of educational opportunities to a broad area. In some cases, these services even transcend school district boundaries. In York County, Pennsylvania, vocational and technical education at the high school level is provided to the entire county through the York County School of Technology (which I can see from my house). There are sixteen public school districts in the county, so my neighborhood is exporting vocational and technical education not only to the rest of our school district but to fifteen others as well.

Private schools also typically have a broader geographic scope than public schools. However, they usually have considerable homogeneity along one or more dimensions. These can include race, as in the case of the private academies organized in the South to evade the onset of court-ordered desegregation; religion, as in the case of church-related schools; or income, as is the case in certain exclusive schools. Income, religious, and racial homogeneity are also often the case in public schools drawn from a defined geographical area, as the Tiebout sorting process described earlier can lead to areas that are composed of relatively similar households.

The expansion in recent years of charter schools and vouchers is also straightforward to characterize in this framework. Charter schools represent an attempt to alter the pattern of trade in educational services.

In some cases, this manifests as an increase in local production, as small charter schools are created and children are removed from a large regional district. In other cases, this manifests as an increase in trade, as specialized charter schools are created to attract similar students from a broad area. Vouchers are simply an export subsidy.

Dimensions of Segregation

> If Levittown was a model of suburban homogeneity in 1950, it is no longer. The clash of dissident internal forces has rendered the community a heterogeneous assemblage of urban families. The rise of working-class elements has eroded the formerly middle-class ethos of the suburb. Furthermore, the Levittown population clearly reflects, perhaps now more than ever, the conflicts between ethnic and religious minorities so long a characteristic of cities.
>
> William Dobriner (1963, 122)

Trade requires heterogeneity among places and reduces the extent of that heterogeneity. When a good or service is not traded, then the heterogeneity can persist. An outcome in which members of different groups reside in different places is a form of heterogeneity called *segregation*. There is considerable popular attention paid to segregation for its own sake, as well as for its possible relation to educational quality and other public policy issues.

Characterizing segregation turns out to be tricky, for the same reason that characterizing urban sprawl is tricky. There is more than one dimension of segregation. For example, one approach is to compare how evenly the members of two groups are distributed within an area. The index of specialization (in this context called the *index of dissimilarity*) is the most popular way to measure this aspect of segregation. A second approach is to calculate the extent to which members of one group are exposed to interaction with members of the other group. If one group comprises 99 percent of the population, then the outcome is arguably segregation regardless of how evenly the two groups are distributed. A single measure of segregation will not provide all of the relevant information, just as was the case in designing measures of sprawl (see Chapter 3).

Segregation is even more difficult to measure than sprawl, however, because there are many different ways to identify groups. If you're like most Americans, you immediately thought of race when forming the groups discussed in the previous two paragraphs, although I never mentioned it. That's one way of defining groups, but there are others, such as income or age, that can also be relevant. In the case of public schools, the importance of parental behavior and motivation implies that perhaps we should focus on parents' education and how that is distributed over space.

As with so much else about metropolitan structure, the pattern of segregation is continually changing. There is a substantial research literature on this topic, which shares a common theme. Even a small initial change can lead to large changes in a relatively short time. In technical terms, there is a nonlinear relationship between variables of interest. One of the most sophisticated recent analyses of racial segregation is by Federico Echenique and Roland Fryer, Jr. (2005). They find that segregation within a school is a nonlinear function of the percentage of students that are black, with extreme segregation resulting as soon as the percentage of students that are black is higher than 20 percent. These nonlinearities complicate the design and implementation of policies to reduce segregation. If there is not much difference in within-school segregation between 20 percent black and 100 percent black, having a goal of moving from 40 percent black to 30 percent black by redistricting or busing won't accomplish much.

The quote from William Dobriner shows how even the paragon of suburban homogeneity, Levittown, New York, rapidly evolved. Because race, education, and income were highly correlated for a long time, it remains an open question whether integration can be a stable situation. The continuing rise of a college-educated black middle class allows us to investigate whether the racial segregation in the United States is an artifact of history or the result of ongoing choices. Patrick Bayer, Hanming Fang, and Robert McMillan (2005) use data from the 2000 census to analyze whether an increase in the middle-class black population leads to greater residential integration. One possibility is that it does as a wider range of housing options becomes available. The other possibility is that it doesn't, as a critical mass of middle-class black households are now able to create, Tiebout style, a neighborhood segregated by choice. Their empirical results are consistent with the latter outcome, suggesting that racial segregation is at least partly by mutual choice.

EFFECTIVE CHANGE: TARGETING SUBSIDIES TO THE UNDESERVING

The persuading approach to public policy requires understanding and adjusting to market forces. This often means that we must adjust what we would like to do with what people and companies are willing to do. For example, the theory of investment under uncertainty tells us that the level of deterioration at which people leave a situation is worse than the level at which they are willing to return. (In the one case, they're willing to wait to see if it improves; in the other, they need to be persuaded that it won't deteriorate too much.) Thus, we need to improve an area "too much" before it will be able to regain its earlier vitality.

A recurring theme is that the most effective approach to changing an area requires targeting assistance not on the most deserving individuals in an abstract sense, but rather on individuals whose behavior will be decisive in fundamentally changing the dynamics of the market. Subsidizing housing for an individual does not guarantee that an area will become attractive for investors. After all, the problem in these areas is that the demand is not sufficient to cause the price to be high enough to stimulate investment.

In Chapter 5, we saw in some detail the way that Cleveland provided subsidies to attract housing investment to the downtown. This is not an isolated instance, as the approach is being used in various ways across the United States. Alan Mallach (2005) provides examples from Richmond, Virginia, Baltimore, Maryland, and Camden, New Jersey. In some cases, the subsidy is provided to the developer in the form of reduced-cost capital. In others, the subsidy is provided to homebuyers in the form of low-interest loans, forgivable loans if a residency requirement is met, or even cash grants.

This hardheaded approach to urban redevelopment requires some difficult decisions, as it is not possible given the limited funds available to apply this method to every part of a city. Mallach cites the case of Richmond, which focused almost all of its discretionary funds into only six neighborhoods beginning in 1999. In Philadelphia, the redevelopment efforts have been assisted by the analytical work of The Redevelopment Fund, a community development financial institution and think tank. The fund created an index of community housing market health and explicitly used it for triage, targeting efforts at both neighborhoods that are in need of subsidy and those where subsidies are likely to have an impact in attracting private investment.

Colleges and other place-based employers, such as hospitals, have also participated in these efforts by providing financial incentives to purchase homes nearby. In New Haven, Connecticut, Yale University gives $7,000 at closing plus $2,000 per year for nine years to employees who purchase in a group of selected neighborhoods (Mallach 2005). The University of Pennsylvania, whose commercial efforts in West Philadelphia we already saw in Chapter 5, also has a program to encourage employees to live in the neighborhood. But it is not just the Ivy League that takes this approach. My own employer, York College of Pennsylvania, provides a forgivable loan of up to $8,000 to employees who purchase housing in a neighborhood adjacent to campus.

While the low pay of faculty and staff at universities is a standard complaint heard by administrators (like me), it is nevertheless true that these employees do not generally qualify for most forms of subsidized housing. Rather, their colleges have made a calculated decision that their funds can help attract other investors into these neighborhoods. This is not just good public policy, but it can also be a necessity for a college to survive in a particular place. It is much easier to attract students and faculty when the campus is in a thriving neighborhood than when it is in a dangerous and decaying neighborhood.

One concern about bringing middle- and upper-income households into urban neighborhoods is the impact on the residents who already live there. In particular, there is fear that they will be displaced as rents go up with the improved amenities. Lance Freeman, at Columbia University, has studied this question and found grounds for optimism. There is considerable mobility in areas that are redeveloping, but not more than one finds in similar areas that are not redeveloping. Americans are highly mobile and low-income Americans even more so. People in the neighborhoods who own their homes stand to benefit as the value of this important asset goes up, and as bank credit for home improvement becomes more readily available. This is one instance of a more general benefit from connecting previously isolated areas with the broader metropolitan area. As seen in Chapter 5, an important part of neighborhood economic success is integration with other trading places. If this integration requires subsidizing those who are already well connected to extend these links, then an approach that at first glance seems immoral could be concluded after further thought to be the only reasonable answer.

Adding the dimension of race makes an already difficult situation even more complicated. Many places try to promote racial integration, for example, with only limited success. One success story is the Cleveland suburb of Shaker Heights, Ohio, which has pursued pro-integrative strategies for fifty years. In the 1980s, residents were concerned that one neighborhood that bordered the city of Cleveland was on a path to become overwhelmingly black. The city created a low-interest loan program to promote the purchase of houses by whites in areas that had a high percentage of black residents and vice versa. In practice, the program was dominated by loans to middle-class and professional white households purchasing houses in the neighborhood of concern. An analysis by Brian Cromwell (1990) found that the loan program achieved its goal of stabilizing the racial composition of the neighborhood. This success comes at the expense of a potential stigma of paying white households to live in integrated neighborhoods. This example is even more telling because of the long history of successful integration in Shaker Heights, illustrating the challenge facing pro-integrative efforts in places that lack such a history.

Even the extent to which an area is considered in need of redevelopment can be affected by race. Two social psychologists, Robert Sampson and Stephen Raudebusch (2004), studied how the perception of disorder in a neighborhood varied by race. They found that among neighborhoods that were otherwise equal, the one with a higher concentration of minority groups was perceived as having a higher level of problems. This finding is not simply the result of white prejudice, as the results were consistent across both white and black respondents. Thus, there is not an abstract measure of disorder that must be corrected, but a more fluid level that depends on the observer and the characteristics of the neighborhood. This implies that an additional level of effort is required to generate sustainable success in declining areas, even beyond the already elevated amount indicated by the theory of investment under uncertainty.

REGIONAL SERVICE PROVISION

We already have the municipal services equivalent of charter schools, home schools, and private schools. Even proponents of regionalism do not advocate eliminating all local autonomy for service provision. Thus, much of the advocacy of regionalism stops short of the complete uniformity aspired to by many efforts in public schools that actively oppose charter and private schools.

What is more troubling, however, is the willful ignoring of the meaning of voluntary efforts by municipal governments to more efficiently provide public services. At the same time that homeowners' associations have arguably increased the balkanization of the metropolitan area, councils of government and regional service consolidation have reduced it. The difference between these initiatives and complete metropolitan consolidation is the voluntary nature of the process. If there are efficiency gains to be had, then municipalities can agree with each other to take advantage of them. For example, the sixty-nine municipalities in York County, Pennsylvania, have been gradually consolidating their police forces. According to a municipal government summit in April 2005, there are now five regional police forces involving twenty-eight municipalities in completely merged services. About two-thirds of the municipalities (including those in regional police forces) have some type of municipal cooperation, such as contracting police services to other municipalities or mutual aid agreements. In addition, there have been multiple joint purchase and other cooperation agreements, as municipalities have found it advantageous to pool their resources to cover the costs of activities such as purchasing police radios. These regional police forces have brought together areas that are naturally aligned, by both geography (including the road system) and outlook. Other agreements have been reached regarding administrative services, planning and code enforcement, emergency services, recreation, and utilities.

These types of initiative are what we should be encouraging. Complete metropolitan consolidation is a crusading move, while voluntary regional consolidation is a persuading move. The result could be quite similar, as complete consolidation combined with the opting out of some private developments leads to a heterogeneous pattern not unlike gradual consolidation of some services with retained independence of others. But the political approach is quite different.

HETEROGENEITY THROUGH HOMOGENEITY: NEIGHBORHOOD ASSOCIATIONS

> In the mass movement into suburban areas a new kind of community was produced, which caricatured both the historic city and the archetypal sub-urban refuge: a multitude of uniform, unidentifiable houses, lined up inflex-ibly, at uniform distances, on uniform roads, in a treeless communal waste, inhabited by people of the same class, the same income, the same age group, witnessing the same television performances, eating the same tasteless pre-fabricated foods, from the same freezers, conforming in every outward and inward respect to a common mold, manufactured in the central metropolis. Thus the ultimate effect of the suburban escape in our time is, ironically, a low-grade uniform environment from which escape is impossible.
>
> Lewis Mumford (1961, 486)

Common interest developments (CIDs) and other forms of neighborhood association are a large and growing phenomenon throughout the United States. By 2005, there were about 274,000 communities with 54.6 million residents living in 22.1 million housing units, according to the Commu-nity Associations Institute. This is a twenty-five-fold increase since 1970, when there were only 10,000 communities with 2.1 million residents. They are not, however, a completely new phenomenon. In older, walking cities, there was social distance even though all income and social classes lived in close proximity. Once carriages became available, the wealthier residents moved a carriage ride's distance from their undesirable neigh-bors. The advent of the horsecar, the electric streetcar, and finally the private automobile made geographic separation infeasible without some augmented measures to ensure isolation. Thus, the gated community is a "back to the future" phenomenon in which uniformed private security officers preventing entry to motorists that do not have a resident to vouch for them have replaced liveried servants preventing entry to the masses living in the alley behind the mansion.

In addition to the long-standing social reasons for restrictions, there are reasons based on the logic of real estate markets. Most mortgages today are bought and sold far beyond the towns in which the property is located. Homebuyers benefit from this activity, as it has permitted low interest rates and straightforward loan approval processes to flourish. For investors to be willing to participate in such a market, though, there needs to be some degree of standardization. A standard set of covenants, conditions, and restrictions (CC&Rs) is one part of making mortgages from a wide range of places into a homogeneous commodity that can then be traded widely.

Despite being identified by their exclusivity, it is wrong to consider CIDs as isolated from the rest of the metropolitan area. Quite to the contrary, their uniform nature requires them to interact with other trading places. For example, residents of high-income gated communities leave to commute to work. Alternatively, residents of senior living facilities import a wide variety of consumption items, including medical services.

A college dormitory represents an extremely homogeneous population, typically consisting of people in a narrow age range who share many other similarities. The dormitory is typically gated or otherwise isolated from the surrounding neighborhood as well, whether for security reasons or to create a campus ambience. Colleges are an export activity for local towns, thus making their decisions about how to house their students doubly important for the local economy. There seems to be no single correct answer. If the dormitories are too isolated from the rest of the town, the college is accused of being an "ivory tower" institution not interested in the well-being of the entire place. If the dormitories are too integrated, then negative externalities ranging from congestion to noise to litter dominate the conversation. These extremes are not unlike much of the discussion regarding CIDs more generally, although many gated communities would probably resent being referred to as dormitories.

Residential homogeneity is not only a phenomenon of explicit restrictions or organizationally provided housing. With the invention of mass transit in the nineteenth century, it became possible for groups to create identifiable enclaves near streetcar stops. The rapid development of differentiated residential areas in Boston in the late 1800s is described in detail in a famous book by Sam Bass Warner, *Streetcar Suburbs*. A contemporary author, Edward Bellamy (1888 [1964], 29), described the results, albeit as an undesirable outcome from his fictional perspective of the classless future of the year 2000: "For it must be understood that the comparative desirability of different parts of Boston for residence depended then, not on natural features, but on the character of the neighboring population. Each class or nation lived by itself, in quarters of its own. A rich man living among the poor, an educated man among the uneducated, was like one living in isolation among a jealous and alien race."

The urban planner of today might believe that mass transit will lead inexorably to mixed-use neighborhoods that incorporate a wide range of social classes. The historical record does not support this belief.

Although the idea of restricted communities is not new, the modern version is a social revolution. Thus, it is not clear what they will look like in thirty years. Just as the initial Levittowns and other new suburbs have evolved both within themselves and in response to society's perception of them, it is reasonable to expect that the current incarnation of gated communities is not the final stage in social evolution.

One dramatic development in modern times has been the growth of retirement communities. These are truly a new phenomenon in history, as it has never been possible in the past to isolate one generation from others for extended periods of time. The early stages of development in suburban neighborhoods often entail a substantial influx of young families with young children, one especially noted during the height of the baby boom. This is a temporary phenomenon, as the early residents age and some are replaced by their younger counterparts, making for a well-integrated area in a relatively short amount of time. Further, by definition this type of homogeneity involves more than one generation, as both parents and children are resident.

The rise in homogeneous housing developments inhabited by older people reflects the breakup of the extended family. After the passage of Medicare, elderly poverty rates declined, making it possible for older households to afford to remain independent. The brilliant insight of Del Webb (and his many rivals and imitators) was that older people preferred to live apart from their families. As early as the 1980s, more than 5 percent of all people over age sixty-five lived in age-segregated communities (Fitzgerald 1986, 210).

The Next Generation: Marriage in Gated Communities

> The strategy of withdrawal by the rich from the vicinity of those less fortunate is the most fundamental shaping force in the development of the modern metropolis.
>
> Jonathan Barnett (1995, 96)

Because the city of tomorrow is influenced by the city of today, we should be concerned about the social implications of CIDs. If the "girl/boy next door" is from a narrowly constructed homogeneous group, then marriage will reinforce the current pattern and tend to lock it in place. The "power couples" analysis by Dora Costa and Matthew Kahn (2000) mentioned in Chapter 5 illustrates that assortative mating based on education is already occurring and that the results have an impact on urban growth.

There are several mitigating factors. First, even in the absence of CIDs, Tiebout selection by households influences the prospects for the future of residents in different suburbs. Second, the postponing of marriage by both men and women means that the accident of neighbors is less decisive for the choice of mate. Third, broader college attendance implies that people are exposed to potential partners from a broader set of social circumstances. When the "girl in the next dorm" replaces the "girl next door" there is still selection occurring, but it comes with concomitant prospects for mixing.

A countervailing possibility is that the availability of social mobility will actually increase social differences. In such a view, those who are able to get away from worse situations benefit, but their flight removes an important potential force for improving a place. William Julius Wilson (1987) attributes the development of the urban underclass at least in part to the ability of the black middle class to move out of segregated neighborhoods following the passage of the Fair Housing Act.

Costs and Benefits of CIDs: A Market Approach

If it were costless to relocate, then market discipline alone would suffice to ensure that CIDs always acted in the interest of their residents. Otherwise, an unhappy resident could relocate or at least use the threat of relocation to obtain a more satisfactory outcome. Realtor fees, mortgage closing costs, and the time costs of search and readjustment all combine to make relocation extremely costly. Thus, it is likely that people remain in situations that they would otherwise abandon, so the market provides only limited recourse. The imperfect and occasional electoral process, when available to CID residents, likewise provides less than perfect relief. A case can be made on this basis for restrictions on what a CID can require of its residents to promote efficiency in the market for residential housing.

One type of restriction is to render the CID similar to a municipal government. Because CIDs are treated as private contractual arrangements, they are not subject to the same limits on their actions as are governments. Susan French (1992) recommends that CIDs adopt a bill of rights to allay fears about future changes. One drawback of this approach is that it might lead to a proliferation of incommensurable CC&Rs, confusing purchasers in a different way from in the absence of a bill of rights.

As was already mentioned, one advantage of a standard set of CC&Rs is that they provide access to the secondary mortgage market, reducing borrowing costs to homeowners. In fact, there is arguably too much homogeneity, as the liquidity advantages of the secondary market could outweigh the costs of CC&Rs that aren't quite to the taste of the residents.

CIDs also serve to reduce uncertainty with respect to the way that an area will develop. Because homeowners have a substantial financial interest in the neighborhood, they are usually averse to any potential for loss. Reduced uncertainty, even if it comes with certain costs, can be valuable, as any purchaser of insurance can attest. CIDs act as a private substitute (or in some cases supplement) to zoning as a form of insurance against declining property values for homevoters.

WINNERS AND LOSERS: THE VIEW FROM ANCIENT ROME

Myron Orfield has made the idea of the "favored quarter" famous with multicolored maps such as those featured in his book *Metropolitics*. This feature of urban life, however, is not of recent or even American origin. Similar to much of our society today, we can trace the roots at least back to Rome. In fact, we can find the origins of urban heterogeneity even earlier than the historical record, in the myth surrounding the founding of Rome.

As related by Tom Holland in *Rubicon* (2003, 18–21), Romulus and Remus quarreled over the name of the city they wished to found. Romulus, who won the argument and killed his brother, based himself on the Palatine hill, while Remus was on the neighboring Aventine hill. From that point onward, the Palatine was the most desirable part of the city, while the Aventine area was at the bottom.

Despite this disparity, the geography of Rome also illustrates the connectedness of the city that continues even to the present. In the valley between the Palatine and Aventine hills was found the Circus Maximus, the common ground for the entire population. Appropriately, it was a sporting venue, again demonstrating that many of our supposed modern inventions have a considerable history.

Before leaving Rome, we can also find there an example of how neighborhoods evolve over time. The Julian clan had originally settled in a small village called Subura (Holland 2003, 22–3). Unfortunately, by the time Julius Caesar was born this area had degenerated into a slum that belied the clan's descent from the goddess Venus. It is hardly surprising that some neighborhoods in American cities, whose families do not have the advantage of Olympian origins, struggle with this same issue.

9 THE WORLD OF TOMORROW

These are the last things. A house is there one day, and the next day it is gone. A street you walked down yesterday is no longer there today. Even the weather is in constant flux. A day of sun followed by a day of rain, a day of snow followed by a day of fog, warm then cool, wind then stillness, a stretch of bitter cold, and then today, in the middle of winter, an afternoon of fragrant light, warm to the point of merely sweaters. When you live in the city, you learn to take nothing for granted. Close your eyes for a moment, turn around to look at something else, and the thing that was before you is suddenly gone. Nothing lasts, you see, not even the thoughts inside you. And you mustn't waste your time looking for them. Once a thing is gone, that is the end of it.

Paul Auster (1987, 1–2)

W E NOW COME TO THE END OF OUR TOUR THROUGH TWENTY-first-century metropolitan areas. It would be wrong, though, to depart without an eye toward the future. After all, a recurring theme has been that there is too much attention paid to the current situation at the expense of future developments. At the same time, there is insufficient understanding that the future will be strongly influenced by the present, which in turn reflects decisions made in the past.

Recognizing that the city of today is the child of the city of yesterday brings with it the recognition that the problems of today have antecedents. The Greeks had long trips to the market, the Romans had congested streets, and Victorian England saw incredibly rapid urbanization of formerly rural areas. It is wrong to act as if these issues sprang into existence at the end of World War II like Athena from Jupiter's forehead. If this book gives the reader nothing more than a better sense of proportion about both space and time, then it is a success from my point of view.

NEVER CAPITULATE, BUT ALWAYS RECAPITULATE

Extremism in opposition to misconception may be no vice, but moderation in pursuit of accuracy is certainly a virtue.

Bruce Seaman (1987, 49)

I began this book by identifying three features of my view of metropolitan areas that are distinct from those of most other writers. First, I emphasize the connections among the parts of a metropolitan area. Now that we have explored this issue both theoretically and empirically, I hope that you have gained a greater appreciation for the complex web of activity in the modern city. These patterns are not limited to some extreme group of metropolitan areas, such as Houston, Los Angeles, or Atlanta, but rather are found wherever serious analysis is combined with detailed data. Attempts to improve the prospects of one subset of the region are praiseworthy, but only if they do so by consciously increasing the connections of the neighborhood to the other parts of the region. Public policy that reinforces autarky only makes matters worse.

Second, I emphasize that mass transit was dominant for only a particular confluence of technological conditions that have not obtained since at least the 1920s. The combination of mass transit and density observed in the late 1800s and early 1900s was not a harbinger of things to come, but rather a temporary anomaly. The private automobile, in some form, will continue to be the dominant transportation mode for the lifetime of anyone reading this book. Rising prices of gasoline will spur both fuel efficiency and alternate technologies for powering cars but will not cause people to abandon the automobile. Public policy that is based on replacing cars with mass transit is not based in reality.

Third, investment under uncertainty implies that durable construction only occurs at discrete intervals rather than in continuous small increments. If we were building cities from scratch today, we might not build them the same way that they currently exist. But given the huge costs of removing and replacing entire cities at once, we instead gradually modify what was there before. We must not mistake gradual change for stasis, however. The slow accumulation of changes over time can have quite dramatic effects, as anyone can attest after attending a high school reunion. Public policy that interferes with adaptive reuse of existing infrastructure is counterproductive.

ENCOURAGING TRADE AMONG TRADING PLACES

What benefit do we get from conceptualizing the world as a set of trading places? The most important implication of this approach is that maintaining and increasing the connectedness of the metropolitan area is fundamental to improving the quality of life for residents. For trade to occur, the gains from trade must exceed the transactions costs. For most urban transactions for the near future, those costs are largely defined by the difficulty of driving from place to place. Policies that increase the ease of driving are therefore a high priority. An important place to start is by correctly pricing the various externalities associated with automobiles, particularly congestion.

Perhaps surprisingly, increasing the ease of trade is also vital for creating and maintaining diverse residential and commercial opportunities. It is not enough for transactions costs to be low, it must also be the case that there are benefits resulting from differences that can lead to mutually desired trade. The fundamental motivation for trade is very simple: people are different. If possible, they will satisfy these differences. One way to do so is to live near people who share residential preferences while working in a profession and at a company that makes full use of one's talents. These two desires are not necessarily satisfied in the same place. If a metropolitan area is sufficiently connected, then a person can live anywhere and work anywhere. We met this idea formally as the Tiebout model. Less formally, we explored various ways that homogeneity and heterogeneity are two sides of the same coin. The reinvention of the CBD as both a residential and business location is predicated on its links to the entire metropolitan area, and the future of other parts of the metropolitan area is only as promising as their trade pattern allows.

TWENTY-FIRST-CENTURY METROPOLITAN STRUCTURE: GOOD OR BAD?

> Thus one and the same thing can be at the same time good, bad, and indifferent. For example, music is good for him that is melancholy, bad for him that mourns; for him that is deaf, it is neither good nor bad.
> Benedictus de Spinoza (1677, Part IV, Preface)

I often tell my students that the correct answer to any question posed by an economist is "It depends." The real issue, then, is knowing what it depends on. Metropolitan structure, as analyzed by this economist, has this stereotypical feature. There are good things about the way we have organized our cities, and there are bad things.

Urban, Suburban, or Rural?

> Long Island, that vast, empty, beautiful open area beyond the city line that Moses had looked upon in 1923, had since been covered – thanks largely to his parkways, his starving of its railroads, his initiation and encouragement of industry-excluding zoning – with a formless, unfocused sprawl of sub-divisions, mile upon endless mile of land-gobbling, single-family, large-lot

developments that were not only destroying the very assets that he prized – its openness, its spaciousness, its beautiful North Shore hills and South Shore marshes and wetlands, its ocean and bay and sound – but were replacing it with communities that were not communities, that had no "downtowns," none of the focal points that alone make meaningful community development possible and that were so spread out that a trip to anywhere – store, church, school, movie, business – generally required a car, so that the lives of its residents were eaten up by the difficulties in getting from one place to another.

Robert Caro (1974, 940–1)

One reason that people have difficulty understanding and appreciating modern metropolitan structure is that the scale of activity leads to a blurring of the boundaries between urban and nonurban land uses. Robert Caro's view, which is the one most commonly expressed by commentators, is that the result is to destroy something fundamentally good and replace it with something fundamentally bad. Unfortunately, this view displays a lack of understanding not only about the current structure of cities but also about their past.

The intermingling of land uses is not original to the United States of the past eighty years. Even in earliest times, there were agricultural land uses within the city limits and urban influence beyond the official boundaries. Not every analyst will go so far as Jane Jacobs (1969), who ascribes the birth of agriculture to the rise of cities. But there is a strong consensus that urban development and rural development have been linked. Proximity to cities has provided farmers with access to markets, a source of fertilizer (surrounding farms were an early form of municipal sewage treatment), and access to technological improvements.

Neither the city nor the countryside can exist independently. Nor can the concepts of urban and rural be defined in isolation, as the contrast from one to the other is fundamental to understanding both. What the railroad, streetcar, truck, and car have done is to make it possible to have a continuum of uses, so that it is often difficult to know when an area stops being urban and starts being rural. Urban growth boundaries are an attempt to impose dichotomous order on this fuzzy situation, but they have difficulty in doing so. William Cronon (1991, 268–9) best summarizes the situation today, even though his words are a description of the American Midwest in the late nineteenth century: "Outward chaos hid a deeper order, the architecture of which was no less real than the bricks and mortar of which more tangible structures were composed. By peeking into that underlying order, one can begin to see the blueprint that made city and country into a single region, economy and ecology into a single system."

The defining characteristic of urban areas is density, and the defining characteristic of rural areas is space. The main benefit of mingling urban and rural is that many people get access to space. Some of this access is in the form of lower housing prices, some in the form of larger houses and lots. People value open space near them but are less concerned with open space farther away. As long as development occurs at a large enough scale for developers to benefit from the willingness to pay for open space, we can expect an efficient amount of parks and other space to be provided. Government action is an alternative approach, which imposes a collective view about the appropriate pattern of development.

The title of this book is not subtle with respect to urban sprawl. I do not find the term helpful for understanding metropolitan structure. The fact that there is nothing resembling an agreed-on definition of the term is evidence that it is not an analytical concept but rather a pejorative. Here is a simple test to apply to any purported definition of sprawl. Apply it to Central Park in Manhattan. In most cases, you will find that it implies that Central Park should be developed. For fun, you can point this out to the definer, who will quickly assure you that he or she didn't mean it that way.

The world is not simply urban or rural. Nor is it static. Deserts become cities, forests are cleared for farms, which in turn become suburbs, farms return to forests, and coyotes reappear in the Adirondacks. "There are more things in heaven and earth, Horatio, than are dreamt of in your philosophy," says Hamlet, and I encourage us all to approach the question of urban structure with similar humility.

Nondrivers in an Automobile World

One problem with a world predicated on moving using a car is what to do if you are not a driver. Three groups that are often identified as harmed by the trading place structure are senior citizens, children, and the poor. Because of their lack of access to cars, these groups of people are argued to be condemned to a life that is unsatisfying due to their inability to move independently from place to place. It is inarguable, in fact almost a tautology, that people without cars have less mobility (relative to others) in a world of cars than they would in a world without cars. It is possible to overstate this negative impact, though.

Older people who don't drive typically have physical or mental difficulties that preclude car use. These same difficulties would often make it hard to function independently in a world built around walking and mass transit. If I am physically unable to drive, telling me that I can do my shopping within a mere quarter-mile walking radius doesn't necessarily improve my life. Similarly, mental challenges, such as memory loss, will make riding a bus a challenge. The big difference in the life of older Americans in the last fifty years is the move to continued independent living, which has raised awareness of challenges that were always there but were dealt with by the adult children who were caring for their parents.

To rename a broad social move toward independent living for older adults as a loss of independence and then to blame this bad outcome on the use of cars and changes in metropolitan structure is a logical fallacy.

The case of children further stems from broad societal changes rather than from cars. I can illustrate this using my own experience. I spent my elementary school years in an automobile-dependent suburb in New Jersey. We lived a few hundred yards from a municipal park that had athletic fields, a playground, and a creek. My friends and I would regularly spend hours playing there unsupervised by our parents. I am now raising a daughter, who is in elementary school, in an automobile-dependent suburb in Pennsylvania. We live a few hundred yards from a municipal park that has athletic fields, a playground, and a creek. If I sent her there unsupervised, it is likely that our neighbors would report my wife and me to a social service agency that would question my fitness as a parent. My daughter has less independence than I did at the same age, but it is not because she is unable to drive. Social norms have changed, and while it might be convenient to blame these changes on cars, it is not convincing.

Finally, we must recognize that some people are unable to afford cars. This is not a large percentage of the population, though. According to the 2000 census, 89.7 percent of households have at least one vehicle. A substantial fraction of the roughly 11 million households without a vehicle is elderly, which suggests that the primary reason for the lack of a vehicle might be something other than lack of money. There are 3 million homeowners without a vehicle, again probably for reasons other than financial.

Nevertheless, not all of the lack of vehicles is voluntary. There are innovative programs in some places to enable car use by people with little money. These programs focus on improving connections between poor people and the rest of the metropolitan area rather than on imposing the anti-automobile preferences of many policy planners. Although such programs are still all too rare, with luck they will continue to spread.

Heterogeneity Good, Homogeneity Bad (or Vice Versa?)

One effect of trade is to reduce differences between places. Another effect of trade is to increase differences, as areas specialize in producing those goods and services in which they have a comparative advantage. Because trade brings both homogeneity and heterogeneity in its wake, we shouldn't expect that altering trade would affect only one side of the balance.

Economists distinguish between a person who is at the *margin* and one who isn't. The economist's margin is not the marginalized or ignored person, but rather the person who may be just on the boundary of undertaking an action. When circumstances change, the people on the margin take action, so they are the crucial people for understanding the impact of any new policy. If you are just on the border between driving your car and riding the bus, then a congestion toll might lead you to ride, while an inframarginal person's modal choice would be unaffected. Regardless of the situation, this heterogeneity among individuals is important to remember. Not every person will be affected by changes in the same way, and not every person will react in the same way. The distribution of preferences among people implies that almost no one gets exactly what they want.

Heterogeneous individuals sorting themselves into homogeneous communities constitute the essence of the Tiebout model. While Tiebout's original insight concerned only different tastes for local government taxes and services, the same force has played out in multiple dimensions. For example, the move to age segregation, although prompted in part by differential demands for public services (emergency medical assistance versus public schools), is not simply a matter of public finance.

Although the vestiges of legal segregation by race continue to fade, we nevertheless find ongoing segregation by choice. On the one hand, this continuing segregation is antithetical to a dream of an integrated society. On the other hand, the opportunity to associate with a similar group also creates a rich diversity for all to enjoy. New York City is richer in having Soho, Chinatown, Little Italy, and Harlem as identifiable places, so long as the differences arise through voluntary choices and not coercion. This activity dates back to the founding of the American colonies. Religious dissenters from England founded a colony in Massachusetts. Dissenters from the orthodox beliefs in Massachusetts went to Connecticut and Rhode Island, while Quakers and Catholics started Pennsylvania and Maryland, respectively. Valuing diversity requires respecting differences, including the choice to live separately.

We have reasons to suspect that there are tendencies to an excess of homogeneity relative to an ideal situation. Euclidean zoning is often blamed for both cultural sterility and excessive driving because it separates commercial from residential land uses. While I sympathize with some of those criticisms, they must be tempered in their extreme forms of promoting jobs-housing balance. First, simple numerical balance does not solve the assignment problem of people to houses and jobs. Second, the expectation that changing land use will usher in a golden age free from cars is not supported by the experience of the past century.

The market for loans is an important source of pressure toward homogeneity. To reduce the risk of a geographically concentrated loan portfolio, it makes sense (and benefits homeowners) for lenders to resell their loans on a national market. However, this requires the ability to compare loans from many places quickly and easily. A common set of conditions on the

loans facilitates those comparisons. The cost advantage of so-called conforming loans reduces the incentive of developers to experiment, even in
the case of an otherwise attractive set of CC&Rs for a CID.

The scale of activity creates a challenge to individuals trying to understand and shape the twenty-first-century metropolitan area. In the spatial
dimension, this challenge is sometimes met with brute force. Pennsylvania, for example, mandates that every municipality must make provision
for every land use within its boundaries. While the impulse to reduce
exclusion is no doubt well intended, it is not clear that the municipal level
is the right area at which to take this approach, given the fragmented
nature of Pennsylvania. The urban growth boundaries found in Oregon
and elsewhere represent a blunt instrument for creating categories to bring
perceived order to the landscape.

A better way to address the issue of scale is to look at another dimension in addition to space. Too much attention is paid to land use and
land-use regulation at a single point in time. In practice, even zoning can
be changed as municipalities and metropolitan areas evolve, so there is
not a good reason to focus discussion on a static picture. A longer time
horizon that explicitly allows for flexibility in development is more likely
to lead to a good outcome. The use of TDRs illustrates how flexibility in
specific cases can be linked successfully to an overall set of constraints.
Even in Houston, famous for its lack of zoning, developers must follow
a set of city ordinances that are specifically aimed at preventing negative
externalities.

TWENTY-FIRST-CENTURY METROPOLITAN AREAS: A CHANCE TO REINVENT THE CITY?

The United States had about 300 billion square feet of built space in
2000, according to a recent analysis by Arthur C. Nelson (2004). To
accommodate the projected uses in 2030, about 427 billion square feet
of space will be needed. About 82 billion square feet will be replacement
of existing space and 131 billion will be new construction. Thus, almost
50 percent of the total space in 2030 will have been built after 2000.

Those are the facts, if the projections are reasonably accurate. What can
vary from person to person is how those facts are interpreted. Nelson's
paper goes on to discuss how this prospective building boom provides an
opportunity for a substantial change in the pattern of growth in the United
States. After all, the chance to build half of a metropolitan area brings
with it the possibility of configuring this space to fulfill the goals of those
dedicated to reversing urban sprawl. A complementary analysis (Muro
and Puentes 2004) describes how smart-growth development can save
about $125 billion in costs to local governments between 2000 and 2025.

These potential savings in public infrastructure spending don't include other hypothetical benefits such as higher productivity and reduced auto travel.

I look at the same data and draw a very different conclusion. About half of the built space that will exist at my full Social Security retirement age (which will be reached in 2031) has already been built. Thus, I will retire into a world that has already been largely constructed. Further, it is not as if the 213 billion square feet of space will be built all at once by developers guided by smart-growth angels on their shoulders. Much of the growth in the relatively near future will continue to be the type of cul-de-sac subdivisions that I can see out my window, advancing from exit 16 of Interstate 83 across the farmland of York County, Pennsylvania. And while saving $125 billion in government spending over twenty-five years is certainly a large benefit, it might not be large relative to the costs of adopting the full set of smart-growth policies.

I will agree with Nelson about one thing, though. The passage of time can lead to substantial changes, and his projections help us to realize the size of the potential changes that could occur even within our lifetimes. Those changes, however, will happen very slowly, as the result of a large number of individual decisions that make sense at the time. Just as it took fifty years or more for the invention of the automobile to lead to its logical conclusion of the trading place economy, any other major change could take many years to become widely recognized. Moreover, those changes will bring with them unexpected challenges, just as the automobile, hailed a century ago as a solution to the public health hazard of horses, created a new set of problems in turn.

THE NEW URBAN HIERARCHY

This is a book about the future of metropolitan areas in the United States. The future is determined in large part by the present, and we have seen how today's issues are often just new manifestations of classic themes.

By 2030, the U.S. Census Bureau predicts that the population of the United States will be about 364 million, an increase of 82 million from its level in 2000. If current practices persist, at least 80 percent of this growth will occur in metropolitan areas. One way that we could (more or less) accommodate all of the increase is to double the size of our eight largest metropolitan areas. An alternative approach that (more or less) accommodates the increase is to double the population of the 225 smallest metropolitan areas, while holding the population of all the others constant. Neither of these extreme cases is likely to occur, of course, but they illustrate the scale of urban growth we can expect during the next twenty-five years.

The growth of metropolitan areas will not be uniform. Some places will grow rapidly, others will stagnate or grow slowly, and some places will even get smaller. Every large city has had at least one period of explosive growth. Even much-maligned Detroit more than quadrupled its population during the early years of the twentieth century.

Although I would love to provide a list of the fifty largest metropolitan areas in 2030, if only so that I could buy cheap land near the surprising ones, I won't do so. The U.S. Census Bureau's projections do provide some guidance about where to expect growth. Two states, Nevada and Arizona, are expected to double in population. Three states, Florida, Texas, and California, are expected to grow by more than 12.4 million people each, which is comparable to the 2000 population of Illinois or Pennsylvania. At the other extreme, Pennsylvania, New York, and Ohio are projected to add only 500,000 or fewer residents, while Washington, DC, is expected to lose more than 130,000 people, 24 percent of its population in 2000. Clearly, some of the likely locations for growing or new metropolitan areas are in the states that will add a great deal of people.

How much land will be consumed by this increase in population? Newly urbanized areas since 1969 have developed at a density of about 1,500 people per square mile. This means that the roughly 66 million urban residents (80 percent of 82 million) would need 44,000 square miles. This area, roughly 28 million acres, is actually less than the 34 million acres converted to developed land between 1982 and 2001. To the extent that the population increase is driven by immigration, we can expect higher density and less land conversion, because immigrants tend to settle in cities.

Japan provides a recent case study in the extent to which dramatic change in conditions affects the relative size of cities. Donald Davis and David Weinstein (2002) study whether the massive Allied bombing campaign during World War II altered the urban hierarchy in Japan by reducing the growth in places that were more heavily damaged. This damage was considerable, with the typical city seeing about half of its built-up area destroyed. Davis and Weinstein find that there was almost no lasting impact, though, in that postwar rebuilding quickly restored the prewar system of cities. Even the extreme cases of Hiroshima and Nagasaki, facing not only destruction but also the ongoing challenge of radiation, returned to their prewar growth trend.

The changes in the United States have not been nearly as sudden or dramatic as the changes in Japan. Thus, I don't expect to see a massive short-term upheaval in metropolitan structure. Instead, we will continue to accumulate small changes that go unnoticed until their combined magnitude forces them on people's awareness.

The increased individual mobility arising from the application of mechanical power to transportation is now almost 200 years old. Urban structure has adapted to this new mobility by increasing spatial reach while keeping transport times roughly constant at levels found since the first cities were built. Don't call it sprawl. Appreciate the advantages and work to reduce the disadvantages in your trading place.

NOTES

I have endeavored to identify sources in the text to help the reader avoid constant checking of footnotes. In this section, I will mention some sources for the reader who is interested in pursuing the ideas further.

I. THE WORLD OF TODAY

There is a vast literature, both scholarly and popular, on metropolitan structure. Survey articles by Anas et al. (1998), Glaeser and Kahn (2004), and Nechyba and Walsh (2004) are a good place to start on the scholarly side. Garreau's book (1991) has been influential in shaping the discussion during the past fifteen years, and it is still a timely introduction to the idea that metropolitan structure has changed. No one can really begin to understand this topic without consulting Fishman (1987), Jackson (1985), and especially Gottman (1961). Bruegmann (2005) is a book that is worth consulting. It appeared as this manuscript was being prepared for publication, but too late to directly influence my work.

The application of trade theory to metropolitan economies is not a new idea, but it has received a renewed emphasis in recent years. The book by Fujita et al. (1999) is an excellent synthesis of the research to that point. With all due modesty, the best textbook treatment of the subject is found in Bogart (1998).

While I believe that my application of the term *trading places* is original, I discovered one other author who uses the term as part of a discussion of metropolitan structure. Marshall (2000) titles one of his chapters "Trading Places." His focus is on the change in the relative roles of the central city and the suburbs, rather than on the connections between them. This sentence summarizes his position: "Whereas once the city symbolized a merciless, soulless world, and the suburbs calmness, family, and nature, the two worlds have almost completely traded places in what they represent" (87).

An earlier version of the sections "What Does a Typical Metropolitan Area Look Like?" "Mental Models of Metropolitan Areas," and "New Metropolitan Structure: Atlanta and Los Angeles (and Cleveland and Pittsburgh!)" appeared in Bogart (2001). Reprinted by permission of the *Case Western Reserve University Law Review*.

2. MAKING THINGS BETTER: THE IMPORTANCE OF FLEXIBILITY

The issue of how best to approach public policy is controversial, of course. For relatively dichotomous views, I recommend reading Kunstler (1993, 1996) in conjunction with O'Toole (2001). The topic of investment under uncertainty is much more rich than my brief treatment can do justice to, and close reading of Dixit and Pindyck (1994) will provide many rewards. Although I disagree with some of Robert Lang's conclusions, the detailed data that he collects in his book (2003) are a treasure for the student of metropolitan areas.

An earlier version of the section "Utopian Metropolitan Structure" appeared in Bogart (2001). Reprinted by permission of the *Case Western Reserve University Law Review*.

3. ARE WE THERE YET?

I am indebted to the incredible book by Peter Hall (1998) for insight into the Greeks and particularly the city of Athens. Paul Bairoch (1988) is also a wonderful source of analysis and anecdote about cities around the world over the entire period of recorded history.

An interesting study of the nature of agglomeration economies of scale is Saxenian (1994). Jackson (1985) includes detailed case studies of the relation between land speculation and mass transit. Moses and Williamson (1967) is a succinct account of the relation between business location and transport technology. Glaeser and Kohlhase (2004) provide an explanation of the implications of the differing costs of moving goods (low) and people (high) for metropolitan structure.

This chapter covers in an abbreviated way material found in most urban and regional economics textbooks. Naturally, I recommend mine (Bogart 1998) as a resource for those that want to pursue the ideas at more length. Evenett and Keller (2002) explore the theoretical basis for the gravity equation.

An earlier version of the sections "Evolving Metropolitan Structure" and 'Specialization in Local Consumption Goods: The Tiebout Model" appeared in Bogart (2001). Reprinted by permission of the *Case Western Reserve University Law Review*.

4. TRADING PLACES

I already noted in the Acknowledgments the debt I owe to Dan McMillen, Howard Maier, and Nate Anderson for access to data. But I'm mentioning it again, because it's a huge debt and worth mentioning more than once.

The index of specialization has been a workhorse for decades. An interesting survey of the early literature on using this index, called the "index of dissimilarity" in this context, to study racial segregation is found in Yinger (1979, 446–7). Duranton and Puga (2000) use the measures I describe here to analyze manufacturing specialization at the metropolitan area level. Holmes and Stevens (2004) present a survey of the variety of measures of specialization. Like most authors, they emphasize the use of the LQ. And like most authors, they focus on metropolitan specialization rather than considering the extent to which parts of a metropolitan area are specialized. Hoover and Vernon (1959) provide a detailed analysis of the pattern of production in the New York metropolitan area.

The seminal work on Zipf's law is Zipf (1949). See Gabaix and Ioannides (2004) for a review of the literature on Zipf's law as applied to city size distributions.

An earlier version of the introductory part of this chapter appeared in Bogart (2001). Reprinted by permission of the *Case Western Reserve University Law Review*. An earlier version of the section "Size Distribution of Employment Centers" appeared in Anderson and Bogart (2001). Reprinted by permission of Blackwell Publishing.

5. DOWNTOWN: A PLACE TO WORK, A PLACE TO VISIT, A PLACE TO LIVE

A book-length analysis of enterprise zones is Peters and Fisher (2002). An older but still influential study of metropolitan competition for firms is Bartik (1991).

The opening of the chapter is based on Gottlieb and Bogart (1998, 12–13). I'm grateful to Paul Gottlieb for permission to use it here. An earlier version of the section "Detailed Analysis" appeared in Anderson and Bogart (2001). Reprinted by permission of Blackwell Publishing. An earlier version of the section "Declaring Victory: When Can a Local Government Stop Subsidizing Activity?" appeared in Bogart and Shatten (2001). Reprinted by permission of the National Tax Association.

6. HOW ZONING MATTERS

Mills (1979) gives a thorough historical review of land-use regulation. He also suggests a combined tax and land-use reform that is even more drastic than Measure 37. Fischel (2001) is the most complete analysis linking political decisions about land use to economic decisions such as household location. Blinder and Rosen (1985) address the question of whether a large discontinuous constraint is more or less efficient than a set of small constraints.

An earlier version of the first part of "Does Zoning Have a Major Impact on Urban Structure?" appeared in Bogart (2001). Reprinted by permission of the *Case Western Reserve University Law Review*. An earlier version of the sections "How Zoning Is Like a Tax," "Zoning and Trade," "Analyzing the Impact of Zoning," and "Toward a Dynamic Model" appeared in Bogart (2003). Reprinted by permission of Edward Elgar Publishing, Lincoln Institute for Land Policy, and Dick Netzer.

7. LOVE THE DENSITY, HATE THE CONGESTION

The release of the latest study by the Texas Transportation Institute is an annual event that generates newspaper headlines around the country. It's a rare bird in that the quality of the analysis lives up to the hype. As with so many other things, the information provided by the U.S. Census Bureau is invaluable, albeit frustrating because it is only available at ten-year intervals. On the other hand, this length of time makes it easier to identify real changes over time rather than fleeting cyclical trends.

The book by Boarnet and Crane (2001) is a thorough investigation of the relation between urban structure and travel patterns. An influential writer on the subject has been Downs (1992, 1994).

Municipal waste is a fascinating subject. The book by Melosi (2001) is a great introduction. Knaap and Nelson (1992) is an important study of the benefits and costs of planning, especially through the use of urban growth boundaries.

8. HOMOGENEITY AND HETEROGENEITY IN LOCAL GOVERNMENT

Orfield (1997) and Rusk (1995) have risen to prominence on the basis of their writings about regional inequalities and how best to correct problems. It is interesting to read Mumford (1961) and Gottman (1961) in this respect and find that many of these issues have been around for more than forty years. The best analysis of the implications of metropolitan consolidation is a classic paper by Bradford and Oates (1974).

For further description of the Minneapolis –St. Paul program, see the paper by Luce (1998). Fisher (1982) simulates tax-base sharing in the Milwaukee area. A highly readable survey of the role of CIDs is McKenzie (2003).

Cutler, Glaeser, and Vigdor (1999) provide evidence on the evolution of racial segregation in U.S. metropolitan areas from 1880 to 1990. Glaeser and Vigdor (2001) extend these results to include data from the 2000 census.

The analysis of implicit tax-base sharing in the Cleveland area originated as joint work with Nate Anderson, although it has not yet been published. For a detailed description and analysis of the income imputation calculations, see Anderson (2004).

9. THE WORLD OF TOMORROW

I find science fiction to be a great source of insight into the world of tomorrow. Ironically, the requirements of fiction to keep the characters and situations relatively believable tend to lead authors to create situations that are both more plausible and better thought through than much social science. If you're interested enough to read this far, you might enjoy Pohl and Kornbluth (1955) and Stephenson (1992). Another book by Stephenson (1995) is also appropriate, as it takes place in a Tiebout world organized quite differently from the one in his previous novel.

Blumenberg and Waller (2003) describe the evidence on car ownership by low-income families and propose various policies to improve their access to the full range of trading places.

REFERENCES

Ambler Realty Co. v. Village of Euclid, Ohio, et al. 1924. 297 F. 307.

Anas, Alex, Richard Arnott, and Kenneth Small. 1998. "Urban Spatial Structure." *Journal of Economic Literature* 36: 1426–64.

Anderson, Nathan B. 2004. "Understanding the Interdependency of Central Cities and Edge Cities." *Journal of Regional Analysis and Policy* 34: 13–25.

Anderson, Nathan B., and William T. Bogart. 2001. "The Structure of Sprawl: Identifying and Characterizing Employment Centers in Polycentric Metropolitan Areas." *American Journal of Economics and Sociology* 60: 147–69.

Auster, Paul. 1987. *In the Country of Last Things*. New York: Viking Penguin.

Baim, Dean V. 1994. *The Sports Stadium as a Municipal Investment*. Westport, CT: Greenwood Press.

Bairoch, Paul. 1988. *Cities and Economic Development*. Chicago: University of Chicago Press.

Baldassare, Mark, and Georjeanna Wilson. 1996. "Changing Sources of Suburban Support for Local Growth Controls." *Urban Studies* 33: 459–71.

Barnett, Jonathan. 1995. *The Fractured Metropolis: Improving the New City, Restoring the Old City, Reshaping the Region*. Boulder, CO: Westview Press.

Bartik, Timothy. 1991. *Who Benefits from State and Local Economic Development Polices?* Kalamazoo, MI: W. E. Upjohn Institute for Employment Research.

Bartlett, Randall. 2003. "Testing the 'Popsicle Test': Realities of Retail Shopping in New 'Traditional Neighborhood Developments.'" *Urban Studies* 40: 1471–85.

Baxandall, Rosalyn, and Elizabeth Ewen. 2000. *Picture Windows: How the Suburbs Happened*. New York: Basic Books.

Bayer, Patrick, Hanming Fang, and Robert McMillan. 2005. Separate When Equal? Racial Inequality and Residential Segregation. Working Paper #11507. Cambridge, MA: National Bureau of Economic Research.

Been, Vicki. 1994. "Locally Undesirable Land Uses in Minority Neighborhoods: Disproportionate Siting or Market Dynamics?" *Yale Law Journal* 103: 1383–1422.

Bellamy, Edward. 1888 [1964]. *Looking Backward: 2000–1887*. New York: New American Library of World Literature (Signet Classic).

Bello, Francis. 1957. "The City and the Car." In *The Exploding Metropolis,* Editors of Fortune, eds. Garden City, NY: Doubleday and Company.

Benfield, F. Kaid, Matthew D. Raimi, and Donald D. T. Chen. 1999. *Once There Were Greenfields: How Urban Sprawl Is Undermining America's Environment, Economy, and Social Fabric.* New York: Natural Resources Defense Council.

Benmelech, Efraim, Mark Garmaise, and Tobias Moskowitz. 2004. "Do Liquidation Values Affect Commercial Contracts? Evidence from Commercial Loan Values and Zoning Regulation." Working Paper #11004. Cambridge, MA: National Bureau of Economic Research.

Bingham, Richard, and Deborah Kimble. 1995. "Industrial Composition of Edge Cities and Downtowns." *Economic Development Quarterly* 9: 259–72.

Blinder, Alan, and Harvey Rosen. 1985. "Notches." *American Economic Review* 75: 736–47.

Blumenberg, Evelyn, and Margy Waller. 2003. "The Long Journey to Work: A Federal Transportation Policy for Working Families." Washington, DC: Brookings Institution Series on Transportation Reform.

Boarnet, Marlon, and Saksith Chalermpong. 2001. "New Highways, House Prices, and Urban Development: A Case Study of Toll Roads in Orange County, CA." *Housing Policy Debate* 12: 575–605.

Boarnet, Marlon, and Randall Crane. 2001. *Travel by Design: The Influence of Urban Form on Travel.* New York: Oxford University Press.

Bogart, William T. 1993. "'What Big Teeth You Have!' Identifying the Motivations for Exclusionary Zoning." *Urban Studies* 30: 1669–81.

———. 1997. "Increase the Gasoline Tax – And Build Roads and Bridges." *Toledo Blade,* March 1, 1997: 9.

———. 1998. *The Economics of Cities and Suburbs.* Upper Saddle River, NJ: Prentice Hall.

———. 2001. "'Trading Places': The Role of Zoning in Promoting and Discouraging Intrametropolitan Trade." *Case Western Reserve University Law Review* 51(4): 697–720.

———. 2003. "Is Zoning a Substitute for, or a Complement to, Factor Taxes?" In *The Property Tax, Land Use, and Land Use Regulation,* Dick Netzer, ed. Northampton, MA: Edward Elgar.

Bogart, William T., and William C. Ferry. 1999. "Employment Centers in Greater Cleveland: Evidence of Evolution in a Formerly Monocentric City." *Urban Studies* 36: 2099–110.

Bogart, William T., and Richard Shatten. 2001. "Declaring Victory? A Market-Based Measure of the Impact of Public Subsidies." In *Proceedings of the Ninety-Third Annual Conference of the National Tax Association – Tax Institute of America,* James R. Hines, Jr., ed. Washington, DC: National Tax Association.

Bradford, David. 1978. "Factor Prices May Be Constant but Factor Returns Are Not." *Economics Letters* 1: 199–203.

Bradford, David, and Wallace Oates. 1974. "Suburban Exploitation of Central Cities and Governmental Structure." In *Redistribution through Public Choice,* Harold Hochman and George Peterson, eds. New York: Columbia University Press.

Briggs, Asa. 1965. *Victorian Cities.* New York: Harper and Row.

Brookings Institution Center on Urban and Metropolitan Policy. 2003. "Back to Prosperity: A Competitive Agenda for Renewing Pennsylvania." Washington, DC: The Brookings Institution.

Bruegmann, Robert. 2005. *Sprawl: A Compact History.* Chicago: University of Chicago Press.

Burchfield, Marcy, Henry Overman, Diego Puga, and Matthew Turner. 2005. "The Causes of Sprawl: A Portrait from Space." Working Paper TECIPA-192. Toronto: University of Toronto.

Cahill, Thomas. 2003. *Sailing the Wine-Dark Sea: Why the Greeks Matter.* New York: Doubleday.

Calvino, Italo. 1972. *Invisible Cities.* William Weaver, trans. (1974). New York: Harcourt Brace Jovanovich.

Caro, Robert. 1974. *The Power Broker: Robert Moses and the Fall of New York.* New York: Random House.

Chay, Kenneth, and Michael Greenstone. 2005. "Does Air Quality Matter? Evidence from the Housing Market." *Journal of Political Economy* 113: 376–424.

Coase, Ronald H. 1960. "The Problem of Social Cost." *Journal of Law and Economics* 3: 1–44.

Coleman, Alice. 1990. *Utopia on Trial: Vision and Reality in Planned Housing,* rev. ed. London: Hilary Shipman.

Costa, Dora, and Matthew Kahn. 2000. "Power Couples: Changes in the Locational Choice of the College Educated, 1940–1990." *Quarterly Journal of Economics* 115: 1287–1315.

County of Wayne v. Hathcock. 2004. 471 Mich. 415, 684 N. W. 2d 765.

Courant, Paul, and Daniel Rubinfeld. 1978. "On the Measurement of Benefits in an Urban Context: Some General Equilibrium Issues." *Journal of Urban Economics* 34: 299–317.

Crane, Randall. 1996. "The Influence of Uncertain Job Location on Urban Form and the Journey to Work." *Journal of Urban Economics* 39: 342–56.

Crane, Randall, and Daniel Chatman. 2003. "Traffic and Sprawl: Evidence from U.S. Commuting, 1985 to 1997." *Planning and Markets* 6. Accessed at http://www-pam.usc.edu/volume6/v6i1a3s1.html.

Cromwell, Brian. 1990. "Pro-Integrative Subsidies and Housing Markets: Do Race-Based Loans Work?" Working Paper #9018. Cleveland, OH: Federal Reserve Bank of Cleveland.

Cronon, William. 1991. *Nature's Metropolis: Chicago and the Great West.* New York: W. W. Norton and Company.

Cutler, David, Edward Glaeser, and Jacob Vigdor. 1999. "The Rise and Decline of the American Ghetto." *Journal of Political Economy* 107: 455–506.

Davis, Donald, and David Weinstein. 2002. "Bones, Bombs, and Breakpoints: The Geography of Economic Activity." *American Economic Review* 92: 1269–89.

Davis, Mike. 1992. *City of Quartz: Excavating the Future in Los Angeles.* New York: Vintage Books.

de la Blache, Paul Vidal. 1921. *Principes de Géographie Humaine.* Paris: Librairie Arman Colin.

Dixit, Avinash, and Robert Pindyck. 1994. *Investment under Uncertainty.* Princeton, NJ: Princeton University Press.

Dobriner, William. 1963. *Class in Suburbia*. Englewood Cliffs, NJ: Prentice-Hall.

Downs, Anthony. 1992. *Stuck in Traffic: Coping with Peak-Hour Traffic Congestion*. Washington, DC and Cambridge, MA: Brookings Institution and Lincoln Institute for Land Policy.

———. 1994. *New Visions for Metropolitan America*. Washington, DC and Cambridge, MA: Brookings Institution and Lincoln Institute for Land Policy.

Duranton, Gilles, and Diego Puga. 2000. "Diversity and Specialisation in Cities: Why, Where, and When Does It Matter?" *Urban Studies* 37: 533–55.

Eberts, Randall, and Joe Stone. 1992. *Wage and Employment Adjustment in Local Labor Markets*. Kalamazoo, MI: W. E. Upjohn Institute for Employment Research.

Echenique, Federico, and Roland Fryer, Jr. 2005. "On the Measurement of Segregation." Working Paper #11258. Cambridge, MA: National Bureau of Economic Research.

Economics Research Associates. 2004. "Economic and Fiscal Impacts for the Proposed NFL Stadium in Arlington, Texas." Prepared for City of Arlington, August 11, 2004.

El Nasser, Haya, and Paul Orenberg. 2001. "A Comprehensive Look at Sprawl in America." *USA Today*. February 22, 2001. Accessed at http://www.usatoday.com/news/sprawl/main.htm on September 23, 2005.

Euclid v. Ambler. 1926. 272 U.S. 365.

Evenett, Simon, and Wolfgang Keller. 2002. "On Theories Explaining the Success of the Gravity Equation." *Journal of Political Economy* 110: 281–316.

Fischel, William. 1985. *The Economics of Zoning Laws: A Property-Rights Approach to American Land Use Controls*. Baltimore, MD: Johns Hopkins University Press.

———. 1994. "Zoning, Nonconvexities, and T. Jack Foster's City." *Journal of Urban Economics* 35: 175–81.

———. 2001. *The Homevoter Hypothesis*. Cambridge, MA: Harvard University Press.

Fisher, Peter S. 1982. "Regional Tax-Base Sharing: An Analysis and Simulation of Alternative Approaches." *Land Economics* 58: 497–515.

Fishman, Robert. 1987. *Bourgeois Utopia: The Rise and Fall of Suburbia*. New York: Basic Books.

Fitzgerald, Frances. 1986. *Cities on a Hill: A Journey through Contemporary American Cultures*. New York: Simon and Schuster.

Florida, Richard. 2002. *The Rise of the Creative Class*. New York: Basic Books.

Flyvbjerg, Bent, Mette Skamris Holm, and Søren Buhl. 2005. "How (In)accurate Are Demand Forecasts in Public Works Projects?" *Journal of the American Planning Association* 71: 131–46.

French, Susan. 1992. "The Constitution of a Private Residential Government Should Include a Bill of Rights." *Wake Forest Law Review* 27: 345–52.

Fujita, Masahisa, Paul Krugman, and Anthony Venables. 1999. *The Spatial Economy: Cities, Regions, and International Trade*. Cambridge, MA: MIT Press.

Fulton, William, Jan Mazurek, Rick Pruetz, and Chris Williamson. 2004. "TDRs and Other Market-Based Land Mechanisms: How They Work and Their Role in Shaping Metropolitan Growth." Discussion Paper, Center on Urban and Metropolitan Policy, The Brookings Institution, Washington, DC.

Gabaix, Xavier, and Yannis Ioannides. 2004. "The Evolution of City Size Distributions." In *Handbook of Urban and Regional Economics*, Volume IV, J. V. Henderson and J-F Thisse, eds. New York: North-Holland.

Galster, George, Royce Hanson, Michael Ratcliffe, Harold Wolman, Stephen Coleman, and Jason Freihage. 2001. "Wrestling Sprawl to the Ground: Defining and Measuring an Elusive Concept." *Housing Policy Debate* 12: 681–717.

Gans, Herbert. 1967. *The Levittowners: How People Live and Politic in Suburbia.* New York: Pantheon Books.

Garreau, Joel. 1991. *Edge City: Life on the New Frontier.* New York: Doubleday.

Gatzlaff, Dean, and Marc Smith. 1993. "Uncertainty, Growth Controls, and the Efficiency of Development Patterns." *Journal of Real Estate Finance and Economics* 6: 147–55.

George, Henry. 1880 [1955]. *Progress and Poverty.* New York: Robert Schalkenbach Foundation.

Giuliano, Genevieve, and Kenneth Small. 1991. "Subcenters in the Los Angeles Region." *Regional Science and Urban Economics* 21: 163–82.

———. 1993. "Is the Journey to Work Explained by Metropolitan Structure?" *Urban Studies* 30: 1485–1500.

Glaeser, Edward. 2005. "Reinventing Boston: 1640–2003." *Journal of Economic Geography* 5: 119–53.

Glaeser, Edward, and Joseph Gyourko. 2005. "Urban Decline and Durable Housing." *Journal of Political Economy* 113: 345–75.

Glaeser, Edward, Joseph Gyourko, and Raven Saks. 2004. "Why Have Housing Prices Gone Up?" Discussion Paper no. 2061. Cambridge, MA: Harvard Institute of Economic Research.

———. 2005. "Urban Growth and Housing Supply." Discussion Paper no. 2062. Cambridge, MA: Harvard Institute of Economic Research.

Glaeser, Edward, and Matthew Kahn. 2004. "Sprawl and Urban Growth." In *Handbook of Urban and Regional Economics*, Volume IV, J. V. Henderson and J-F Thisse, eds. New York: North-Holland.

Glaeser, Edward, Matthew Kahn, and Chenghuan Chu. 2001. "Job Sprawl: Employment Location in U.S. Metropolitan Areas." Center on Urban and Metropolitan Policy, Survey Series. Washington, DC: Brookings Institution.

Glaeser, Edward, and Janet Kohlhase. 2004. "Cities, Regions, and the Decline of Transport Costs." *Papers in Regional Science* 83: 197–228.

Glaeser, Edward, Jed Kolko, and Albert Saiz. 2001. "Consumer City." *Economic Geography* 1: 27–50.

Glaeser, Edward, and Andrei Shleifer. 2001. "A Reason for Quantity Regulation." *American Economic Review Papers and Proceedings* 91: 431–5.

Glaeser, Edward, and Jacob Vigdor. 2001. "Segregation in the 2000 Census: Promising News." Center on Urban and Metropolitan Policy, Survey Series. Washington, DC: Brookings Institution.

Gottlieb, Paul, and William T. Bogart. 1998. *The Downtown's Economic Revival: Cleveland's Recent Success and Next Steps.* Cleveland: Center for Regional Economic Issues.

Gottman, Jean. 1961. *Megalopolis: The Urbanized Northeastern Seaboard of the United States.* Cambridge, MA: MIT Press.

Governor's Office of Smart Growth. n.d. "Driving Urban Environments: Smart Growth Parking Best Practices." Annapolis, MD: Governor's Office of Smart Growth.

Hall, Peter. 1998. *Cities in Civilization: Culture, Innovation, and Urban Order.* London: Weidenfeld and Nicolson.

Hamilton, Bruce. 1975. "Zoning and Property Taxation in a System of Local Governments." *Urban Studies* 12: 205–11.

———. 1976. "Capitalization of Intrajurisdictional Differences in Local Tax Prices." *American Economic Review* 66: 743–53.

———. 1989. "Wasteful Commuting Again." *Journal of Political Economy* 97: 1497–1504.

Hanson, Gordon. 1998. "Market Potential, Increasing Returns, and Geographic Concentration." Working Paper #6429. Cambridge, MA: National Bureau of Economic Research.

Haughwout, Andrew, and Robert Inman. 2002. "Should Suburbs Help Their Central City?" In *Brookings-Wharton Papers on Urban Affairs 2002,* William Gale and Janet Rothenberg Pack, eds. Washington, DC: Brookings Institution Press.

Higbee, Edward. 1960. *The Squeeze: Cities without Space.* New York: William Morrow and Company.

Hohenberg, Paul, and Lynn Hollen Lees. 1985. *The Making of Urban Europe 1000–1950.* Cambridge, MA: Harvard University Press.

Holland, Tom. 2003. *Rubicon: The Last Years of the Roman Empire.* New York: Anchor Books.

Holmes, Thomas, and John Stevens. 2004. "Spatial Distribution of Economic Activities in North America." In *Handbook of Urban and Regional Economics,* Volume IV, J. V. Henderson and J-F Thisse, eds. New York: North-Holland.

Hoover, Edgar M. 1968. "The Evolving Form and Organization of the Metropolis." In *Issues in Urban Economics,* Harvey Perloff and Lowdon Wingo, Jr., eds. Baltimore, MD: Johns Hopkins Press.

Hoover, Edgar M., and Raymond Vernon. 1959. *Anatomy of a Metropolis: The Changing Distribution of People and Jobs within the New York Metropolitan Region.* Cambridge, MA: Harvard University Press.

Howard, Ebenezer. 1902 [1946]. *Garden Cities of To-Morrow.* London: Faber and Faber.

Howard, John. 1941. "What's Ahead for Cleveland?" Publication no. 10. Cleveland, OH: Regional Association of Cleveland.

Hoyle, Fred. 1967. "Welcome to Slippage City." In *Element 79.* New York: New American Library of World Literature (Signet Classics).

Immergluck, Daniel, with Timothy Hilton. 1996. *Breaking Down Barriers: Prospects and Policies for Linking Jobs and Residents in the Chicago Empowerment Zone.* Chicago: Woodstock Institute.

Initiative for a Competitive Inner City and CEOs for Cities. 2002. *Leveraging Colleges and Universities for Urban Economic Revitalization: An Action*

Agenda. Accessed at http://www.ceosforcities.org/research/2002/leveraging_colleges/index.htm on May 9, 2005.

Isserman, Andrew. 1980. "Estimating Export Activity in a Regional Economy: A Theoretical and Empirical Analysis of Alternative Methods." *International Regional Science Review* 5: 155–84.

Jackson, Kenneth. 1985. *Crabgrass Frontier: The Suburbanization of the United States*. New York: Oxford University Press.

Jacobs, Jane. 1961. *The Death and Life of Great American Cities*. New York: Random House.

———. 1969. *The Economy of Cities*. New York: Random House.

Keats, John. 1956. *The Crack in the Picture Window*. Boston: Houghton Mifflin.

Kelly, Barbara M. 1993. *Expanding the American Dream: Building and Rebuilding Levittown*. Albany, NY: SUNY Press.

Kelly, Eric Damian. 1993. *Managing Community Growth: Policies, Techniques, and Impacts*. Westport, CT: Praeger.

Kelo v. New London. 2005. 125 S. Ct. 2655.

Knaap, Gerrit, and Arthur C. Nelson. 1992. *The Regulated Landscape: Lessons on State Land Use Planning from Oregon*. Cambridge, MA: Lincoln Institute of Land Policy.

Kohlhase, Janet. 1991. "The Impact of Toxic Waste Sites on Housing Values." *Journal of Urban Economics* 30: 1–26.

Kolankiewicz, Leon, and Roy Beck. 2001. "Weighing Sprawl Factors in Large U.S. Cities." Accessed at http://www.sprawlcity.org/studyUSA/index.html on August 3, 2005.

Kunstler, James Howard. 1993. *The Geography of Nowhere: The Rise and Decline of America's Man-Made Landscape*. New York: Simon and Schuster.

———. 1996. *Home from Nowhere: Remaking Our Everyday World for the Twenty-First Century*. New York: Simon and Schuster.

Lang, Robert E. 2003. *Edgeless Cities: Exploring the Elusive Metropolis*. Washington, DC: Brookings Institution Press.

Leinberger, Christopher B., and Charles Lockwood. 1986. "How Business Is Reshaping America." *Atlantic Monthly* October 1986: 43–52.

LeRoy, Greg, Sara Hively, and Katie Tallman. 2000. "Another Way Sprawl Happens: Economic Development Subsidies in a Twin Cities Suburb." Washington, DC: Institute on Taxation and Economic Policy.

Levinson, David. 1997. "Jobs and Housing Tenure and the Journey to Work." *Annals of Regional Science* 31: 451–71.

———. 2003. "The Next America Revisited." *Journal of Planning Education and Research* 22: 329–45.

Levinson, David, and Ajay Kumar. 1994. "The Rational Locator." *Journal of the American Planning Association* 60: 319–32.

Levinson, David, and Yao Wu. 2005. "The Rational Locator Reexamined: Are Travel Times Still Stable?" *Transportation* 32: 187–202.

Luce, Thomas. 1998. "Regional Tax Base Sharing: The Twin Cities Experience." In *Local Government Tax and Land Use Policies in the United States: Understanding the Links,* Helen Ladd, Ben Chinitz, and Dick Netzer, eds. Northampton, MA: Edward Elgar.

Mallach, Alan. 2005. "Restoring Neighborhoods, Rebuilding Markets: New Directions for Struggling Cities." NHI Shelterforce Online, Issue #140. Accessed at http://www.nhi.org/online/issues/140/strategies.html on September 6, 2005.

Marshall, Alex. 2000. *How Cities Work: Suburbs, Sprawl, and the Road Not Taken.* Austin: University of Texas Press.

McHone, W. Warren. 1990. "Highway Accessibility, Location Rents, and the Efficiency of Metropolitan Area Tax Base Sharing." *Growth and Change* 21: 46–55.

McKenzie, Evan. 2003. "Common-Interest Housing in the Communities of Tomorrow." *Housing Policy Debate* 14: 203–34.

McMillen, Daniel. 2001. "Nonparametric Employment Center Identification." *Journal of Urban Economics* 21: 242–58.

———. 2003. "Identifying Subcenters Using Contiguity Matrices." *Urban Studies* 40: 57–69.

McMillen, Daniel, and T. William Lester. 2003. "Evolving Subcenters: Employment and Population Densities in Chicago, 1970–2020." *Journal of Housing Economics* 12: 60–81.

McMillen, Daniel, and Stefani Smith. 2003. "The Number of Subcenters in Large Urban Areas." *Journal of Urban Economics* 53: 321–38.

Melosi, Martin. 2001. *Effluent America: Cities, Industry, Energy, and the Environment.* Pittsburgh: University of Pittsburgh Press.

Mills, Edwin. 1979. "Economic Analysis of Urban Land Use Controls." In *Current Issues in Urban Economics,* Peter Mieszkowski and Mahlon Straszheim, eds. Baltimore, MD: Johns Hopkins University Press.

———. 1992. "Sectoral Clustering and Metropolitan Development." In *Sources of Metropolitan Growth,* E. Mills and J. McDonald, eds. New Brunswick, NJ: Center for Urban Policy Research.

Moses, Leon, and Harold F. Williamson, Jr. 1967. "The Location of Economic Activity in Cities." *American Economic Review (Papers and Proceedings)* 57: 211–22.

Mumford, Lewis. 1961. *The City in History: Its Origins, Its Transformations, and Its Prospects.* New York: Harcourt Brace and Company.

Muro, Mark, and Robert Puentes. 2004. "Investing in a Better Future: A Review of the Fiscal and Competitive Advantages of Smarter Growth Development Patterns." Discussion Paper, Center on Urban and Metropolitan Policy, The Brookings Institution, Washington, DC.

Natural Resources Conservation Service. 2003. "2001 Annual Natural Resources Inventory: Urbanization and Development of Rural Land." Accessed at http://www.nrcs.usda.gov/technical/land/nri01/urban.pdf on September 2, 2005.

Nechyba, Thomas J., and Randall P. Walsh. 2004. "Urban Sprawl." *Journal of Economic Perspectives* 18: 177–200.

Nelson, Arthur C. 2004. "Toward a New Metropolis: The Opportunity to Rebuild America." Discussion Paper, Center on Urban and Metropolitan Policy, The Brookings Institution, Washington, DC.

Nelson, Robert. 2001. *Economics as Religion: From Samuelson to Chicago and Beyond.* University Park: Pennsylvania State University Press.

Noll, Roger, and Andrew Zimbalist, eds. 1997. *Sports, Jobs, and Taxes: The Economic Impact of Sports Teams and Stadiums*. Washington, DC: Brookings Institution Press.

Orfield, Myron. 1997. *Metropolitics: A Regional Agenda for Community and Stability*, rev. ed. Washington, DC: Brookings Institution Press and Lincoln Institute for Land Policy.

O'Toole, Randall. 2001. *The Vanishing Automobile and Other Urban Myths: How Smart Growth Will Harm American Cities*. Bandon, OR: Thoreau Institute.

Pashigian, Peter, and Eric Gould. 1998. "Internalizing Externalities: The Pricing of Space in Shopping Malls." *Journal of Law and Economics* 41: 115–42.

Peiser, Richard B. 1989. "Density and Urban Sprawl." *Land Economics* 65: 193–204.

Peters, Alan, and Peter Fisher. 2002. *State Enterprise Zone Programs: Have They Worked?* Kalamazoo, MI: W. E. Upjohn Institute for Employment Research.

Pickrell, Donald. 1992. "A Desire Named Streetcar – Fantasy and Fact in Rail Transit Planning." *Journal of the American Planning Association* 58: 158–76.

Pohl, Frederik, and C. M. Kornbluth. 1955. *Gladiator-At-Law*. New York: Ballantine Books.

Poletown Neighborhood Council v. Detroit. 1981. 410 Mich. 616, 304 N. W. 2d 455.

Porter, Michael. 1995. "The Competitive Advantage of the Inner City." *Harvard Business Review* May–June 1995: 55–71.

Real Estate Research Corporation. 1974. *The Costs of Sprawl: Environmental and Economic Costs of Alternative Residential Development Patterns at the Urban Fringe*. Washington, DC: Council on Environmental Quality.

The Reinvestment Fund and the Metropolitan Philadelphia Policy Center. 2001. "Choices: A Report on the State of the Region's Housing Market." Philadelphia, PA: The Reinvestment Fund.

Riordon, William. 1905 [1963]. *Plunkitt of Tammany Hall: A Series of Very Plain Talks on Very Practical Politics*. New York: E. P. Dutton.

Robinson, Kim Stanley. 1988. *The Gold Coast*. New York: Tom Doherty Associates, Inc.

Rusk, David. 1995. *Cities without Suburbs, second edition*. Washington, DC: Woodrow Wilson Center Press.

Rybczynski, Witold. 1995. *City Life: Urban Expectations in a New World*. New York: Scribner.

Sampson, Robert, and Stephen Raudenbush. 2004. "Seeing Disorder: Neighborhood Stigma and the Social Construction of 'Broken Windows.'" *Social Psychology Quarterly* 67: 319–42.

Sanders, Heywood. 2005. "Space Available: The Realities of Convention Centers as Economic Development Strategy." Research Brief, Metropolitan Policy Program, The Brookings Institution, Washington, DC.

Saxenian, Annalee. 1994. *Regional Advantage: Culture and Competition in Silicon Valley and Route 128*. Cambridge, MA: Harvard University Press.

Schneider, Wolf. 1963. *Babylon Is Everywhere: The City as Man's Fate.* Ingeborg Sammet and John Oldenburg, trans. (from German). New York: McGraw Hill.

Schrank, David, and Tim Lomax. 2005. "The 2005 Urban Mobility Report." College Station: Texas Transportation Institute, The Texas A&M University System.

Schumpeter, Joseph. 1950. *Capitalism, Socialism, and Democracy, third edition.* New York: Harper and Row.

Schwartz, Joel. 1976. "The Evolution of the Suburbs." In *Suburbia: The American Dream and Dilemma,* Philip Dolce, ed. Garden City, NY: Anchor Press/Doubleday.

Scott, Allen. 1988. *Metropolis: From the Division of Labor to Urban Form.* Berkeley and Los Angeles, CA: University of California Press.

Seaman, Bruce. 1987. "Arts Impact Studies: A Fashionable Excess." In *Economic Impact of the Arts: A Sourcebook.* Washington, DC: National Conference of State Legislatures, 43–75.

Serrano v. Priest. 1971. 5 Cal. 3rd 584, 487 P. 2nd 1241.

Shoup, Donald. 2004. "The Ideal Source of Local Public Revenue." *Journal of Regional Science* 34: 753–84.

Siegan, Bernard. 1972. *Land Use without Zoning.* Lexington, MA: D. C. Heath and Co.

Silverberg, Robert. 1973. "Getting Across." In *Future City,* Roger Elwood, ed. New York: Pocket Books.

Simons, Robert, William Bowen, and Arthur Sementelli. 1997. "The Effect of Underground Storage Tanks on Residential Property Values in Cuyahoga County, Ohio." *Journal of Real Estate Research* 14: 29–42.

Sleeper, Sally, Henry Willis, Eric Landree, and Beth Grill. 2004. "Measuring and Understanding Economic Interdependence in Allegheny County." Technical Report TR-200-HE. Pittsburgh, PA: RAND Corporation.

Spinoza, Benedictus de. 1677. *The Ethics.* R. H. M. Elwes, trans. Champaign, IL: Project Gutenberg.

Stephenson, Neal. 1992. *Snow Crash.* New York: Bantam Books.

———. 1995. *The Diamond Age.* New York: Bantam Books.

Sudjik, Deyan. 1992. *The 100 Mile City.* London: Andre Deutsch.

Swindell, David. 1996. "Public Financing of Sports Stadiums: How Cincinnati Compares." *Policy Insight* (February 1996). Dayton, OH: The Buckeye Institute for Public Policy Solutions.

Tiebout, Charles M. 1956. "A Pure Theory of Local Expenditures." *Journal of Political Economy* 64: 416–24.

Tsuru, Shigeto. 1963. "The Economic Significance of Cities." In *The Historian and the City,* Oscar Handlin and John Burchard, eds. Cambridge, MA: MIT Press.

USA Today. September 6, 1996. "Ballpark construction's booming." 13C–14C, 19C–21C.

Vesterby, Marlow, and Kenneth Krupa. 2001. "Major Uses of Land in the United States, 1997." Statistical Bulletin no. 973. Resource Economics Division, Economic Research Service, U.S. Department of Agriculture.

Warner, Sam Bass. 1962. *Streetcar Suburbs: The Process of Growth in Boston, 1870–1900.* Cambridge, MA: Harvard University Press/MIT Press.

Weiss, Marc A. 1987. *The Rise of the Community Builders: The American Real Estate Industry and Urban Land Planning.* New York: Columbia University Press.

Weitzman, Martin. 1974. "Prices vs. Quantities." *Review of Economic Studies* 41: 477–91.

Wilson, John. 1987. "Trade in a Tiebout Economy." *American Economic Review* 77: 431–41.

Wilson, William Julius. 1987. *The Truly Disadvantaged: The Inner City, the Underclass, and Public Policy.* Chicago: University of Chicago Press.

Worley, William S. 1990. *J. C. Nichols and the Shaping of Kansas City: Innovation in Planned Residential Communities.* Columbia: University of Missouri Press.

Yinger, John. 1979. "Prejudice and Discrimination in Housing Markets." In *Current Issues in Urban Economics,* Peter Mieszkowski and Mahlon Straszheim, eds. Baltimore, MD: Johns Hopkins University Press.

Zipf, George. 1949. *Human Behavior and the Principle of Least Effort.* Cambridge, MA: Addison-Wesley.

INDEX

Burchfield, Marcy, 58, 59, 199
bus, 5, 49, 129, 146, 148, 150, 152,
    185, 187, *see also* mass transit
business, viii, 2, 8, 9, 10, 16, 25, 33,
    40, 41, 42, 43, 44, 49, 55, 90, 94,
    95, 96, 97, 98, 99, 104, 105, 113,
    122, 126, 139, 146, 154, 156, 159,
    160, 161, 163, 183, 184, 194, 203,
    205

Caesar, Julius, 145, 157, 180
Cahill, Thomas, 39, 199
California, 59, 82, 118, 130, 131, 138,
    152, 168, 190, 206
Calvino, Italo, 1, 2, 7, 199
Capitalization, 127, 159
car, 5, 7, 8, 17, 18, 32, 40, 41, 42, 49,
    66, 71, 80, 122, 146, 149, 150, 151,
    152, 153, 154, 155, 156, 182, 184,
    185, 186, 187, 196, 198, *see also*
    automobile
Caro, Robert, 142, 184, 199
Census Bureau, 3, 5, 20, 57, 67, 77,
    81, 86, 87, 91, 94, 112, 138, 147,
    148, 149, 165, 167, 172, 186, 189,
    190, 195, 196, 201
Census Transportation Planning
    Program, 81
central business district (CBD), 8, 9,
    16, 40, 41, 42, 44, 45, 46, 49, 52,
    71, 75, 76, 77, 79, 82, 84, 88, 91,
    92, 93, 94, 102, 108, 109, 110, 129,
    145, 146, 147, 153, 158, 183, *see
    also* downtown
Central Park, 185
central place theory, 43, 46, 47, 48,
    79, 129
CEOs for Cities, 96, 202
Chalermpong, Saksith, 152,
    198
Chatman, Daniel, 147, 199
Chay, Kenneth, 159, 199
Chen, Donald, 2, 198
Chicago, 9, 15, 30, 34, 43, 46, 47, 65,
    67, 69, 76, 91, 95, 96, 137, 149,
    197, 199, 202, 204, 207
Chu, Chenghuan, 14, 91, 201

city-state, 3, 20, 21, 118
Cleveland, vii, xi, 3, 4, 10, 12, 13, 14,
    15, 18, 19, 24, 25, 29, 60, 65, 69,
    72, 77, 78, 81, 82, 87, 91, 92, 93,
    94, 98, 100, 101, 102, 103, 106,
    111, 112, 113, 114, 115, 116, 133,
    164, 166, 168, 173, 174, 193, 196,
    198, 199, 201, 202
Coase, Ronald, 134, 199
Code of Hammurabi, 22
Coleman, Alice, 29, 199
Coleman, Stephen, 201
college, xi, 8, 31, 48, 80, 95, 96, 97,
    102, 109, 110, 172, 173, 177, 178,
    199, 202, *see also* university
common interest development (CID),
    176, 177, 178, 179, 188, 196, *see
    also* neighborhood association
community development financial
    institution (CDFI), 98, 99
commute, viii, 5, 8, 10, 11, 12, 13, 18,
    19, 32, 36, 37, 40, 50, 51, 53, 54, 65,
    80, 81, 82, 83, 84, 85, 86, 103, 109,
    110, 114, 124, 129, 144, 145, 146,
    147, 148, 149, 154, 155, 167, 177,
    199, 202
commuting quotient, 82, 84
concurrency, 157, 158
congestion, viii, 8, 11, 18, 23, 44, 49,
    56, 62, 66, 105, 109, 113, 128, 139,
    143, 144, 145, 146, 147, 148, 149,
    150, 151, 152, 153, 154, 156, 157,
    158, 168, 177, 183, 187, 195, 200
Connecticut, 20, 173, 187
construction, viii, 1, 6, 17, 26, 34, 35,
    44, 90, 99, 100, 101, 105, 109, 111,
    112, 115, 116, 117, 126, 136, 138,
    142, 150, 151, 152, 154, 155, 182,
    188, 205, 206
consumer surplus, 107, 108, 151
Copernicus, 40
Costa, Dora, 110, 178, 199
Courant, Paul, 124, 199
Crane, Randall, 10, 147, 154, 196,
    198, 199
creative class, 108, 109, 110, 200
Cromwell, Brian, 174, 199